PIECES *of* ME

Felicity Nicole

NYX PUBLISHING

First published in 2023 by Onyx Publishing, an imprint of Notebook Group Limited, 11 Arden House, Deepdale Business Park, Bakewell, Derbyshire, DE45 1GT.

www.onyxpublishing.com
ISBN: 9781913206529

A CIP catalogue record for this book is available from the British Library.

Typeset by Onyx Publishing of Notebook Group Limited.

This book is the author's interpretation of their upbringing and life. All names have been changed to maintain their privacy.

I dedicate this book to my son, Evan. May you see that nothing is impossible, regardless of your circumstances. We, sweetie, are built to move mountains, and you will do so when it's time for your calling. Stand strong, never give up, and keep chasing your dreams. It will always be me and you, kiddo. I love you.

The warrior rises amidst her pain, suffering,
And aching in her heart.
She had no one to believe in her
But the belief she discovered within herself.
She is resilient, quiet, and has a heart of gold,
And those she allows into her sacred space feel special
For they are graced with the wisdom, truth, and light that she emits
As a healer to the many souls she has touched.
Her pain will be seen by those that recognize it in the eyes, the window
to the soul,
But her light will always remain bright.

The warrior rises amidst her pain,
Awaiting the next chapter of her life.
Will it be one of freedom?
One of pleasure?
The days when the sun shines the most on her freckled face,
She feels utter peace and contentment
For she no longer needs to battle
Her sword is down
She stands with her arms wide open
Allowing the breath of life to swirl in and around her ever-spiritual soul.

PART I
THE PIECES

1

The Crystal Ashtray

———

IT WAS THE CRYSTAL ASHTRAY that was the ultimate catalyst.
I'm asleep in my twin bed. Or at least pretending to be. I've pretended
so often, cocooned in my protective barrier of duvet, that sometimes
I even fool myself.

Someone shifts in the bunk bed across from me with an angry snap
of the blanket. I think it's my brother, David, who is in the bottom bunk.
I could look, but David doesn't like me much. He tries to avoid me most
days. And if he *is* awake, he knows just as well as I do exactly what's going
on in our living room.

David is twelve-and-a-half years old. Almost a teenager, he likes to
say. He and his friends are all about girls. They don't drink yet, but they
will. That's what teenage boys in our neighborhood do, preparing to drink
themselves into a stupor as grown men. I'm only ten, but I know that to
be a fact. Our baby brother, Tommy, who is eight and sleeping in the top
bunk above David, already knows that, too.

I don't pay much attention to the words being thrown around out
there. Only the screaming. She—my mom—always pushes too hard when

our dad comes home from wherever he's been. Usually, he's been indulging in women and drugs, but of course, I don't know that yet.

He used to be a Thornton man, but he doesn't live here on any sort of a regular basis anymore. He hasn't for as long as I can remember. If he ever believed in being neighborly or taking care of his family, he's beyond all of that now for sure. His wife seems happy enough with this life of all take and no give, the cycle of hollow absence followed by precarious, charged presence, but it's not good enough for him. Maybe he thinks that it's boring. Or maybe I'm wrong and he doesn't question it. Maybe it's simply what he was taught. After all, his father was an alcoholic who abused women, too.

Most days, I think of him as an "almost dad". I see him in snapshots: I'm sitting on the couch with him watching television, but mostly, I'm watching him; I ask about the "silly cigarette" that smells funny in his hand just to make him laugh; I'm looking down at the cheap necklace set he handed to me at the front door with a, "I thought of you."

If we ever sat around the table and had dinner together like a family, the snapshot of it never found its place in my mind. He doesn't take me to the movies, nor does he take David and Tommy to ballgames. He doesn't tinker around the house. If he even notices that his wife and kids are living like cockroaches, knocking on the neighbor's door when the plumbing goes out to ask to use the bathroom or take a sponge bath in their utility room sink, it isn't of interest to him.

We aren't of interest to him.

And when he *does* come home? Well, it barely qualifies. He's a stray cat, out all night, strung out on whatever he can shove up his nose. He's Spanish and plays the part well: pinky ring, gold chain, and a wad of cash. He likes the look.

His day job is as a bridge and building foreman for a large railroad company in the Midwest, and his night job... well, I won't find out about that until much later.

David takes another tug at his blanket, and Tommy whispers something. Or maybe he's crying. I could reach up and grab Tommy's hand if I wanted to; that's how close my twin bed is to my brothers' bunk bed in the room that we've been sharing since we were all born.

We have a sister, too. Dawn is twenty-two, twelve years older than me. She has her own room because of how much older she is than us. There wouldn't be enough room for my twin bed in there with her, anyway.

Dawn is waiting for the boy of her dreams to walk her out of our front door for good. I never ask her why she doesn't just leave by herself. It's not like we ever have enough food to eat or room to breathe in this house. But I don't ask because I already know. It's familiar. It's home.

That's the four of us: David and Tommy in the bunk bed, me in my twin, and Dawn in her room. Tommy and I are closer than Dawn and I or David and Tommy, probably because we're the youngest in the family, but we all remember that we're family every once in a while. David will let me tag along to play baseball with him and his buddies on the field down the street, and Dawn will see the pregnant calico stray in my arms and help me make a bed in her closet so that the kittens can be born in peace. We're a tribe: nothing alike, but stuck to this house like old flypaper.

Dawn buries herself in boyfriends (I know this because she and Mom fight about all the guys she brings home—guys who are *bad*), David wants to shut all of us out, I'm shy and stubborn, and Tommy clings to my mother like a baby chimpanzee. We cohabitate—no, *cosurvive*—in the minefield that is our home, a less-than-one-thousand-square-foot box on railroad ties, our various coping strategies operating at full power.

It's how we live.

There's a loud bang in the living room. Our bedroom door wobbles but doesn't open. It's a thin door. Tommy's head went straight through it once, during some rough-and-tumble with David.

"Wheezy."

Dawn's voice.

Tommy reaches down from the top bunk, and I finally raise my head. "Wheezy" is an old nickname that Mom gave me as a baby, when upper respiratory infections plagued me. Everyone calls me Wheezy.

The screaming in the living room is escalating, and I can sense that Tommy is scared. We assume Dawn is in her bedroom, but she tells us later that she was watching television with her boyfriend. That's her yelling now. "Stop it!"

Feet move across the living room floor like boxers during a match, inching closer to our bedroom door.

Now, David is up, and I hear him let out a deep breath. *"Fuck!"*

My heart pounds at this exclamation and I leap out of bed with David and Tommy. Our heads are leaning against the door, listening, straining to decipher the meaning from the commotion, when it flies open, almost knocking us to the floor.

Our father runs in. There are sprays of blood splattered all over his shirt, and his chest heaves as he breathes raggedly. He doesn't say anything or even look at us (no comfort or explanation) but just keeps moving through our bedroom to the one he's supposed to be sharing with our mother, grabs a black duffle, and shoves some things inside.

I don't watch him for long. Instead, I'm looking at my mother. She's propped up on the floor, her beautiful blond hair streaked with red. There's blood dripping down her face, too.

And her head is split wide open.

Our crystal ashtray (the one she fills with cigarettes a couple of times a day) is on the floor just to the side of her, and, on its rim, a crack is perceptible. Cigarette butts dotted with more of her blood spill on the floor.

I walk to the bathroom, calmer than I should be. I can hear Dawn on the telephone with the police. She tells them we'll need an ambulance.

I unroll some toilet paper—a *lot* of toilet paper—and walk back out. Dawn's boyfriend is leading Dad and his black duffle out of the house. I ignore my father entirely.

I bend down next to my mother and dab at the blood, a steady, pumping stream that isn't going to be stopped by a little girl and a wad of tissue. Tommy sits beside me. He's crying.

I don't think Mom's a fool for letting Dad hurt her like this. I simply wonder how I can help her feel good about herself when it's all over. I could tell her that she's a good mom; that none of this is her fault. I could remind her of the time that I brought the stray cat home and how, even though she could barely feed us, she scrounged up money for cat food because she saw how much it meant to me.

For now, I don't say anything. I just dab at the hole in her head that's gushing blood like a volcano at a science fair.

"Wheezy!"

Dawn yells louder than I think she should, but I guess she's been trying to get my attention for a while now. She tells me to grab what I need because we're going to be sleeping at Maggie's next door for the rest of the night.

I look up at Dawn and then down at the red tissue that I'm holding against our mother's head. I vaguely hear Dawn say it will be okay and that the ambulance is coming, but everything feels dreamlike, wishy-washy, far away.

She pulls Tommy up by one arm and me by the other and tells Mom to keep holding the tissue against her head. She'll be right back.

Mom is sobbing. "Why?"

My mouth feels dry and my head light as I'm pulled away.

Dawn's boyfriend is standing outside the house with my dad, waiting, when we walk out. David is there now, too. The three of us fall in behind Dawn—David, me, and Tommy—like a train. I'm thinking that when Dawn finally does leave home for good, it'll be hard—very, very hard—but at least I'll get her cubbyhole bedroom. I'll fill it with every stray cat and bird I can rescue, and my mother will let me have them because by then, the screaming in the living room will have stopped for good and her worn-out nerves will have reached their breaking point. She'll spend her days at our antique kitchen table smoking cigarettes and trying to figure out where the money is going to come from now, or how she can stretch food for the week with four children. The feral animals living in my bedroom won't even be on her radar. Most days, a simple homework question will be met with a stop sign of a hand, and that will be a shame, as she's always been so good at giving advice and wanting us to do our best.

Maggie is already waiting for us at her front door. Her daughter, Sara, who is a couple of years older than David, is standing next to her. They don't say much.

What *can* they say?

Sara says Tommy and I can have her bed. We don't argue. I don't know where she's going to sleep or what David is going to do, but we follow her to her bedroom and Tommy snuggles right into her bed. Maybe he falls asleep.

Then, I do what I do best: I pretend.

I can hear the sirens, soft at first, then louder and louder still, alerting the whole neighborhood of where they're going.

Sara and David are watching from her bedroom window. I could watch with them, but I don't. I want to lie here, pretend that I'm asleep, and listen to them talk about what's going on at our house.

The paramedics are leading our bleeding mother to the ambulance and the police are talking to Dad. David and Sara wonder if they'll arrest him or just let him go. David says they'd better arrest him. I think it doesn't matter.

At some point, I fall asleep to the sound of the sirens, my head swimming and my body feather-light.

Dawn comes to collect us the next day, when Mom and her stitched-up head are home from the hospital. I don't know where Dad is, but this will soon be nothing out of the ordinary. He'll slowly begin to fade away from us from this point—further away than he even was before. I won't really know much more about him until years later, when he confesses from his deathbed to all of the shady things he's done.

One of the neighbors brings over a meatloaf the night after our dad almost killed our mother with the crystal ashtray. We sit at the antique dining room table and dig in like it's Sunday dinner. We don't talk about what happened the day before.

We go to bed earlier than usual. David crawls into the top bunk and Mom cuddles with Tommy in the lower bunk. Apparently, she has no interest in her own bedroom tonight.

She says, "Goodnight, Wheezy. I love you."

I say, "Okay."

I can't say the words back. Not to her. Not to anyone.

2

I Love Lucy *Is to Blame*

———

S O, HOW DID WE END up here?
What I can tell you is that I have real tough woman genes flowing
through my veins, but being as tough as steel comes at a cost. I
was born into a family tree of women who are strong, resilient, and
steadfast, yet these same women have battled immense struggle,
judgment, and abuse. And as we know, these things create ripple effects—
huge, generational ripple effects—if the cycle is not recognized and
consciously stopped.

But unfortunately, this cycle went unnoticed by my family, and so
the home I entered was one of serious trauma and baggage. It was reactive
and survival-oriented and characterized by motherly coldness.

To understand this fully, let's take a look at my maternal
grandmother's (my beloved Nan's) upbringing.

My grandmother was a war bride from England.

My Great Nan lost her husband when my grandmother was three
years old due to complications from diabetes (we assume during WWI,
since he was stationed in Palestine and buried in Tel Aviv), and from then,

Great Nan was on her own in raising her two kids. Great Nan was a seamstress and nanny for the wealthier families in the surrounding villages (fun fact: one of her little charges was Stephanie Beacham, the now-well-known actress), and so Nan would stay in the kitchen area of grand houses as her mother cared for different families.

From what I've picked up over the years through stories, Great Nan was a tough, stern woman with zero tolerance for disrespect. She once knocked my grandmother off her chair during dinner because she mouthed off to her, and she placed her fourteen-year-old son in military school after he attempted to punch her. Nan has since told me stories of walking miles to and from school, running a stick alongside the picket fences that lined the rolling hills in the country as her sole entertainment.

Even though she was raised by a strong mother, my grandmother had a meekness about her. She struggled with standing up for herself (something I related to for a long period of time), and was always picked on in school as a child.

Their little family moved a lot during WWII to escape the German invasions. They often had to turn their lights off when the raids were happening. At one point, my Great Nan tried to send my grandmother to Australia (like hundreds of other British families were doing) but, by the grace of God, this didn't happen. (It was later discovered that these British children were sold off to slave labor.)

Nan eventually came to the United States as a war bride, marrying into a wild family of Polish origin. Some years ago, I came across her food ration cards from the Depression and photos of her on the Queen Mary when she was coming to the United States. All of those men, women, and children squeezed together on the ship like a can of sardines… insane. To this day, standing strong at ninety-three, she still holds onto all of these memories of her journey to a better life in America.

Meanwhile, my grandfather (Pa, to us) grew up on a farm in

Goodman, Wisconsin, with about a dozen siblings. His mother didn't speak a lick of English, and her days were spent caring for all the kids and her husband. The stereotypical gender roles were prevalent in their home. From what I understand, Pa's father was an alcoholic farmer, and not the kindest of husbands. Even still, my grandfather's stories of his childhood were the best to listen to. He would manage to spin growing up on a farm during the Depression while poorer than dirt as fun, with anecdotes centered on sharing a farmhouse with twelve siblings. His story about him ice-skating on a frozen pond with just one ice skate was one of my favorites.

Pa hopped on the New Deal that Roosevelt implemented to plant trees throughout Wisconsin before heading to Europe for WWII.

My grandparents met in an English pub when she was fourteen and he was seventeen (yes, he was seventeen in the war, lying about his age in order to serve). My grandpa's version of when they met is super-sweet, while my grandmother's version shines a light on his wild side. While *he* said he used to pick her up for a date to go dancing, *she* maintained he ended up dancing with all the "fast" women instead. Regardless, there was an obvious connection between the two of them, and he later asked her to marry him, after which he brought her to Chicago, where a number of his relatives lived after World War II. I've heard her say more than once that she would have stayed in Europe if she could do it all over again.

Nan and Pa initially settled in the Jackson Park area of Chicago, but they ultimately bought a little brick home in Dolton on the southern outskirts of Chicago. Chicago bungalows lined the streets, kids played freely, and the parents kept an eye out for each other's children. It was a safe place for my mom and her sister to grow up.

Nan walked everywhere with her little girls. The milk delivery man would walk by daily with his pushcart. Overall, the picture is very foreign and wholesome. Yet from what I have gathered over the years, my mom and her sister did not feel they had the strongest relationship. I can recall them coming over and celebrating birthdays and such during my adult life, and my aunt's husband and kids are fantastic, yet there was always simply something off with the both of them. It was like there was some sort of distance or resentment that neither one wanted to address.

Soon enough, Pa became an alcoholic (a running theme in my family history, apparently) to the point where Nan had to go and physically pull him out of bars. He ultimately became extremely ill, and she told him that if he continued to drink like he was, he was going to die.

In the end, with his wife's ultimatum and with the diagnosis of his serious condition, Pa got his shit together.

Now, I look back on my times with Nan and Pa as the one source of stability and loving kindness in my youth. Sundays were a respite from the daily misery of my home life: they were for donuts, McDonald's, or some kind of special treat from Nan and Pa. My Pa, a tiny Polish man with a big heart and the ability to make anybody laugh, would putter around the house during these days, fixing any little thing that my mom needed help with. He taught me how to rake leaves, plant a garden, and mow the lawn.

Good job, really, as the Lord knows my father was never going to be there to do any of that with me as a child.

I don't know too much about my mom's childhood, but what I do know is that she was always tremendously artistic. I have this mental image of her sitting crisscross applesauce on her bed, hairbrush in hand, sweeping back the long hair of a young neighbor. She did the hair and makeup of all the girls who lived on her block in Dolton. She could think outside the box and devise all sorts of artistic creations. She'd also always wanted to be an attorney, but that was ultimately derailed, and she ended up settling with just a GED.

Creativity was my mother's one love language, I think. Thank God she had some kind of personal outlet and way of positively expressing herself. Looking back now, it still makes no sense to me that the same woman who painstakingly crafted a whole array of garments and gifts with delicate attention and ease was the same woman who often greeted me with, "What the fuck do you want?", "Don't ask me for anything," or, "I'm not fucking taking you anywhere."

As she entered her high school years, she became more defiant and entrenched herself in a rebellious friend group (hello, teenage me!), and although she wasn't into drugs, she certainly was partial to thrills.

Enter my smooth-talking, dark-haired, passionate young father.

Back then, Dad was handsome and Mom was beautiful, and that was enough for them. Always dressed to impress and wearing his dark hair slicked back, my father looked a bit like Ricky Ricardo from her favorite TV show *I Love Lucy*. (Later, when things went south, my Nan jokingly blamed their doomed romance on this show. If it hadn't been for my mom's crush on Ricky, things would have probably gone very differently.) He certainly appeared to be the ticket to an exciting new world, and it was a different world, alright—just not the one Nan and Pa had wished for their daughter. Dad held the company of some men who were in the Spanish mob... and perhaps did more than just hang out with them. He liked women and drugs more than anything on Earth.

Dawn has told me that, when she was young, while other kids her age were practicing the alphabet, she'd started imitating my dad by pretending to roll joints out of receipts.

Father of the Year.

The fact he was so heavily involved in such shady, unsavory crowds is probably unsurprising upon inspection of his childhood. He was born into the middle of a large Hispanic family in San Antonio. At some point, they moved to Thornton, Illinois (the quaint, humble town where I would grow up), and my grandfather, who worked for Material Service Corp. (owner of the Thornton Quarry, one of the world's largest limestone quarries), made enough to keep the family in beans and rice and himself in booze... and that's about it. My grandfather was a mean drunk who beat his wife and died of a heart attack at the age of fifty, while my dad's mom (I never call her my grandmother because we didn't have the slightest familial bond) was a hateful woman who never offered to help us.

I think their pack of kids, including my dad, learned to just stay the hell out of their parents' way and basically raise themselves. They all got out of that house as quickly as they could.

Anyway, I digress.

My beautiful, blond, outgoing mother, Erin, didn't bring home my handsome Hispanic father, Richard, until she was already pregnant at age sixteen with Dawn. After their courthouse wedding, they moved in with Nan and Pa, who made some attempt to compensate for my father's feral childhood and teen years by raising him into manhood and teaching him the skills he'd never been taught.

A few years later, while still in their late teens, my parents rented a small apartment in Thornton, and the thrills wore off quickly. My mom was back and forth to Nan and Pa's house with her baby girl (Dawn) in the face of my father's rages. Dawn would often stay there for days at a time during the first four years of her life. My mom would experience many bouts of my father's rage before he finally bashed her head open with the crystal ashtray—the final hurrah after more than two decades of aggression, infidelity, and walking on eggshells.

Dawn has more memories of Dad than I do, and sometimes, I pressed her for details of what our parents were like when she was young. They were living with Nan and Pa when Dawn was born, and Dawn says, flat out, that Nan and Pa pretty much raised her until she was four, when our parents had enough money to buy a house. She recalls lots of parties and people coming in really high or drunk after that.

The sad truth is, alcohol and drugs were staples in my parents' apartment. At around the time she was improvising my father's joint-rolling with receipts, Dawn remembers nights full of people coming in and out; of waking up to strangers passed out on their modest furniture and in the corner on the floor.

I don't think my mom was involved in illicit drugs. Nicotine and caffeine were as far as her vices went. Even looking back now, I don't think there are any two objects I associate more with my mom than a cup of coffee and a cigarette. These were her trademark props, and the visual and olfactory concoction these two create in my mind's eye instantaneously bring back a ream of memories.

And we know how much little girls love to idolize and imitate their moms!

One summer, when I was about ten years old, I was (of course) running around with the neighborhood kids when I saw Mom take one of her cigarettes and leave it in her ashtray, only partially smudged out.

Well, I'd say it's pretty obvious where this one is going!

Completely impulsively, when my mom was off somewhere else, I grabbed the cigarette from the tray and started running to the back of the house with it. I was loosely planning on examining it a little (these little things had always intrigued me)... and seeing if I had the balls to smoke it. Only I didn't manage to make it without being spotted. Thankfully, one of the older neighborhood kids caught on to what I was doing, snatched the cigarette out of my hands, and scolded me. Strangely mature for what were still pretty young kids, I know, but there we have it! I guessed I wasn't going to be trying any of my mom's cigarettes anytime soon.

So yes, my mom wasn't exactly on the substance abuse train. Rather, I think she spent most of those nights babysitting the partiers and making sure nobody died. She was clinging to her merry-go-round for dear life.

Later, for thirteen grand, my parents bought a two-bedroom, one-bath house in Thornton. The modest size of the house suited them just fine... until David came along, and then me and Tommy. Then, they needed another room, so my parents turned the garage into their bedroom. They had to walk through our bedroom to get to it, which was a privacy issue for all of us, especially David, who would have built walls around his part of the bunk bed if he could. It was a dumpy little house that my artistic mother made as beautiful as possible. Not clean, mind, but well-decorated. She had a talent for decorating. She could take nothing and turn it into something beautiful, and that's exactly what she did as she bought used furniture. There was an antique wood dining table with thick carved legs, chipped and stained a bit, that she draped with the prettiest tablecloth; the dining room chairs were rickety, but did the job; she put a few area rugs over the worn wood floors and had Nan and Pa over for Sunday dinner.

It was near the end of my father's life when I learned he'd been involved with some incredibly shady people doing shit that would make the strongest soul quiver when their death was near. This explains so much, and not just the wads of cash he often carried, but also the random stuff he'd show up with during my childhood. At one point, somebody was paying him off in food stamps, and he would give those to my mom. Or a microwave. Or odd pieces of furniture. Even a big-screen theatre-style TV. I can still remember the conversation regarding the latter between my parents:

Dad: "It's for the kids."

Mom: "Richard, where did this come from?"

Dad: "Don't worry about it."

Mom: "Richard, *they* have kids."

Dad: "He owed me money, so I took it. Fuck him. He owes me

money."

My father's Joe Pesci approach to his side-hustle felt very gangster. When people didn't have the money to pay him back, he took what he felt was his.

Talk about filling our home with bad energy.

As would perhaps be expected considering the hand she was dealt, my mother couldn't be bothered with any of us most of the time when we were growing up. She loved us, but I always felt like a burden to her. Maybe it was her depression shining through, or maybe she was just overwhelmed at her life unraveling at a scarily fast pace. Regardless, she interacted with each of us differently, helping to groom us into specific roles.

My mother did have enough energy to apply cosmetics almost every day, however. From her teenage years to the very last day of her life, she was fond of flashy hair and makeup. When my dad nearly killed her with the crystal ashtray and she was hauled off to the hospital, she was furious that her makeup wasn't done, and later that day, when her best friend came to check on her at the hospital, she found my mom sitting Indian-style in the ER, head gashed wide open, trying to reapply her makeup. During my teenage years, my mom would spend a couple of hours in the morning puttering around, going back and forth from applying makeup to making coffee to back to tweaking her makeup.

Mom might have been too overwhelmed and checked out to clean the disgustingly dirty kitchen floors, or to bother with days' worth of dirty dishes piled in the sink, or to figure out why our single bathroom faucet wasn't working, or to help us with our homework, or to even just ask us how our school day was, but by God, would she fix her hair and makeup no matter what.

Of course, even really young kids can do chores like wash dishes and scrub floors and dust furniture, but they need training, or at least a role model, to do that. My mother, however, had zero interest or inclination when it came to equipping us with these skills. Instead, she passively skated through life and essentially left us to fend for ourselves.

Around four years before I was born, Dawn recalls my mom driving along in her beat-up Chevy Malibu, the windows down, plumes of cigarette smoke wafting outside and all throughout our old family beater. Batting her dramatic, long, false eyelashes and with her big blond bouffant wig blowing in the breeze, her two little kids bounced around in the back seat. It was the seventies, so nobody was worried about seatbelts or secondhand smoke. God knows where my mom was taking my two older siblings.

My older brother, David (an infant at the time), started to cry.

"Take care of that baby. Make that baby stop crying," my mom snapped, barely turning toward Dawn. "Put that bottle in his mouth."

At the age of eight, my sister was forced into a caregiver role. It's no wonder she ended up becoming quite controlling in her adulthood.

With my mother dumping a lot of her own duties onto Dawn and Dawn spending so many years as the only child, my sister remained somewhat separate from the rest of us siblings throughout our childhoods, and this wasn't helped by the fact that she never really had the opportunity to *be* a child. From the moment she entered this world, she was surrounded by drugs and booze, and was affected by an absent father and a mother who spent her days chasing him. As a little girl, if Dawn engaged in normal, important childhood behaviors, such as twirling around playfully or burying herself in a book, my father would always nip it in the bud and demand she stop or put the book down and take care of the house or David.

While Dawn and I may have had our differences since, my heart aches to think of that lonely, reprimanded little girl with the weight of the world on her shoulders.

David, meanwhile, was the golden child who could do no wrong in my mother's eyes. The running joke was that it was because he was the only breastfed baby. Yet my father made no effort to have any semblance of a relationship with him, and was actually pretty hateful toward him at times. Maybe it's that Mom saw the potential in David: he did grow up to be the most financially successful of any of us.

Meanwhile, my younger brother, Tommy, was quiet and withdrawn, and he still is to this day. His "role", so to speak, was to play peacekeeper and hide when faced with confrontation. However, when pushed enough, he would (and still will) lose his shit and go AWOL. I can think of a few times when Tommy had David up against the wall by his throat in a fit of rage. Overall, though, during our childhood years, Tommy was usually easy to be around. He was the baby of the family, and everyone coddled him to some degree. He and I always had a better bond than the rest of my siblings—even the bond that I had with my sister back in the day. Tommy and I are eighteen months apart, so we shared similar friend groups and would often pal around.

And me? I was Felicity the Screwup. The troublemaker. The one who was going nowhere fast and couldn't do anything right.

From very tender ages, my and my siblings' roles were sealed.

Every morning in our little Thornton home, my mother got up and made breakfast for my dad. My dad would then dutifully head off to work after polishing off his meal, and when he came home, my mom always had dinner ready.

Quintessential. Seamless. A white picket fence, all-American setup.

Right?

Wrong.

The truth was, every moment that my father happened to decide to come home, the air was charged with electric, nervous energy. Every other member of the family was constantly picking through a minefield, walking on eggshells, terrified of being the culprit for setting off a new bout of fury.

Well, most of the time we were. Sometimes, my mother just couldn't help herself. She'd get a bee in her bonnet about something and follow him from room to room, griping, as us kids sat around nervously, waiting for the baby to blow. My dad for sure gave Mom plenty of reasons to complain, but this was something different. She was pushing his buttons; goading him; itching for a fight.

As it happened, he didn't stick around the house for long, especially after Tommy came along, and as his presence—no, his *visits*—grew more and more few and far between, the stream of druggies that had up to that point always infiltrated our home swiftly minimized to a trickle.

Now, with a new babe in arms, my mother was left to maintain some kind of bare-minimum functional home while my dad continued to lead a double life and come and go as he pleased. At night, my dad dressed to the nines and headed out the door for an evening of getting drunk, getting high on heroin and cocaine, and screwing hookers at seedy bars in a neighboring town. My dad's mom was a bartender at one of the bars, and she'd often leave nasty voice messages to my mom on the answering machine. My mom also sometimes got calls from my dad asking her to come get him, often opened with, "I really screwed up this time."

My parents did this dance until I was ten—until the crystal ashtray incident, when it came to a screeching halt.

So, this was our little family. Our circumstances and temperaments created the perfect storm for disaster, and we were well on-board the merry-go-round of generational dysfunction.

Welcome to our home.

3

Unlikely Friends

————

ONE OF THE FIRST MEMORIES I have (and it's a pretty shocking one) dates back to when I was around two years old.

We were in Washington Square Mall in Homewood, Illinois. Tommy was practically a baby, and so was carried around in my grandmother's arms as we made the rounds, while Mom walked ahead and David and I skipped along behind. (This was the same mall from which David had stolen a *Star Wars* figurine, I remembered fondly—though he didn't do this successfully. Mom had to go back to the Kmart, return the stowaway figurine, and make David apologize.)

I was still absent-mindedly skipping along when, before I knew it, I felt something heavy on my head.

A hand.

Before I knew what was happening, the hand had spun me around and I was suddenly walking in the opposite direction, away from my family and with a mysterious gentleman who, I perceived, had long hair.

Thankfully (though that is, of course, the understatement of the century), my mom, spotting this short exchange in her peripheral, span around and immediately saw me walking away with this tall stranger. Then, Nan, also spotting the same thing, stalked up to the man and, with her one free arm (the other was holding Tommy), swung her purse at the back of the man's head. He whipped around, his eyes widened, and he ran out of the mall, leaving me behind with my family.

So, yeah, from the get-go, there was never really a dull moment with me and my family.

You may think such an experience would have made Mom hold us even closer, but nope. My mom babied both of my brothers but did *not* pamper us girls. That traditional male patriarchal vibe of serving the men of the house and not the women was chiseled into my brain from a very young age. Mom would make coffee for my brothers, serve them dinner, and do their laundry, even as they approached manhood, while all Dawn and I would receive was a perfunctory, "You know where the kitchen is."

Bottom line: my dad was busy indulging his vices, and my mom was consumed by her demons. So, we kids were something of a wolf pack, pretty much left on our own.

While we were grade schoolers, the three of us younger kids all hung out together, and Dawn and David's friends also spent time around our house pretty often. Our house was like Grand Central Station with their friends. I think my mom enjoyed the vibe, and she was a phenomenal woman in the eyes of the neighborhood kids. There were no rules there, and as long as my dad wasn't home, everybody could come in and feel relaxed. If Dad *was* home, however, there was a good chance that he'd be pretty coked out, which made everyone feel uncomfortable.

My brothers and I would run all over our neighborhood playing army, baseball, and football. I was just part of the mix with my brothers and the neighborhood boys. Of course, that inevitably became uncool for my older brother—he didn't want me cramping his style—so, when he ditched me, it became just Tommy and me who ran around together.

I really do hold many cherished memories from my childhood. One such memory goes a little like this. (Spoiler: it's another mall memory!)

In the south suburbs of Chicago, we had River Oaks Center and Lincoln Mall, and we were regulars at the latter. During one trip with Mom, Nan, Tommy, and David (I was around five or six years old), I was having a dandy ol' time looking at the stores when—drumroll, please!—I was treated to some white Nike sneakers with a purple "swoosh".

I was absolutely ecstatic.

You have to remember that my family's economic standing wasn't exactly amazing, so to have these gorgeous, squeaky clean, *purple* shoes was just a mind-bogglingly amazing experience. I hopped around that mall on Cloud Nine, beaming at strangers and bopping along with the rest of my family. I was so excited, in fact, that once we were home, I hopped into our living room/dining room (still with my new sneakers on), lifted our phone, and dialed "0" for the operator. As soon as I heard a distant voice on the other end of the line, I launched into an excitable spiel about my new shoes.

After what was probably a good couple of minutes of this, my mom came into the living room, took the phone off me, and apologized to the operator. All the while, I could tell she was trying to hold back a massive laugh, so I knew I wasn't in serious trouble. I'd just been so excited about my new shoes!

As for our family's extreme dysfunction, I simply didn't know anything better when I was growing up. I thought that this was what all families were like. I thought it was standard for things to be terrible most of the time. The *real* dark side to my family was the lack of empathy and unconditional love and support that normal families give to one another. My family's way of expressing support and love felt more like a tug-of-war. I would "tug" seeking love, and they would retaliate with hurtful words. My older brother would tell me straight up that I was an idiot, and while this was obviously the kind of behavior that a parent should have nipped in the bud, my dad was physically absent and my mom was vastly emotionally unavailable. So, there was no one nurturing or overseeing the relationships between any of us... meaning things (unsurprisingly) tended to devolve into *Lord of the Flies* as we grew up.

Looking back, it seems it may have been this lack of care, attention, concern, and love at home that contributed to my tendency to bring vagrant animals home. That, and being an empath. Animals gravitate toward empaths, and from half-dead cats to abandoned baby birds, I was always finding creatures to love, like a little dysfunctional Snow White. I remember bathing a cockapoo at around the age of eight, which sums it up!

It's clear there must have been an awareness deep inside of me— something inbuilt, instinctive—of what a love exchange (a *real* love exchange, without ulterior motives or the influence of underlying trauma and toxicity) looks like. The menagerie of cats I collected over the years was a manifestation of the hurt little girl searching for the love that she wasn't receiving at home.

And this empathy wasn't reserved for animals only. I remember being about eight years old and always telling my mom that I wanted to join forces with Peace Corps and bring food to people in third world countries. "I want to bring a ton of McDonald's to all the starving children in Africa," I said seriously, heart pounding with fervor and excitement. From the get-go, I knew, deep down, in my very essence, that I felt an impossibly strong pull toward a life of helping and healing people, in whatever capacity and through whatever means they needed. I didn't question this at the time, but looking back now, I find it a little mind-blowing that I so clearly knew and understood what my soul's purpose was at such a young age. Even today, I actively plan to go to Africa and volunteer at animal sanctuaries once I have a little more time and fewer demands on my hands. My heart and soul crave that raw, unfiltered life geared entirely toward nurturing, healing, and helping. No mortgage, no expectations, no fancy clothes or makeup or hair. Just a life filled with doing what makes my soul feel fucking amazing. *That* would be the dream.

For now, though, what I called "home" (our little cream-colored cottage on Brownell) housed a whole load of chaos, both physical and emotional. Pretty much every surface was covered with a layer of grime, and we fought every day over anything and everything. David would start out by playing, roughhousing on the couch, and the next thing I knew, I'd be seriously getting my ass kicked. And I was much the same: I'd turn around and kick my little brother's ass without any hangups. It was the status quo. It was our normal.

As the icing on the cake, food was scarce at the best of times. I can laugh about it now—the thick wedge of government cheese sandwiched in between two pieces of claggy white bread and a big glob of mayo—but we lacked most of the basics, and had to get creative when it came to feeding ourselves. We had Kool-Aid but no sugar. Peanut butter but no jelly. Cereal but no milk. It was a constant shitshow of clutter, an empty fridge, and angry kids. I honestly believe every single one of us functioned in survival mode. And when we *did* have food in the house, it was gone in a flash. We learned to snag it and binge before someone else did, creating a lovely food insecurity and emotional eating pattern that I struggled with for years.

My mother did have certain recipes that she could prepare well, but the food and money scarcity we constantly faced, combined with her general lack of empathy, helped to create something of a jungle; a Darwin-esque feeding atmosphere. Mom typically made a big pot of mostaccioli on a Monday that was meant to last the week, but when it was gone, it was gone. David would routinely dive into this (or any other meal available) with a selfish frenzy, without a care for how much might (or might not) be left for the rest of the household. On Sundays, when my grandparents came over, my mother would try to prepare a more special dish (a roast, some chicken, or, occasionally, pork chops), so sometimes, our leftovers from Sunday dinners would make it into the weekly food options. But when the fridge was empty and one of us expressed hunger, my mom would just snap back, "I don't know what to tell you. There's no food."

Well, she wasn't wrong. And, of course, as an adult looking back, I can empathize with the bleakness of her situation. But to young me, it sounded like my mother just didn't care.

The emotional neglect in our own home was significant for every one of us, and so my siblings and I all latched onto different coping skills: Dawn ran through guys; David turned to alcohol; Tommy tried to just get along; and I checked out, rebelled, and pushed boundaries.

And nurtured my little animal friends, of course.

It was what had to be done.

There was, however, another, rather unexpected, layer to my life outside the battle for survival at home. A certain gift, or insight, or power, that granted me access to what appeared to be a complete other realm— and a set of some rather unlikely friends. These friends were unlikelier than a stray cat or struggling baby bird. And, interestingly, it was this very gift that allowed me to make immense breakthroughs much later in life, when all seemed lost and I was stumbling through a dizzying vortex of dead ends.

My first experience of this was the Christmas after my dad left, after the crystal ashtray incident. It was about four in the morning, and I had crept to the great room to sneak a look at the Christmas presents. My father may have been chintzy with funds all through the year, but he did give my mother money at Christmastime, and what a lovely sight it was that year! The Christmas tree was twinkling in front of our big picture window with presents spread all underneath.

I spotted a My Pet Monster right away. That had to be for Tommy. *And what's this? A beautiful dollhouse, for me!* I dropped to my knees in excitement to get a closer look. Was that a little bear family living inside?

As I was checking everything out, I happened to look up at the window.

Above the philodendron plants that my mom had nestled in our six-paned old picture window, there was an image forming. I stood, squinted hard, rubbed my sleepy eyes, trying to focus on what was appearing in front of me, when an image formed.

At first, it was a fuzzy haze of black and gray shadows... and then it became clear. An old man in a black suit with a white-collared shirt and thin black tie was peering through the paned window. He was bald, with the exception of a ring of white fuzzy hair all around the circumference of his head.

I stood frozen in our tiny room, more caught off guard than afraid. His funeral attire and emotionless face didn't alarm me... until the old woman in a black suit appeared next to him. Her silver hair was pulled up into a bun, and she was staring straight at me, except she didn't really have eyes: just two sunken black holes. Her stern energy scared the everliving daylights out of me, and I let out a bloodcurdling scream and started to run to my sister's room before quickly ducking into my brothers' room, leaping right on top of David. "Help me, help me, help me!"

My mother, asleep in her bed in the room next to us, came through the door in a frenzy. "Wheezy, what happened? What's going on?"

I was shaking from head to toe uncontrollably, unable to spit out exactly what I'd seen. The words eventually became legible enough for my mother to make out that I had seen people. This prompted her to swiftly check all the doors and windows before following up with question after question as she attempted to determine the details of what I had seen. At first, she assumed it was Nick, the neighborhood Rambo, but I kept telling her, "No, Mom, it was two people, and they were *old*! Very old! She had no eyes, and she was so angry that I was up, Mom, she really was!"

Still perplexed, my mother curled up in bed with me to try and comfort my little trembling body.

I knew that what I had seen was much more than a teenager's prank. This was real.

Mom asked again the next morning exactly what I had seen, and I kept telling her that the woman had sunken-in eyes. No, *no* eyes.

Shortly after the incident, our neighbor, Donna, suggested going to the historical society to see if we could find any information about the house (built in 1910) and its original owners. To my surprise, my mom was open to believing me, and thought maybe I had seen a ghost, since we had experienced other unusual activity in our home. My siblings didn't think I was making it all up, either.

Seeing the old man and woman outside our picture window hadn't been a nightmare. It hadn't been a hallucination. It was the first (and not the last) time I remember seeing people who had already passed over to another realm. And I would one day discover that this was one of my greatest gifts of all.

And the spiritual goings-on didn't stop there.

Throughout my childhood, our home had an open door. All were welcome. Conversations flew around our rickety old dining room table regarding religion and politics, plumes of cigarette smoke hanging in mid-air. Some familiar faces, such as Father Burke and Sister Kay from our parish and school, would regularly pop in to chat with my mother. Looking back on those drop-in visits from the priest and the nun now, I wonder if maybe my mother consulted them about some of the strange goings-on in our house.

Outside the large picture window of our small, cream-colored cottage was an oft-windy sidewalk leading to our front door, and this was the most spiritually active area in our home. No matter what time of day it was or what you were doing, anyone might catch a glimpse of what looked like someone walking up to the front door. It happened so frequently that I can't count the number of occurrences on both my hands and feet. We'd see everything from quick, dark shadows to more fully colored, woman-like images, to figures who made eye contact with whomever was coming to visit.

This didn't creep any of us out. In fact, we kind of joked about it. We might have been dysfunctional, but we were insanely adaptive and resilient.

Nan's first experience along these lines occurred when she was sitting on the sofa sipping her coffee with my mom. She looked out the window, and as I saw the shadow of someone walking outside, I thought, *Oh, here comes Judy.*

Nan got up to answer the door, to find no one there.

Another time, my aunt had come over for coffee, and we were all hunkered down in the great room, gabbing away, the Christmas tree lit and a fire in the woodburning stove, when my aunt and I both saw a beautiful young woman with long blond hair walking down the sidewalk. We both thought that it was David's girlfriend and, excited to see that she was visiting, my aunt got up to answer the door, to find there was nobody there.

I'd continue to see shadows throughout my childhood and teen years, oftentimes in the form of people walking past my hallway and standing in my bedroom. Surprisingly, I wasn't freaked out by this, unlike a lot of the people who came into our home. As an empathic kid, I just didn't know how to process what I was seeing and feeling.

I find it likely that the house itself contributed something to the bad mojo surrounding our family and, in turn, the abundant spiritual activity around us. Hang in there with me; I'm keeping it real. Our house had always been a spiritually active place, and I was (and continue to be) spiritually gifted, but the activity really seemed to pick up after my father moved out.

My mom put up a crucifix on one of the walls of the great room, and, on more than one occasion, when the rack became so heavily burdened with coats that the crucifix was no longer in sight, the coat rack *moved out of the way of the crucifix*. Many of us in the family saw this happen at different times. The coat rack wouldn't just wobble around a bit; it looked like it was being dragged several feet, accompanied by the sound of scraping along the wooden floor. It would spook some visitors in the house to the point where they would literally grab their shit and go.

At one point, a cedar chest was placed in the corner of that same great room, just opposite the coat rack, and when Mom placed a tray on top of it with a pitcher, we saw the whole thing lift up and go back down.

Mom's solution was to move the cedar chest to another place in the room, and the problem was once again solved.

What's a bit of a shame is that by my late teens to early twenties, I'd shut down my ability to see spirits simply because it by this point scared the shit out of me, unlike in my childhood. That didn't mean those gifts had left me, though. They remained, lying dormant, growing in potential all the while, waiting for me to call on them at my time of need.

And I did.

4

Child of the Eighties

————

WHEN MY DAD LEFT, I was ten years old and suddenly wetting the bed at night.

I felt like I'd been abandoned by both of my parents, and my mother never seemed to consider that maybe, just maybe, I needed help. That maybe I needed to speak to someone. Considering the circumstances behind his leaving, you'd think it might have occurred to her that everyone in that house was in need of some trauma counseling, herself included.

School, at least, was an escape, but I struggled with the work. I'd ask my mom for help with the homework, but she was not at all interested, prepared, or emotionally up to it herself. "Figure it out yourself, Felicity," was always her cutting response.

My teachers knew that Dad wasn't in the picture anymore, and they did what they could for us. I was at least with good people during those hours of the day. Whenever my mother came for the parent-teacher conferences, my teachers always remarked on how welcoming, kind, and open I was with new students. That empathic vibe showed up early on, even if I didn't know exactly why I felt so inclined to reach out to others, and I'm still like it to this day, always trying to take people under my wing and help them. Coaching, mentoring, and healing were all natural fits for my gifts and personality; it just took me a while to put all of that together.

Tommy was eight when my father left, and, to be honest, I don't know how much he took in after he was gone. What I *can* say with certainty, however, is that he struggled, as I did, both emotionally and intellectually. Clearly, though, Mom wasn't going to seek any help or support for any of us academically, so Tommy, much like me, skated through school, just about getting by. Looking back, this shared experience probably further strengthened our bond.

From this point and until I was in my later high school years, I saw Dad very seldomly and at random times. He'd just pop in out of the blue, and his infrequent appearances usually had to do with finances. The house was always falling apart and nearly devoid of groceries, and I'm sure that my mom begged him for help. She was technically a stay-at-home mom after Dad left, earning a tiny amount by babysitting the girl across the street from us.

I can picture Dad standing in the living room during one of these random visits, Tommy and I fawning for his attention—"Dad, Dad, look what I can do!"—as we danced around his feet, hoping for acknowledgment. My father would always stand over my mother, dressed to impress and holding open a wallet stuffed full of cash, and hand her a few meager bills just to shut her up. It was a financial exchange that was clearly meant to display his power over her.

One time immediately after the split, I remember him picking the three of us younger kids up and taking us to a Pizza Hut. The bill was about twenty-five dollars, but he opened his fat wallet and threw down two or three hundred. He always had to be flashy, like he was some kind of high roller.

Basically, our family unit (if you could even call it that) was built on a rocky foundation of performativity from my father, blissful ignorance from my mother, and self-preservation from all of us. We were dysfunctional. Burdened. Reactive.

But that didn't mean we couldn't create our fun.

Summertime as a whole brings back reasonably fond memories, not just of my childhood escapades (more on those shortly), but also of my mother. Maybe she was more relaxed, or maybe her anxiety dipped a little when we weren't in school (even if we were pulling crazy stunts outdoors), but either way, some of the positive memories I have of my mom are directly related to her wonderful creativity.

When it comes to my father, I honestly have very few childhood memories of him. You know, from before the time he tried to kill my mother. I have glimmers of him smoking funny cigarettes while watching TV westerns; foggy memories of him getting ready for work at five-thirty in the morning, the blow dryer running and Mom making breakfast while Dad got his stuff together.

I do have this one particularly strange, hazy memory of my parents taking us to the drive-in movies. My dad had a conversion van, and we opened the back doors and sat on rubber mattresses in the back. Of course, as an adult, remembering that he owned a creepy conversion van with mattresses in the back raises all kinds of questions, but as a kid, it just seemed like a fun way to watch a movie.

And that's about the extent of my childhood memories of my father. I've had enough psychotherapy, eye movement desensitization and reprocessing (EMDR) therapy, and cognitive behavioral therapy to know that my lack of memories with my father is genuine and not the result of memory loss. My dad was just not around when we were little. No kissing the kids on the forehead as he went to and from work. No playing catch in the front yard. Nothing remotely *Leave It to Beaver* in my memory bank. And my adolescence wasn't much better. After Dad tried to bash Mom's head in with the crystal ashtray, he bugged out. My parents divorced (only to remarry much later down the road), and they never lived in the same house again.

But back to Mom.

Some of the positive, shining memories of my mother center around Halloween. She made the coolest costumes on the planet. Every year, we'd trek to Joanne Fabrics and flip through the pattern books, looking for the perfect idea. The year that I was in fifth grade, all the other girls at school were planning on standard, predictable costumes, like cheerleaders, but as my mother and I searched the patterns, I landed on a butterfly costume. It was random—just something that I thought would be completely different from everyone else—and my talented mother made sure it was. She took the pattern and ran with it. She never followed the instructions precisely. She cut out large foam wings, made a silk yellow cover to go over them, and adorned them with sequins. I put on a black leotard, black tights, and a headband with antennas. Unsurprisingly, my mother excelled at face painting, and she painted my face beautifully with matching colors to look like a butterfly.

All the kids wore their costumes to school, and someone from the South Holland newspaper was there and asked if I would pose for a picture with some friends. "This is a cool costume. I'll make sure this picture gets in the paper," he promised. I never liked being the center of attention, but posing with a couple of other kids made me feel more comfortable.

My picture in my fabulous butterfly costume was indeed printed in the newspaper, and the memory is strongly imprinted in my memory—

young Felicity with her antennas and makeshift butterfly wings. It was during these opportunities for creativity that my mother came alive and I received a semblance of the love and care I always craved. That version of my mother—lit up, absorbed by her latest project—is utterly radiant in my mind.

It was also around this time (in about the fourth or fifth grade) that I started gluing myself to my South Holland schoolfriends. I didn't like being home: it seemed so ugly, depressing, and unloving in contrast with their homes, which were like a breath of fresh air. I can recall a few memories of going to Andrea's house when Mrs. Perkins had homemade cookies on a plate for her kids to enjoy. This blew my mind: I was lucky if we had a stale bag of Chips Ahoy! cookies somewhere in our house.

One evening, I was invited to stay for dinner at Jenny's house, and we had pizza. No big deal, right? But it was the *feeling* that drew me in. I felt so awkward and shy as we gathered around her kitchen table. Placed next to my plate was a knife and fork, and *napkins*! I couldn't wrap my head around this. Talk about boujee! We never even had paper towels because they were so expensive. What's more, there were conversations about everyone's day. My family rarely ate at the table together, and if we did, conversations were few and far between. Our family was just so disconnected, and my mother didn't seem to have the ability to tune into my or my siblings' emotional needs. The feeling of love and support for one another in my South Holland friends' families was something that otherwise didn't exist in my life.

These mini revelations were what made me start putting the pieces together about our home. The Catholic school in South Holland that Mom had enrolled me in was like Mayberry to me, and this whole new league of homes that I was being introduced to—homes that were clean and had food—was just mind-blowing to me.

Some of my friends' homes were incredible, and not only in comparison to my own dilapidated dwelling. One of my friends had a bowling alley in her basement, which sums it up pretty well. The contrast between our houses couldn't have been much more different, and yet I never felt unwelcome or like I wasn't good enough to be in their space.

It began to dawn on me that not even the other people in our own modest neighborhood lived the way we did. At least, not the main bulk of them. The single mom next door to us had two kids a little older than I, and she had a good job (as an administrative assistant, or something) that allowed her to provide decently for her family. I'd been in their home plenty of times, and whenever she came home from work, she always got busy cooking dinner, and their home always smelled amazing.

Basically, *everybody else had homes that felt like home.*

I was a cheerleader during these early middle school years and developed close bonds with several of the South Holland girls. We had fun, wholesome relationships, and were always having sleepovers, which meant I always found a friend's house to stay at so I didn't have to be home. We'd stay up late watching MTV and *Saturday Night Live*. Those were the Adam Sandler, Chris Farley, Mike Myers, and Dana Carvey days of *SNL,* and we had a blast, beached out in the basement, eating chips, giggling at Wayne and Garth, and running to the bathroom in the basement that had *toilet paper.* (In my own home, there were plenty of times we had no toilet paper and had to use coffee filters.)

I truly do believe that if I'd held onto those early friends a little tighter, my path would have been a little straighter. But instead, I was destined for a hard road filled with some of the same harsh lessons that my mother had been forced to learn.

For now, I was happy with my South Holland friends and siblings. When I wasn't hanging out with my South Holland friends, Tommy and

I expanded our creative relationship. We'd spend hours playing cops and robbers, making forts out of sheets and hiding from the killer. We would also play house. I would dress him up in my mom's favorite makeup, for which she would yell at me. He's always been kindhearted, and would put up with me pulling him in all sorts of directions when we were kids.

As I've mentioned, Tommy and I also spent a lot of time with our grandparents, who swept us both under their wing as much as possible. David refused to engage in this way, but Tommy and I were always doing something together, either with friends or Nan and Pa. Even into adulthood, he is the only sibling that I have maintained any semblance of a relationship with. Our memories together are abundant. We (as in, me, Tommy, David, and the neighborhood kids) all played baseball and broke windows and injured ourselves countless times. We were rough and tough; creative and loud. Some of our antics would curl a modern mother's hair, but I was a child of the eighties, the last of the resilient generations, and we ruled! Despite all our family crap, I really do have some of the best childhood memories purely due to the sense of freedom and trust that was afforded to us. We ran all over Thornton like we owned it.

With that said, we spent a fair amount of time running to the ER, most often for Tommy—like the time he and my brother David found some antique swords, which they of course put to the test. Naturally, Tommy took a sword to the eye. Or the time that Tommy and his friend found a BB gun and integrated it into what was probably a fine game of cops and robbers. I remember Tommy rounding the corner of our block with a hole in his cheek. Another time, when Tommy was about ten, he was running around the back of our small cottage (Mom had created a little patio outside the French doors to her converted garage bedroom, in which there was a little patio table and low surrounding shrubs), and

Tommy rounded the patio just as the next-door neighbor (Steven) came striding from the opposite direction. Steven was in high school at the time and was a very solid six foot two. He caught Tommy right in the head and knocked him out cold. Of course, he promptly picked Tommy up, rushed him inside, and put him on our kitchen counter. "Wake up! Wake up!"

I was crying like crazy, mostly because my selfish little self was worried about what this was doing to my upcoming birthday plans. "I'm not going to have a birthday! I hope he's alive for my birthday!"

Of course, Tommy did go to the hospital… again. Full concussion.

Bottom line: we definitely put my mother through the wringer.

Weirdly, there were a few times when our Thornton neighborhood seemed almost within reach of the Mayberry reality I'd seen in my new South Holland school. When Pa was over, he could sometimes get parents and kids alike involved in a grand game of baseball. I can also remember a huge game of flashlight tag when even my mom and sister played along with all the other parents and kids. It was great fun running through all the yards at night, dashing behind bushes and throwing ourselves flat on the ground, trying to avoid being caught by the beam of the flashlight. We loved games like that, especially on summer nights: Ghost in the Graveyard; Friday the 13th; pond hockey in the winter. But what made our neighborhood activities truly magical was the forest preserves. On either end of our street, there were two of the largest forest preserves in Cook County. Deer, raccoons, coyotes, skunks, turkey vultures, and other such creatures were common sights right in the middle of our block, and the possibilities for adventure within the woods were enormous.

We took full advantage of our freedom.

Of course, as small children, we were frequently warned to stay out of the woods. My mother and the local cops all warned us that it wasn't safe and that people lived there. Even still, some of the older neighborhood kids would go into the preserve and build forts and tell us what they came across in there. They swore to us that people really were living in huts in the woods.

Context: in the sixties, the nearby Wampum Lake area had been a popular out-of-the-way party location for folks looking to get stoned and have sex, and the whole preserve (just on the south side of Chicago) continued to offer plenty of cover for people on the fringe of society.

We made little ventures into the edges of the forest preserve despite the many warnings. I mean, it was perfect for our army games! We'd patrol the nearby woods daily in our homemade army fatigues, black shoe polish smeared across our faces and hands to camouflage our bodies. We ran through the neighborhood, dodging pretend bullets from our toy semi-automatic weapons, and what a blast we had! We'd run calf-deep in drainage ditches and murky streams of water before diving face-first into those cesspool streams to hide from the other team.

How none of us got leptospirosis or parasites from that icky water is a mystery.

It was when I was in about seventh grade that a group of about seven of us decided to hike from Thornton Woods to South Holland. This was clearly not an adult-sanctioned activity, but we were, as usual, left on our own to run wild and free.

Of course, we donned our army fatigues, and some of the boys painted their faces, and with that, we grabbed our backpacks and stuffed them with food and useful supplies (rope, spray paint, knives... all that jazz).

The preserve was a combination of denser woods and open prairie, with big hills and slopes. We came to a huge ravine, tied our handy rope to trees at the top, and made our way down the steep side.

It was at the bottom of the ravine that we came across manmade huts and crude altars.

Yes, altars.

Now, this should have served as a big fat *TURN BACK NOW* sign, but we'd heard rumors of occult happenings, so this evidence didn't come as a total surprise. One girl in the neighborhood had even had her cat sacrificed. Her parents gave off a weird vibe, so I don't know if there's a chance they were genuinely involved in something dark. Whatever the reason, someone nailed the poor cat's carcass to the front door and rubbed blood on the door. Creepy as hell.

Anyway, I guess this occult presence was part of the intrigue we had, and it was this intrigue that made us determined to go the rest of the way.

We paused to have lunch, and, as we were sitting around talking, eating, and surveying the landscape, we discerned a big man in a white shirt walking around. The boys in the group started getting rowdy and yelling at the man, goofing off and hollering... until we all realized that the large man had a gun in his hand.

Silence.

We hunkered down and zipped it, and without any of us having to say anything, we knew the expedition had come to an end. We shut the hell up and skulked back the way we came as quietly and swiftly as possible... to realize the crazed man was pacing quickly behind us. One by one, we made our way up the ravine, turning around in turn and pulling the other kids up. Once we were safely back in our neighborhood, we reported the fellow to one of the local policemen.

"I told you guys not to go in there. It's not safe," was his response.

Lesson learned. That was the last time we travelled deep into the preserve.

My point? We were a creative bunch of kids when it came to entertainment. "Boredom" didn't exist in our vocabulary. We were an "out the door after waking and home when the streetlights come on" generation. We'd devour dirt by the mouthful in a good game of tackle football, and one summer, we even had the harebrained idea to film a homemade horror movie. (Remember, it was the late eighties, so we thrived off late-night thrillers like *Nightmare on Elm Street, Friday the 13th,* and *Creepshow*.) My mother, always the designated artist, chose to do our makeup and painted our faces to resemble the characters from *Night of the Living Dead*. One neighbor kid came as a zombie army dude, and my *Friday the 13th*-obsessed older brother, David, was, of course, Jason Voorhees. By the end of the day, we were all filthy, sweaty, and in desperate need of a Silkwood shower, but we weren't doing *anything* until we'd watched the recording. It was time to watch the gang from Thornton, Illinois, make movie magic!

Well, needless to say, it was bad. And by bad, I mean horrible. There was no sound, the costumes were terrible, and our acting was horrendous. Nonetheless, it will forever be in my heart as one of the coolest fucking childhood memories I have. We took an average summer day in the eighties and turned it into a horror movie because we could!

Very soon (sooner than I realized), I'd miss those carefree, sun-flecked days of pure, unrestrained childhood, not burdenless or without its shadows, but joyous all the same. Regardless of how fucked up some of my childhood was in hindsight, these memories are tinged in a golden light in my mind's eye, and for those moments when I felt untouchable I will be eternally grateful.

However, the truth was, sadly, that things were about to get rockier as we each coped with our trauma in our separate ways, and, perhaps inevitably, our family dynamic only got more fractured as we grew older and navigated our own paths and pain points.

For now, though, we were kids frolicking in the sun, getting into trouble and clinging onto every morsel of freedom and childhood thrill we could get.

5

Can You Hear Me?

————

NOT ALL OF US WERE able to let loose like this in the years after Dad left, and these next few years only served to further cement the roles that had been passed down to us. And Dawn was no exception to this.

If there was a motherly duty to be done, such as combing my long hair, it fell to Dawn. These motherly acts didn't quite lead to me giving her motherly respect, however. I still pulled typical Annoying Little Sister numbers, like reading her diary and stealing gum from her purse.

Saying that, contrary to this caregiver role, I don't have many memories of Dawn living at home with us as a family. I just remember her train wreck of a revolving door of men that was on a constant rotation in and out of the house. Dawn liked boys to the point where my mother was always shooing them off our front doorstep like stray animals, and Dawn and my mom fought constantly about the boys who came around to see her. Which was no wonder, as Dawn had terrible taste in guys. It ran something along the lines of a sleazeball car salesman trying to sell you a lemon. Her men had one thing on their minds, and I'm pretty sure they accomplished that thing every time.

And so that was pretty much Dawn's life as a teenager. It felt like she spent her days waiting for a guy to deliver her from our den of wolves.

David, meanwhile, struggled hard throughout his childhood and teen years. He grew into an angry, disconnected teen who drank his nights away and became verbally and physically abusive towards me.

These behaviors probably weren't helped by the fact that the dynamic between my father and my two older siblings revolved around them asking for help and my father telling them no—a word that was foreign to me and my younger brother. For some reason, my father was insistent on making Dawn's and David's lives difficult. I think David saw the writing on the wall fast and chose not to engage much with our father until much later in life, and this preferential behavior from my dad was probably the root cause of a lot of the animosity that began to brew between the sibling pod post-crystal ashtray incident. David grew up working, as did all us siblings, but the difference was that while our father would hand money over to us two younger siblings without much care, he'd never dream of volunteering a single cent to David. This more than likely contributed to David's bad temper.

Allow me to illustrate.

One day, in Bratty Little Sister mode, I completely ignored David's request for me to keep my hands off his clothes. He worked a lot as a teenager and would buy nice stuff, and so I loved to fish through his closet, admiring the clothes that hung on the wire coat hangers. I was about fourteen at the time, and my only pocket change was coming from neighborhood babysitting, which didn't amount to much, and my father wasn't in the picture buying his way into my heart during this time. So, I decided to muster the courage to snag one of his argyle navy blue V-neck sweaters.

I looked on point for the early nineties: big baggy sweater, big hair, and tight-rolled jeans. I was cruising the hallways of my freshman year in style that day.

When classes were passing midday, David and I happened to cross paths in the hallway, very unexpectedly. I rarely saw him at school. I was a freshman, and he was a senior doing morning-only classes on a work program, which meant he left at noon each day to go to his job. I'd thought I was going to skate out of this one, but, boy, was I mistaken! He glared at me so hard down the hall that I knew I was going to get the shit kicked out of me when I got home.

And that's exactly what happened.

He came home in such a rage (maybe fueled by alcohol, I'm not too sure) that before I knew what was happening, he already had me pinned up against the wall and thrown right into a mirror that was on my dresser. The glass shattered, and my forearms were all cut up and bruised the next day.

The kicker was my mother's response: "You had it coming."

Okay, maybe I'd had *something* coming for disrespecting his personal space, but what the fuck!

The bottom line is, my home life and family had no boundaries. We did what we wanted, when we wanted, because my mother never taught us what a fucking boundary *was*.

The following day at school, I wore long sleeves to hide what had happened. My girlfriend at the time started to poke fun—"Roll those sleeves up, Felicity"—and as she began to push up my sleeves, she jumped back, eyes wide, as she took in the sliced, tender flesh. Astonished, she demanded to know what had happened, so I told her, and before I knew it, she'd pulled me into my counselor's office and made me tell him everything.

Of course, Social Services were contacted immediately, and my mother and brother had to come up to the school for a meeting. It should have been obvious that my brother's aggression was out of control, but my mom excused it all. "It was just brother–sister stuff. Felicity was provoking him. She had it coming."

Unbelievable.

My mother literally laid the foundation for what the remainder of my high school years looked like.

The truth is, my relationship with my older brother was, and will always be, complicated. Even today, any chance he or his wife has to belittle me and make me feel "lesser than" they take full advantage of. And the dynamic that David and I had growing up set the stage for how I expected to be treated by my first husband.

Yet my mother's bond with David continued to grow, even with all the drunken bullshit he put us through growing up. Piles of vomit on the hallway floor leading to the bathroom? No real blowback from my mom. The cops dropping David off because he was too drunk to drive home? Oh, well, boys will be boys. Tommy and I coming home from grade school to see the Thornton PD raiding our home because David happened to be in the wrong place at the wrong time? Nothing. No matter what he did, my mother always held him in high esteem. And this remained the case later on in life: they'd have coffee and do their bills together on Sunday mornings, and, during the week, he'd come home from work and tell her about his day.

Then again, not all was as it seemed. The funny thing about their relationship was how self-serving it really was. When we were all working adults, he rarely helped our mother out financially like Tommy and I did (even when she really needed the help), nor was he tuned into her emotional needs. "How was your day, Mom?" are words that perhaps never came out of his mouth. Focused entirely inward, he talked about himself and what *he* wanted to do.

And, in the midst of all these shenanigans with David, I was about to traverse a much darker path than that which would probably have been predicted for me during my Catholic school years.

I've thought long and hard about what took me down that road. Were these generational patterns that I didn't have the power (at least at those critical moments) to leap away from? Were my difficult experiences part of a soul contract? Of predetermined karmic lessons I needed in order to grow and learn?

I don't have the answers to these questions, but what I do know is that my life took a pivotal turn at the commencement of my high school years.

High school meant transitioning to public school, and at first, I still had the same core friends from Catholic school, who were doing well academically. I'd also met a cool girl called Alicia in a class, and she, Jenny (another girl I got along with) and I became a threesome. Alicia and her mother lived with her aunt and family during the time I knew her, and they were all very friendly people.

Things were also looking up on the (previously non-existent) romance front. The summer prior to freshman year, I must have grown into my looks a little more, because for the first time ever, I noticed boys checking me out and speaking to me flirtatiously. This was foreign to me, but I soaked up every ounce of it nonetheless, and I soon had someone I called a boyfriend.

Brian and I met in the middle of my freshman year. He was a junior, on the basketball team. He was cute, and smelled *really* good. We'd chat on the phone and hold hands in the hallway. Peak romance.

All couldn't stay amazing forever, though. My mom was incredibly overprotective, and when she found out about Brian, she put her foot down. I assume she was so insistent because Dawn had been a bimbo back in the day and my mom had been a teen mother herself. She didn't want that pattern to repeat with me. So, she went to the extreme and grounded me from seeing him.

We improvised by getting my brother's girlfriends to bring him over to see me and introduce him as their cousin. As if my mother would buy their story! She laughed and replied, "Nice try, girls."

Hellbent on overcoming this obstacle, Brian and I figured out a "safe" time to see one another (immediately after school), and during this precious timeslot, I'd either go to his house or he'd come to mine while my mother was out working.

He was my first kiss, which occurred in my bedroom during one of these afternoons. For that brief moment in my world, I felt like things were in my favor and normal. I was doing okay in school, I had a good friend group, and I had the cutest boyfriend a girl could ask for. What more could I want?

A week or so after my first kiss, I woke up with a mild fever and sore throat. My mother popped me on the sofa to ride it out. Now, historically, my mother had not been very attentive to our health. For instance, my menstrual cycle was horrible all my life, with very intense cramps, heavy flow, diarrhea, and vomiting each cycle. (Little did I know I would be diagnosed with PCOS and premature ovarian syndrome in my late adulthood. Explains a lot!) Because of this, I would miss school each month for a few days, and yet she was always dismissive whenever I complained of my symptoms. So, I'd be left to load myself up on whatever painkiller we had and pray I had sanitary napkins or tampons, because sometimes, she wouldn't buy them after I ran out. Similarly, if we were sick with a fever or other cold symptoms, she would have us ride it out for a few days before calling our pediatrician. And so now, with a fever and sore throat, I lay on the couch for a full week, running a ridiculously high temperature and hardly taking in any food, before she took me in to see Dr. Shapiro.

I'm sure you can guess what I had! Of course, it was mono. That's right—the blood test came back, and I was down for the count with mono for a good four months.

This hit me hard. I slept all the time and hardly had an appetite. Frankly, I don't know if your body ever fully recovers from mono. I still go through a good few days of needing to sleep to recover from life even now.

It was from this point that my life started to pass right by me, and this included my friend group diminishing because my best friend made out with my boyfriend. This didn't surprise me all that much, and besides, some new friends were on the horizon.

I met Nancy late freshman year, although we didn't really begin hanging out until my sophomore year. But as soon as we got close, I suddenly started meeting more and more new people and pulling away from my middle school friends... and partying. Nancy's house was a total party house. Teenagers and young adults hung out there all weekend long, smoking and drinking way too much. Nancy's mom figured that if we were going to party and drink (which was a given), we might as well do all that under her roof, where she could keep something of an eye on our activity. And it wasn't just Nancy's house that was bustling: after my father left and David was in high school, our house maintained the status quo ground zero for friends. This meant that at any given time, my home was filled with really cute teenage boys who were most certainly bad for me. And I loved it!

Of course, my mom saw right through me. My fourteen-year-old self would prance around, showing off. She kept me as far away as possible as much as she could, and, to be honest, I would have done the same in her position: his friends were *rowdy*. No one sold drugs or was in a gang, but they were rough around the edges alright. "Get drunk, screw girls, and get into a fight or two" type dudes. Their presence energized me. They'd flirt with me and tease me. No one ever crossed a boundary (well, without my consent, of course!), but I, a girl who up until that point had never gotten much attention, lapped up every bit of attention I got.

As I write, it wasn't that long ago that I saw a meme with a photo of Lip from *Shameless* (anyone else remember him?!) and a caption underneath saying something like, "It's sad this is the reason why I've spent thousands of dollars on therapy: to *not* date hot men like this." And this made me wonder: why *is* it that historically, us women gravitate toward "bad partners"? That is, men that are emotionally unavailable and "bad news", but have that sense of thrill?

Obviously, there's quite a few schools of thought you could go with here, and I'm not a psychologist, so just humor the insight of a mere devout people-watcher.

The first way we could explain this is by blaming it on a lack of good male role models during our formative years. The second one could just be low self-esteem in general. Or maybe it's more biological. Maybe there's something about the perceived risk, excitement, and danger associated with the "bad boy" archetype that, for some caveman-esque reason, we just can't get enough of.

In the majority of cases, I think this lust or craving comes down to two main causes: us seeking what we already know, and us looking for validation from something that provides a "kick" and instantaneous gratification when we're not getting the validation we need from inside ourselves.

Regardless of the "why" behind this phenomenon, it's pretty crazy when you think about the fact that every single woman I've known has secretly (or not-so-secretly!) desired this type of man at some point in their life. And yours truly was the perfect example of this during her high school years. I had the *biggest* crush on the stereotypical "bad boy". He was your typical rebel child: he'd smoke, ditch class, and generally push the boundaries whenever and however he could. Plus, he was super-hot. Basically, he was everything all us dysfunctional girls were lusting after.

Another perfect example is my father. My dad was the literal "bad boy" template. My mother was the wholesome young woman with lots of potential and the dreams and work ethic to go with it, but her Achilles heel was finding the "bad boy" quality hopelessly attractive. And we all know how that one ended!

I bring this up because this is a recurring theme I've consistently noticed during my work with women. It seems so many of us are still in the cycle of gravitating toward the bad boy, chasing the instantaneous gratification that comes from an impulsive, fiery, reckless fling with someone we *know* is trouble. And while I don't judge where anyone is at in their life or the relationships they seek or create for themselves (we're all on our own respective journeys), I do think it's important to identify any negative patterns such as this and to establish whether this is occurring because of some deep healing work we still need to do. In my (uneducated but experienced!) opinion, we women can often fall into the trap of glamorizing our teenage self and, in turn, making decisions with our "teenage brain", and if that's the case for you, it's important you reacquaint yourself with your adult archetype. I myself have done this with several of my clients, and every time I get a woman who was previously lusting after a "bad boy" successfully "acquainted" with her adult self and ask her what she *now* seeks in a partner, the answer is always radically different to that which she was desiring before. All of a sudden, they go from wanting—*needing*—someone daring, reckless, and changeable, to someone stable, consistent, and loving.

Once this change has occurred, my parting message is always the same: keep that inner teenager in check, and learn to nurture her in ways that *aren't* picking the "bad boy". They always thank me for this later on down the line when they're in a settled, loving relationship, or happily single.

But back to our story.

While I was stepping into my rebellious phase, Dawn was turning a new corner of sorts. She'd met the person who is now her husband of twenty-five years (and counting!), and, thank *God*, he was pretty much a one-eighty from the guys she'd been dragging into our home throughout the years. Dawn and Scott were both working at a fast-food chain restaurant (one that his father happened to own) when they met, and their relationship developed at lightning speed. She moved into his home in the blink of an eye, and then he went off to the police force and she maintained her norm of working management at her local Arby's.

Scott is and was a good guy. He was an athlete and powerlifter, and a big, beefy blond. He had a child from a previous marriage, and I think that prepared them for their own family they ended up having further down the road.

This also meant that even though Dawn certainly continued in her motherly role to us siblings, she was now more like the cool mom. It quickly became the norm for me and Tommy to go to her house, watch the Bulls game, and spend the night. We'd feast on chips and soda and laugh at the jokes Scott would tell us. They were good to both of us, and I absolutely loved going over to their home for weekends away. We could swear while watching scary movies and stay up late listening to the town gossip from Scott's viewpoint as a cop based there. I'd smoke with Dawn and she'd question me about boys and drugs, trying to establish whether I was doing something I shouldn't be.

Even when I began to rock the boat and pull away from everything that a functional teen does (school, friends, work, etc.), Dawn still embraced me, and I loved her for that. I truly believe she knew that our mom was just not giving enough to us, and she tried her best to fill that void.

And the greatest part? The best days with Dawn and Scott were yet to come, when she became pregnant with their first child. Expecting my niece, Heather, was like God offering our family this beautiful gift of second chances.

Not all was sunshine and rainbows, however.

As time went on, I was getting more and more deeply involved with a particular group of teens and young adults, and, together, we'd go to Cherry Hill (a forest preserve right behind the South Holland Oasis) to hang out and drink. I wasn't a huge drinker (never have been), but I tagged along for the socializing. What drew me in most of all was all the new faces. This was a whole different crowd. Maybe not the *best* crowd to hang out with (the majority were stoners), but for whatever reason, this intrigued me more. I wouldn't call them friends, really; I simply coexisted among them all. Nobody was a good friend; they were all just bad influences. It's obvious when looking back now that hanging out with them was most definitely just my way of screaming louder for help, and when my mother still ignored me... well, things only went further south.

Because of this, I'd push the envelope a little farther with every gathering. I started smoking pot with them, even though I was scared to do it and knew it was terribly wrong, as a big "fuck you for not listening to me". Meanwhile, while I was trying to psych myself up to hit a joint, my chums were casually dabbling in ecstasy, acid, and cocaine.

I didn't go there, but it's safe to say it was a rowdy bunch.

It's a shame, really, as we were just wasting our lives away, doing drugs and listening to the Grateful Dead and Phish. A few of them have already passed away during recent years, all at such young ages, and it's heartbreaking to know they didn't break the cycle of disruption.

To top it all off, by this point, school was pretty non-existent for me, and I'd pushed the bar so far that I knew my habitual truancy would catch up to me at some point.

And David was also continuing to spin out of control. He and his friends were wild and constantly drinking, whether at our house or someone else's. And David wasn't a mellow drunk. He was angry. Abusive. On the plus side, though, he had a beautiful, wealthy girlfriend from the other side of the tracks who we *adored*. Tina was family to us, and they dated for quite a long time, even though how David treated Tina was appalling. Even my mother attempted to set him straight when she observed his treatment of her, but, in classic David fashion, he would shut the door on the world and lock himself in his bedroom.

I can only assume that they had good times in between the moments when he talked to her like she was a piece of shit on his shoe, but I never witnessed this for myself.

Regardless, Tina and I became close. We were always palling around doing fun girly stuff, from painting our toes and watching *Sex and the City* to slightly risky daytime excursions, like the time we decided at age eighteen to get tattoos and ended up in a dodgy-ass tattoo parlor with tigers (yes, real tigers) and an alligator in a glass-covered tank in the basement. (Suffice to say we got out of there fast, although not as quickly as we should have!)

She came to pick me up one Saturday morning (we were going into the city to bum around that day) and she popped into David's room before we left (I assumed to say good morning).

She never mentioned to me that she'd just broken up with him.

When she dropped me off that evening, my mother asked "how it went". Her question baffled me—Mom never asked how my day had been—so, of course, my suspicious response was, "Why are you asking?"

That was when she explained to me that Tina had broken up with David.

It sounds silly, but I was heartbroken. I felt like she'd broken up with us, too, and I almost felt angry with her for abandoning me (as I saw it). I mean, wasn't this how relationships were? As a woman, weren't we meant to be beaten emotionally and verbally? Why did Tina think she was better than us?

My awakening was still far, far away. For now, I couldn't understand why she'd walked away from us, and that still-raw abandonment wound my father had inflicted reopened and swallowed me whole.

Later in high school, my dad started coming around more. Often, I'd come home from hanging out with friends to find him sitting on the couch with Mom.

"Oh, me and your mom have just been out to dinner," he'd casually say by way of explanation.

As if *that* was normal.

Maybe there was some intimacy going on. I don't know. As dysfunctional as they both were, they were like magnets: they just couldn't stay away from each other.

But my dad hadn't changed his ways.

My father had, to put it bluntly, zero respect for human life. He treated everyone, including his wife, like garbage. Whenever he picked me up to drop me at a friend's house, I surveyed his creeper van, scanning my surroundings for something that would help me to recognize and connect with him. What I discovered was his glove department box usually homed a gun, which I will assume was loaded.

So much for some father-daughter bonding.

One time, when we were cruising the streets of Riverdale on our way to Halsted Street to get some grub, Pops pulled it out. "Sit tight, Felicity. Is your door locked?" he asked as he placed the weapon on the dash of the van, eyeballing a group of men circling our vehicle.

Not creepy at all.

While he might not have been a good egg for a good chunk of his life, he gave the best advice I've ever received: "Don't loan anyone money unless you're willing to shake 'em down."

My father's path was rugged and sketchy, that's for sure. How he managed to stay alive for as long as he did is beyond me. Funnily enough, though, it was easy to wrap this guy around my little finger. In my high school years, my friends and I would head to his Chicago apartment when we needed some money. Dad was always good for that (he learned he could at least buy some kind of a relationship with me), and I used him for all I could get.

At that point, our relationship just revolved around money. I had checked out emotionally and wasn't a great student, and so if I didn't get what I wanted, I could be a brat. My brothers say I was a real bitch during this time, and I probably was. Anyway, back in the day, pagers were cool, and I learned that if I paged him "911", he'd call back immediately. "Hey, Felicity. What's going on?"

"Dad, I need money."

That was the foundation of our relationship for years: my friends piling into somebody's car and trekking out to the South Side to pick up cash. The funny part is, contrary to what you might expect, we weren't up to anything bad. We'd just use the money to go get fast food or go to the movies.

One Saturday night, we headed out to Daddio's (the nickname we had for my father) for party money to find that he, too, was glammed up and smelling good. My sharp eyes quickly surveyed the room, again attempting to see if I could catch a glimpse of who the hell my father was, when I spotted toys laying around. "What's this?"

"Oh, they're Diane's kids' toys."

"Who the hell is Diane?"

"She's a waitress at Tiger's place."

"Okay, and why are there toys, Dad?"

"Felicity, I'm dating her. The toys belong to her kids." He grinned. "You want a stepmom?"

What the hell? "But you were at *Mom's* just last night."

"She's a waitress where I hang out. She means a lot to me."

"She's looking for an easy ride, Pops, plain and simple, and if you can't see that, you're a fucking idiot." Pause. "But can I get one hundred dollars for tonight? Thanks."

So, that was mine and Dad's relationship. And now, my own version of his sketchy path was about to get sketchier.

One day, I was just coming off another school suspension when my friends Samantha and Grace picked me up for school. I hopped in the car to find they were already stoned. They asked if I wanted any.

"Absolutely!"

I took a hit.

Now, these two girls were beautiful, popular, and "going somewhere", as the school staff would tell my mother. And we were all higher than a kite right before the school bell was due to ring.

We arrived at school and I headed to the dean's office for a slip authorizing my return to classes. I was sitting there, stoned, waiting for the dean to sign my slip, when she noticed my eyes were completely bloodshot.

Oh, fuck.

I bluffed that I'd been crying, but she obviously didn't buy it and proceeded to drill me. I was like a vault and didn't crack, so she asked how I'd got to school. I explained that Samantha and Grace had picked me up, and that was it: before I knew it, both girls were called down, and they spilled the beans.

Everyone's parents were called, and they all made a point of explaining how I was the problem and going nowhere. *These* girls were going places, and *Felicity* was a bad influence. My mom didn't try to sort out the truth; she just agreed with them. It was all on me. "You're not going anywhere, and you're costing me time off work."

While these might sound light lighthearted teenage stories, this was actually a dark time for me. I felt such a deep emptiness, and truly believed I would never amount to anything. So, with no real connections at high school, I just stopped going. I didn't skip to do drugs, however. I'd quit all that after an experience that shook me quite a bit: I was smoking with Deanna, another new friend, when I had my first out-of-body experience. It was literally like my spirit took off to experience a whole new dimension. We were at the house of a girl I didn't know, but she understood exactly what I was going through and guided me through my experience. Maybe she was an angel and this was meant to be. Who knows? Regardless, when in a normal, sober state, I'm able to see everyone's egos—it's all out there, visible to me—so put drugs or alcohol on top of that sort of ability, and it's like throwing kerosene on a fire.

What I felt rocked my foundations enough to prompt me to turn a new leaf.

From then on, I'd ditch school just to hang out with my brother's friends. Amy and I would go watch soaps on TV or go shopping, yet I never felt like I could fully relax during our outings because I knew Amy had a plan (she was working nights at a hospital and was planning to be a paramedic), while I... well, I had no plan. I was flying by the seat of my pants.

What I *did* have was some boyfriends. Once I reached around eighteen, my awkward, gangly appearance did a one-eighty, and the guys who'd tormented me for my looks before that point were suddenly paying an interest. Yet no matter how pretty I was, deep, suicidal thoughts plagued me. I was deeply lonely and depressed.

Maybe that's part of why I turned to sex. I reckon it's not as simple as that, though. I think the main reason for this phase I went through was simply the fact that *I wasn't taught how to be in a relationship,* and certainly not about the importance of boundaries and self-respect. In truth, I had no idea how or why someone should have sex or say "I love you", or what commitment to someone else even looked or felt like. I was raised to be completely feral (to put it bluntly).

Perhaps unsurprisingly, when I finally lost my virginity at the age of seventeen, I did it just to get it over with. In fact, I remember I was really scared. No one had ever discussed with me what intimacy was, what to expect from it, how it would feel, or what I was supposed to do. I was absolutely clueless, and was basing my first experience off of what the guy's expectation of me should be.

Now, writing this as a forty-five-year-old woman, I fully know and understand the sacred bond of sex; how much of an energy exchange it truly is; how important and intimate it is and should be. Fast-forward post-divorce and intense therapy (spoiler alert!), and the adult Felicity (as in, the *real* adult Felicity) understands that a woman's body is a temple to only be shared with someone who respects this sacred bond; that my wisdom and self-worth is built up through myself, and nobody else; that there are and should be sexual boundaries in such a deep-rooted energetic exchange.

But I didn't know this as a teenager. So, for the first decade or so of my adult life, I used sex as a weapon and as a way to boost my self-confidence, and in the process, I allowed men to use and disrespect me. And why? Because I didn't know any better and I had no one to turn to.

Basically, after dropping out of high school, I was just existing. I had no job or parental guidance, but I *was* dating a gorgeous young man that I'd met at a party. He was rich, and I fit his ideal, but in the end, I met a girl at a barbecue and discovered she was dating him, too. So, of course, I moved on.

I hadn't finished my high school degree and I wasn't in college. I had no self-respect or love for myself. I was just hanging out with a bunch of college kids every weekend during my visits to my boyfriend's dorm at his college, a group of boys and girls in one giant bed partying and drinking. They often used ecstasy, which made me feel a little like I was babysitting one big sexcapade for three years.

This life was not moving me forward out of my emptiness, and the only thing I could think of that might was prayer. Throughout those years in Catholic school, prayer had never really meant anything to me, but now, in my college years, I was so fucking lost that I finally started praying in earnest. I was sensing people's emotions all the time and not understanding how to deal with them, I was in debt and felt that I would never dig myself out of that hole, and I had no vision for a hopeful, joyful life. I was drowning in an ocean of desperation, and quickly found myself clinging to prayer like a life support.

6

Tailspins

———

WE ALL NEED SOMETHING IN our world to guide us. For me, prayer got me through some dark times, and later, courage helped me to push through so I could get from where I was as a kid to where I am now.

And I wasn't the only one on a spiritual journey.

In my senior year of high school, around the time when I dropped out, Dad started going to church. He also bought some condos near Mom, one for him and some others for his family members. And, likely due to this new proximity to my dad and us both opening ourselves up to the power of prayer during this tumultuous time, our relationship began to shift. Dad had found God, too, and I had finally started to see hope for myself.

This also meant that, when I was eighteen, I finally looked around at our filthy home, and my self-starter genes kicked into high gear. *If nobody else is going to clean this place, I guess I'll do it,* I thought.

And that was the start of me forging my own path.

As a high school dropout, I finally got fed up with the feeling of going nowhere, and I knew that fixing that lack of a high school diploma was my first hurdle. So, I grabbed hold of the reins of my life and jerked it back onto a path with a future. I called a local junior college to figure out how I could finish my high school degree, requested my transcript from my high school... everything. And, just as I'd promised myself, I enrolled in junior college and finished off the credits I needed in order to complete high school.

Just like that, I had cleared the first hurdle.

I was on a roll, and I immediately signed up for a night class to begin college. Night classes were more comfortable for me: I've always been something of an old soul, more easily connecting to people who are quite a bit older than myself, so the thought of attending daytime classes with a bunch of actual peers overwhelmed me. Plus, I needed a ride, which I could only get from my dad at night. At my house, you learned to drive when you'd saved enough money to buy a car and pay for insurance yourself, and I just wasn't there yet.

The night of my first class, my dad dropped me off, and I distinctly remember thinking, *Here goes nothing.* I was scared to death, crippled by self-doubt and fear over my stepping out of my comfort zone.

And yet the most amazing thing happened in that sociology class: *I enjoyed what I was learning.*

In fact, I fell in love with the subject. And guess what? *I was really good at the work.* In high school, I'd been bored and unattended to, but now, in junior college, I was fascinated by the topics.

I worked my ass off and attained a great GPA in the process.

This proved to be game-changing for my mindset. It was an incredible rebirth experience for me. I quite literally felt like a whole new person. I was focused and determined to make something of myself, and, what's more, my first college instructor really *believed* in me as a student. With my gaze set on an eventual degree in family counseling, I took every psychology and sociology course that he taught. However, I was more than a little embarrassed when I walked into his class: I had really blossomed physically, and every time I entered the classroom, my instructor said, "And here comes Miss America." This comment made me seriously uncomfortable. It still does now, when I think back on it.

Nonetheless, I thought he was a wonderful teacher, and I looked up to him very much.

At one point, he invited me to go on a study program abroad. Excited at the opportunity, I eagerly asked my mom if I could go.

The answer was disappointing but not surprising.

"No. And keep your eye on that man. I don't like him."

She didn't know him, but I had pointed him out on-campus a few times and said that she should meet him. I was so excited that somebody actually believed in me, and yet my mom continued to assert, "I don't like him."

Then came a day when I was sick and missed a test. My instructor asked me to meet him in his office to retake it, and, upon walking into his space, he said, "Felicity, do you see how we all turn our heads when you walk into the classroom?"

He didn't physically step outside boundaries, but his words were like a punch in the gut.

I just took my test, mute, and left. I felt deflated.

Damn, Mom was right.

That was a letdown, but all in all, I knew it was my time to blossom and that I shouldn't let it get me down. School was my job, so I had to learn ways to study effectively—something that I hadn't managed to do in high school. Memorizing details was difficult, but I outlined all the chapters in my textbooks in a way that helped the information to click and stick. I also made new friends; we even studied together. Organized study was a new thing to me (study groups had *not* been a part of my high school experience!), but I learned to write papers and found satisfaction in expressing myself well.

I also took theatre, and the world of the arts was opened up to me as a result. My theatre professor will always hold a place in my heart for this. With my class, I went to see some amazing plays in Chicago (including *Angels in America*), studied Chicago-based playwrights (such as David Mamet), went to Second City, and discovered that I simply loved the arts. I learned about classical music and soaked up the emotion and moods from a host of composers.

At this point in my life, the sky was the limit. It was beautiful. *Could I finally be figuring out that each of us can rewrite their story?*

I also learned that I really did suck at math (and still do), but that that was okay. I was so encouraged by and excited about this new me who was rebuilding who she was and enjoying the schoolwork, the freedom, the responsibility... everything about this new phase of life.

Meanwhile, my dad was going to church regularly and beginning the (long) process of making amends. He volunteered often at his church and helped the Polish-Mexican community there in many ways. He also started coming to Mom's house more—but she had some real long-term animosity towards him, and, at least on the surface, didn't much like having him around. I can still picture my mom sitting in her red chair next to the phone, a cup of coffee in hand, his name on the caller ID and his voice reverberating through the room. "I'm not answering it," she'd mutter as she let the answering machine pick up.

And yet the next thing I knew, he was coming around again and they were going to dinner or she was fixing a meal at the house. It would have killed me if my ex kept turning up like a bad penny the way Dad did, though I really do think he was just trying to set things right. He bought groceries and fixed things around the house (the stuff he didn't do when we were growing up) and routinely asked Mom what she needed, but she'd resist his help and push back. He offered to move her out of that broken-down house, and her response was, "Richard, this is *my* dump." He offered to buy her a new car, and she said, "Richard, I'll get my *own* car."

Besides my mom's constant self-contradiction, things were slowly becoming a little more harmonious. Mom and Dad were at home spending more time together, and I was on a path that was actually *leading* somewhere.

I felt on top of the world.

And then, everything was thrown into a complete tailspin: Pa was diagnosed with lung cancer.

My sister had a very small child at that time, and everyone else in my family had a day job outside the house, so it was basically arranged *for* me that I would be the one to take care of Nan during this time, who was utterly shellshocked. Now, if I had to do it over again, I'd still help her in a heartbeat, but the key detail here is that I wasn't permitted to have my own say in the matter. This meant that when my life (inevitably) changed radically so I could help her, I felt powerless once again. It was as though I had lost my agency overnight. My days had gone from pleasantly busy and challenging to being completely at the whim of others. Daily, I'd be told, "Nan is picking you up, and you're going to the doctor with them," and that would be that—and Nan would sometimes pick me up and say, "You're coming home with me tonight." No questions asked.

Shouldering my allocated role yet again, I began to serve as Nan's travel buddy and advocate. I was like a fly on the wall during doctor appointments, absorbing everything the physicians were telling her. I can only imagine how scared and uncertain she must have felt during this part of her marriage. Nan and Pa were approaching their fiftieth wedding anniversary, and had spent their whole adult lives together.

This routine continued for a good year while my grandfather was ill, and I was constantly back and forth to and from their house, keeping Nan company and helping her in as many ways as I could.

When Pa eventually passed away, Nan was beside herself. She was in her seventies and had never once lived alone, and so after the funeral and a big luncheon at her house, she came to stay with us for a few days.

I was nineteen, and Pa was my first experience with death. In all honesty, I do not recall many of my feelings surrounding his passing. What I do remember is that he was the father figure my dad hadn't been during my critical years. He was the source of so much fun during my childhood. He was also a man of many quirks—he didn't even know his home phone number (he had it written down in his wallet)—and of much selflessness: he was always doing something for somebody to stay busy.

One thing I did learn through his death was *always save voice messages*. Life is too short, and I miss hearing my grandpa's voice, along with the voices of those I have lost since.

I was literally there, beside him, when he crossed over. He endured what felt like a long battle with lung cancer, and, on the morning he passed, I was cruising around my grandparents' house, getting myself ready for the day, when I came to the dining room threshold, right next to my grandmother, and stared in awe as my grandfather was led by what looked like an angel.

It was ethereal.

As with a few of my other spiritual experiences, I was scared to death, and begged my father to come back home with me so I could sleep that night. I was afraid to be alone. Yet the distance of time has given that powerful image of my grandfather passing a feeling of poignancy that will never leave me, and while I may not have understood my spiritual gifts back then, I have since come to a place of understanding that maybe one of my life purposes here is to help people cross over, since there have been a few more times when I have experienced this beautiful moment.

At this point, though, I was still fearful of this gift... yet I could feel these spirits were coming to me for a reason. Did they need to be crossed over? Was it so-called unfinished business?

As a young adult, I shuddered in all-engulfing fear when they came to me.

When my grandmother somewhat recovered from her shock, she (perhaps as a new coping mechanism) jumped into her new routine of taking care of my mother and us young adult kids. This strong front wasn't foolproof, though: Nan always made her way into one of our beds each Saturday night.

Basically, Nan was heartbroken to have lost Pa, and so before I knew it, I was (obviously) picked to move in with her.

In truth, I believe I wasn't given the space to grieve like I should have been, and this was because I was charged with the role of caring for Nan in the throes of her mourning—a decision which, in retrospect, I must be honest and say I don't fully see the necessity of. She was healthy and in her seventies. Sure, she will have needed emotional support while reconciling her new future (one without Pa in it), but I'm not convinced all the sacrifices I made were wholly necessary.

Regardless, for about four or five months after Pa passed, I spent every week with her, still going to class at night, before coming home on the weekends. My grandmother was perfectly capable of caring for herself, but she was very lonely, and so she'd drag me all over the place. The grocery store. The mall. Restaurants. Nanny loved to have lunch out, and honestly, I didn't really mind it. Running around with her kept me busy during the day.

Even still, homesickness was setting in. I missed my normal routine and freedom. I'd met a couple of cute young boys who'd asked me out on study dates, and I couldn't accept because I always had to go straight home with Nan. The one time I said yes, he came to pick me up from

Nan's, and I never saw him again. This made me feel weirdly sick and heavy with embarrassment.

I loved Nan, but I was beginning to find the fact that I was being made to burden the whole load frustrating, to say the least. So, I finally began to complain over my newfound duties. "Why me?" I lamented to my family. "Why can't David or Tommy do it?"

"You just do it," Mom snapped.

Undeterred, I pled with my brothers. "Come on, somebody give me a break." I felt this looming negativity in my life. It seemed like every time the sun began to shine on me, something happened to blot it out and set the storm clouds brewing.

Of course, these pleas got me nowhere... until (and I don't know what the exact catalyst was) I threw a big temper tantrum. "It's not fair! I know she's having a hard time, but I want to be at home!"

After this, I was finally allowed to move back home, at which point I signed up for a full load of college classes. I applied for financial aid, and my father initially covered the rest of the cost. I also got a job. Looking through the local shopper ad paper, I'd found an employment ad for a local kennel, and, reasoning that I liked animals, I thought I'd give it a shot.

Little did I know that this job, which had so casually and unassumingly entered my radar, would mark yet another incredible turning point for me, both personally and professionally.

Clearly, by opening my mind to prayer, being willing to take risks, and understanding that I *deserved* to craft a future that was gratifying and precious, I increased my surface area for serendipity. And this very job was serendipitous indeed.

7

A New Calm and a New Calling

———

NEEDLESS TO SAY, I GOT the job, and my role ended up being about so much more than just working with animals. I learned how to foster relationships with coworkers and clients, and I gained a crazy amount of knowledge about myself and the animals. That first job was an integral part of the growing of the "new me", and it helped me to fully recognize a) how deeply passionate I was about helping others and b) the intensity of my bond with animals.

At this high-end boarding kennel, people brought in their dogs when they were going on vacation, and, as expected from a minimum wage job, I did basic chores like coming in early to let the dogs into the runs, cleaning the kennels, washing toys and bedding, feeding the dogs, and administering medication. While doing these meagre tasks, I really learned how to get in tune with the dogs' energy and help them through their boarding stays. Some were scared to death, and, through my calming energy, I was able to build trust with them and comfort them. Some dogs were just complete assholes, of course, but I learned their vibes as well, learning how to connect with them, respect their space, and calm them down.

I also had the joy of taking care of some outstanding, finely trained dogs during this time. The kennel owner was a miniature poodle breeder, and I often took care of her beautiful show dogs. I was also working at the kennel during 9/11, and some airport security dogs were boarded there. The security agent might call and say, "I need about a week's worth of food packed up. We're going to be at the airport," and we'd have to immediately hop to. It was a tense time, to say the least, but I had the privilege of caring for those highly trained dogs and helping get them ready for their next stint out on duty.

I also learned fast when working with animals that you get a lot of lost souls coming through the door: outcasts, former drug abusers, alcoholics… lots of the same personality types with the same baggage. So many of these character types aren't very social with other people, but make strong empathic connections to animals. It's funny how those of us who fit this description focus all our healing capabilities and intuition on healing the scared stray dog, and yet we find tapping into these same skills to heal our *own* wounds far too challenging.

Regardless of the baggage *I* carried with me, my skills in relating to people and sensing their concerns grew stronger and more refined as I worked in the kennel and, later, in the veterinary industry.

I loved it. I worked there for about four years, and only missed work once because of illness.

What's more, my dad was in the process of buying a new car, and so gave me his old one. Turned out I was earning enough from the kennel job to cover the insurance, and so I (finally!) got my driver's license when I was about twenty-one. Unfortunately, the car only lasted about a year before going kaput, but I remained steadfast in my view that I was succeeding in taking care of myself and growing into adult responsibilities.

I later took on an additional nighttime job to help with expenses, and because the role it intrigued me! If any of our boarders fell ill, we took them to South Holland Animal Clinic (the clinic down the street run by Dr. David Nielson and his staff), and I heard that the clinic needed someone for nighttime kennel help. So, after clearing the second job with my kennel boss, I took the position, which was mostly just cleaning catteries and caring for the hospitalized patients. This didn't quite quench my curiosity, so Dr. Nielson often caught me listening at the door in the lab area as he examined his furry patients, and whenever he sauntered back through the threshold and into his office, I'd scurry away, hoping I wasn't in trouble for eavesdropping. But he never shamed me for this. On the contrary, he encouraged me. He saw my eagerness to learn, and so invited me into the exam room and asked if I'd like to hold the animal being examined.

His technician, Denise, also loved my keen interest, and so I became her shadow, picking up every possible skill and bit of knowledge I could. Denise loved to teach and was really thorough in educating me on how things used to be done back in the day. I learned how to intubate a cat; how to do blood smears; what cancer cells looked like.

I thrived on the new challenges, and the fun atmosphere of Dr. Nielson's clinic certainly helped. He was patient and young, and I suspect he viewed me as somewhat of a daughter figure. That is, until I started working full-time and spreading my wings in earnest. From that point, I got smart *quick*, and was quickly offered a sort of hybrid role whereby I'd work as a tech on the floor for one of my shifts every week so the clinic tech could have a day off.

This was a *massive* step in the right direction, as an understatement, and it marked the beginning of me really starting to not only connect with our clients in a very real and personal way, but to prove that I *did* have the knowledge, skills, and confidence to do this... and to do it well.

I distinctly remember that one day shortly after this promotion, we had a castration and a spay due to take place. I, of course, had my cheat sheets at the ready for all the medication dosages and formulas (I was terrible at math, remember!), and the day went really well... except we soon discovered that the castration was for a stray cat that was absolutely infested with fleas. We gave him an oral cap so we could kill all the pests within a twenty-four-hour window, and we of course hadn't previously informed the owner we were going to do this (we'd only discovered the fleas right before the surgery, once the cat had already been sedated). So, spotting an opportunity, I decided I was going to be the one to communicate this to the owner.

This doesn't sound like a big deal, but it's important owners are informed of any changes of plan with regards their pet and their treatments ASAP. So, it was critical that this was conveyed in the correct way. Some owners don't respond well to such changes in plan, so I knew it was my time to shine. Time to look poised, professional, and competent.

I headed to the waiting room (a pretty small room, by most clinics' standards), where around ten people were sat, and briskly but gently explained, "The castration has been completed successfully, and he is doing very well! We also took the liberty of cleaning his ears and giving him a good claw clipping, and since we also spotted fleas, we went ahead and sprayed him with the fleas."

Suddenly, I noticed that the room was buzzing with polite but barely concealed laughter. I shot a glance at my colleague, who was across the room also trying to keep in her laughter.

"What's so funny?" I called lightheartedly across the room, suddenly nervous.

"Wheezer"—yep, Dory called me "Wheezer"—"you just said you sprayed their cat with fleas!"

"*Oh!*" I burst out laughing. "That's not what I meant. My apologies! This is what we *actually* did..."

Way to go, Wheezy! You had *one* job.

I probably had about two thousand moments like that throughout my time working for the veterinary industry. My words will always be jumbled up in my head because my brain is always on fire, and my mouth just sometimes can't catch up and put things together coherently! It's a good job that I've learned to embrace these moments and just have a giggle at myself. Professionalism isn't perfection, after all!

We also had one dog that we regularly saw at the clinic who was the cutest little red Pomeranian. His owner was one of the smartest women I'd ever met. She was a little older than me, black, and from the south side of Chicago, and from what I can recall, she was super-well-connected and -educated. I massively admired her grace and how she carried herself. She seemed regal, almost.

Her dog, Miles, had developed diabetes, and we'd debriefed her on his new care routine: how she was to administer his insulin, and how critical it was that she came in weekly so he could get his insulin stabilized. Unfortunately, however, Miles ended up developing ketoacidosis, which happens when a diabetic's insulin gets too high and results in ketones in their urine. This often proves fatal, and, when diagnosed in a pet, they should ideally be sent straight to a twenty-four-hour emergency clinic.

Now, we were *not* a twenty-four-hour emergency clinic, but as soon as Dr. Nielson received word of this, it was already a done deal. Miles would remain within our care, and we would do whatever we could to get him to pull through. End of story. (In all fairness, Dr. Nielson lived next door to the clinic, so between me and him, it was a given that we would do everything we could to save Miles.) And so began a routine of me coming into the clinic every three to four hours every single day (with the exception of the evening and nighttime, when Dr. Nielson would take over) to check Miles' glucose and give him the IV fluids he required.

This sounds like fun and games—a big adventure to see whether we can save the glamorous lady's dog—but Dr. Nielson was quick to remind me, "Remember to steel yourself for coming in one day and him not being alive."

I balked at this. Did he not have the same faith that I did?

"Felicity, this is a very serious illness," he pressed on, "so I don't want you to be upset if it turns out he didn't make it through the night okay."

Talk about pressure! But he did have a point. Perhaps I'd approached the whole thing a little too optimistically. Then again, we had everything in order, and Miles was completely set up for survival. I was definitely thinking positively.

That Saturday morning, I let myself into the clinic, as always, greeted the dog and Dr. Nielson (in that order, probably), asked how he had been doing (again, the dog, and then Dr. Nielson), and set about checking his blood glucose, administering his insulin, handfeeding him, taking him out for some exercise, and just generally giving him a lot of TLC (I'm talking about just the dog this time). I never just came in, completed the checks, and left; I'd spend some real quality time with Miles, chatting to him, walking with him, and relaxing with him for a good hour or two.

I was committed to my job. And, of course, I loved animals. So, it was a no-brainer to go this extra mile(s. Ha). In my heart, I knew this was the only "right" way to go about my job and use the trust this little guy's owner had put in me.

So, what was the end result?

I'm so thrilled to say Miles survived the weekend and beyond. And so, it was official: I had "passed" my first intense case with flying colors! I was well on my way to proving myself and my abilities, and I was just getting started.

Sometimes, though, the course of action we needed to take with an animal wasn't always immediately obvious. One evening, an older man came in with a large carrier housing a twelve-year-old cat. Once he got to the examination room, he plopped the carrier onto the table and said, "I want to euthanize my cat, and I don't want to be present for the moment."

With that, he signed the paperwork, paid for the procedure, and left.

Now, it is a broad but rather accurate stereotype that in the veterinary industry, we all have pretty soft hearts (especially when it comes to our furry friends), and so this entire experience left me utterly stupefied. How could he just plonk his pet of twelve years on a table, sign his death warrant, and leave without a glance behind the shoulder? I felt equal parts heartbroken and incensed. And the grim reality was that we now had a job to do, and so Dr. Nielson and I proceeded to pull this thirty-pound cat from his tiny carrier (which, as you can imagine, was a whole ordeal in and of itself. The carrier was *way* too small for such a large animal). By the time we finally got him out (Dr. Nielson physically grabbed onto the cat while I pulled the carrier), I found myself faced with a *beautiful* white-and-gray tabby cat that, besides being a little pissed at being wiggled out of a teeny tiny carrier, looked... perfectly fine.

He sat sagely on the exam room table as we completed all the routine checks and came to a very definite conclusion: there was absolutely nothing wrong with him. Well, besides the fact that he was most certainly obese (which, unfortunately, isn't uncommon for house cats).

I looked up at Dr. Nielson. He was already looking at me, and, judging by his expression, he was just as conflicted as I was.

I addressed the elephant—sorry, cat—in the room. "Are you going to do this?" I asked. "There's *nothing* wrong with this cat. The owner just clearly doesn't want it."

I don't know this for sure, but I can most certainly imagine that there are *thousands* of clinics out there who've faced this exact same situation many times over. Which is so fucked up, because *legally*, as soon as the owner has signed that paperwork and handed over the fee, we're obliged to provide the requested service. No ifs, ands, or buts. Yet as Dr. Nielson and I met each other's gazes and looked back down at the gorgeous tabby before us, I think we both knew we just couldn't do it. Euthanasia is of course usually offered as an ethical service, and is there to end unnecessary suffering, yet was there realistically any way we could provide *this* service ethically? Sure, paperwork had been signed, but I think we'd have both felt as though we were exploiting our positions and power if we'd gone through with it. Not to mention the fact that, as empathetic animal lovers, it would have been absolutely soul-destroying to do.

So, it was arranged that Kid would move downstairs into the basement with all the other stray cats. Not the most ideal of situations for the poor thing, but he'd be alive and breathing and well looked after, and in that moment, that was all that mattered.

Well, it didn't take long for me to completely fall head over heels for Kid. But there was a problem: he was so morbidly obese that he was physically unable to defecate. This meant we had to put him on a weight loss diet, administer IV fluids and a stool softener, and perform enemas.

Despite this rigorous (and invasive) treatment schedule, Kid's temperament remained one of the loveliest I've ever seen in a cat, and he gradually intermingled with the other cats in the basement. Yet it seemed Kid was too far gone. Our weekly rounds of IV fluids and stool softener soon didn't cut it, and we began having to administer these treatments once every two days.

I believe that by doing all of this and being as attentive as possible, we ended up increasing Kid's lifespan by a good couple of months or so, but the little weight he lost just wasn't enough. When you're overweight to a point where you can't defecate or engage in normal physical activity, there's not much more you can do.

So, we spent as much time with him as we could as we forlornly waited for the inevitable.

In the end, Kid became jaundiced and experienced liver failure, and so by that point, we made the very painful but necessary decision to euthanize him so he didn't need to be in pain or distress more than needed. The whole team had gotten incredibly close to and invested in him and his health journey, and so this was very difficult on all of us. He was so beautiful and sweet-tempered, and I think we all struggled to process it for a while.

Kid was put to sleep in the company of the team—the people who had loved and cared for him for the past several months. The ashes were spread in Dr. Nielson's backyard.

I share these stories to show just how varied and challenging some of the situations we were faced with were, and to really demonstrate how I was able to develop my professional skills so quickly. This was no standard admin job. This was constant high-stakes problem solving, meaning you had to bring your A-game all the time.

When I wasn't working my two jobs or going to college, I cleaned the house from top to bottom, lit a fragrant candle, and maybe added a plugin air freshener... or hung out with my dad. Things between us had suddenly started to click on an even deeper, more honest level. He loved the blues, and my siblings, friends and I would go hang out with him and my uncle at the Chicago blues bars—Legends, Kingston Mines, wherever. During these nights, we'd all have fun drinking, laughing, enjoying the music, and feeling like we were living life to the fullest. Dad always called if he had tickets to the local concerts Buddy Guy hosted every January at Legends—which he always did, what with January being his birthday month. We saw some awesome shows together during these excursions:

Joe Cocker, The Rolling Stones (a few times), The Fabulous Thunderbirds, Koko Taylor, and Buddy Guy himself!

Dad also called when he had tickets to the Chicago Bulls games, and *that* was when they were in their heyday! Scottie Pippen, Michael Jordan, Dennis Rodman... the works.

We went to a *lot* of Bulls games. It was heady; standing room only. Dad would always get a drink (I'd have some pop or water), they'd turn out the lights, and all of us screaming, excited fans would be sandwiched together so densely you wouldn't have been able to hear a gunshot next to you. We had so much fun, my liquored-up dad gawking at women all the while, and the drive home always scared the shit out of me. I know he wasn't overly drunk, but we did weave in the lane enough times to make me grip the edge of my seat in panic! The Chicago Stadium Club, located on the second floor of the United Center, was a members-only restaurant bar, and during one of the Bulls playoff games, we found ourselves roaming the floor that housed the Stadium Club when we were approached by a crowd of people. As we entered this crush, I was in awe of a few of the celebrities that I was casually brushing shoulders with.

We were squeezed together, body to body and barely moving, when the hostess of the club approached us to compliment me on my looks. She suggested I work at the Stadium Club because I was so beautiful. She was probably just making conversation with the people stuck in front of her post, but either way, my overprotective father shut that down in the blink of an eye. He may have been willing to help me in any way that I needed, but, much like my mom, he was privy to mistrust and fear of the unknown, which meant that between the two of them, they would have allowed a whole lot of opportunities to pass me by purely due to their own fear, if they'd had it their way.

Dad still helped me out financially around this time so I could pursue some of my positive goals, though, and it was that financial help that marked the beginning of a more sincere relationship between us. He offered to help with paying off my college tuition, making a car down payment, and paying off my debt.

Funnily, that debt payoff really pissed off my mother. I'd hate to say she wanted to see me struggle, but I do believe she was jealous that my father was helping me when he'd shortchanged and harmed her so much in the past.

I also think part of it was the fact that I actually stood a chance of achieving something.

"Richard, why are you doing that?" she'd demand whenever he offered me some more help. "Let *her* figure it out."

Whenever I was proud of a project or success in class and I shared it, she'd knock me down for it. Her bitterness just wouldn't allow her to be supportive or to celebrate my successes.

Still, I was making big moves. While working these two jobs, I finished my associate's degree at junior college and had my eyes set on a BA in psychology from a four-year university. Chicago had so many great college options, and I fell in love with the brownstones and ivy leagues at DePaul University, but predictably, my mom shut down the idea of me going into the city for my university studies, even though I was *already* in the city with girlfriends every spare weekend. She was deeply afraid for me. Now, when fears and anxieties surface for me or my clients, I ask the question, "Do I own these, or were they handed down to me?" and I sort of wish I'd asked myself this at the time. But instead, I caved and enrolled at Purdue University Northwest, just across the border in Hammond, Indiana.

It was during my time at Purdue that a professor, Megan, finally picked up on my previously unknown learning disabilities. She said, "Something is going on with your brain." I struggled to process her simple directions, and this had clearly flagged something for her, so she reached out to have me perform a slew of tests.

After some investigation (and to my surprise), it was revealed that I had an auditory processing disorder and dyslexia.

All this time, these conditions had been part of my academic struggles. All this time, I'd been made to feel incapable, not good enough, and lazy when my brain just worked a little differently. Throughout my young academic career, I'd been labeled "the girl who's not going anywhere", and it had taken *years* of skating through classes and getting into college for someone to be attentive enough to me as a student to identify these struggles.

I was awash with relief, encouragement, and validation. The professor said that all things considered, I'd learned to compensate for these struggles pretty well, but you do what you gotta do, right?

It felt so good to put a name to some of my issues and to be offered solutions.

Encouraged by this revelation, my goal was a degree in marriage and family therapy (I'd ditched the psychology idea), so I took classes on that degree track two days a week, from eight-thirty in the morning to about three or four in the afternoon.

By this time, I'd left the kennel over a disagreement with my boss (I'd worked there for around four years by this point), but I was still holding down two jobs. On my non-class days, I was working full-time as a dog groomer and at the animal clinic. I was going strong, and felt invincible. And the animal clinic has recently brought to our family a very... *unexpected* gift.

I was working at the reception of the Dr. Nielson's clinic one day when I young South Holland cop walked in cradling a twelve-pound, blue-nosed Pitbull puppy. The officer's expression was urgent and pained, and he immediately launched into an explanation. "I've been passing this puppy in the street for the past two weeks. She's been chained up in a backyard, and look how tiny and sweet she is!" He held her up so I could get a full look.

She was cute, alright. Maybe even the cutest thing I'd ever seen. And I'd seen a *lot* of cuteness during my time at the clinic.

"I never *once* saw her be given any food," the officer continued, "and when I went to enquire with the owner, she couldn't care less. So, I took her. Will you guys take her from me and find her a home?"

This guy was one of my favorite kinds of people.

Just by looking at her from where I was sitting behind the reception desk, I could tell she was unwell.

Of course, we took her in and immediately performed a physical exam. We also tested her for canine parvovirus (basically a really serious virus that's fatal to dogs in the vast majority of cases), for which she (heartbreakingly) tested positive. We immediately put her in isolation, which, in our case, was in the basement, with the cats. (Parvo is highly contagious from dog to dog, but cats can't contract it.) From this point, we had to maintain a *super*-strict hygiene regiment. Of course, hygiene is of number one priority in a place like a clinic anyway, but we were now handling a dog with parvo *and* other dogs throughout the day, so we had to be sure we were using all manners of cleaning products (including bleach) constantly so that the other dogs who were not immunized against parvo wouldn't contract it from us.

That's not to say that caring for this little baby was an inconvenience. On the contrary, she was the sweetest little thing in the world, and was afraid of her own shadow. And we quickly got into the rhythm of things: I'd go down to the basement in the morning to see to her, and as soon as she heard me, she'd dart behind the garbage cans in fear, she was so accustomed to being nervous. We forged on with the treatment for the parvo, however, and she seemed to be recovering well. It isn't uncommon for sufferers of parvo to experience lots of vomiting and (very) bloody diarrhea, but she wasn't doing so bad.

Within a matter of weeks, she began bouncing back *fast*, and before we knew it, she was able to exercise in Dr. Nielson's backyard when the weather was good with no problem whatsoever. You could see the backyard from one of the windows in the reception, and it wasn't uncommon for me to glance outside while I was working the desk and find her sitting there right under the window, watching me with her beautiful, big blue-gray puppy eyes. For some reason, this adoring look reminded me of Forrest Gump and how he'd always say, "Jenny, I always love you!" so we ended up naming her Gennie (with a "G" so that it was clearly connected to "Gump". I don't really know. The logic made sense in my head at the time), or "Gen-Gen".

In short, the clinic now had its own puppy, and my God, was she the cutest. She was absolutely crazy and super-playful, but still maintained that really sweet and placid temperament. We just adored absolutely everything about her. Our lunch breaks quickly became the absolute best: we closed the clinic from noon to 3PM to account for any surgeries, and so this became Gennie's playtime, when she was *really* let loose. She'd zoom around the clinic, a bottomless supply of boundless energy, and we'd play ball with her in the backyard and chase her around the place. I was spending a healthy chunk of my money on toys, collars, and leashes. I was absolutely hooked. It was puppy love!

Naturally, within a very short space of time, I developed one goal: get Dr. Nielson (and my mom) to agree to let me take her home. I'd already been permitted Chessie, a chocolate brown domestic shorthair cat that someone had rescued off Cal-Sag River, a couple of years before (my mom had, very firmly, said no, but I'd snuck her in anyway and pulled this off for a good week before she even noticed), so now, it was Mission Gennie. But I'd have to be clever about it. I was *not* ballsing this one up. Gennie would be mine, end of. She needed a good home, and I couldn't let her go to just *anybody*.

And I had a plan to make that happen. Sort of.

I'd fallen into a routine of sorts during the weekend where I'd pop into the clinic, let Gennie out of her cage, and play with her for a while (I felt *extremely* guilty just leaving her there all weekend, with no interaction), and one such weekend, I decided I was going to try to sneak her home. Just so she could spend the weekend with us rather than being in the clinic alone. No big deal.

Now, it's worth noting at this point that during this time, we already had two Shih Tzus and two cats (Chessie being one of them), so while it might sound crazy for anybody to *ever* think they could just "sneak in" a whole-ass Pitbull puppy (who was next-level energetic, at that), I kind of reasoned I'd be able to sort of... hide her in plain sight. You know, like I did with Chessie.

So, it was the Friday evening of the weekend that I decided I'd chance bringing her home, and, according to plan, Gennie was strapped in the passenger seat of my car, her big pink puppy tongue lolling around and her tail whipping back and forth in excitement.

"Here we go, Gen-Gen! You're going to be spending the weekend with me!" I chirped.

I opened the passenger door, watched with pride as she excitedly hopped out and immediately set about exploring my front yard... and then, I froze. My mom was standing at the front door, arms folded, slowly shaking her head.

Shit, fuck, shit.

Okay, be calm.

"Hi, Mom!" I trilled. "How are you? This is Gennie, the stray puppy that I've been taking care of! Isn't she cute?"

Not a crack of a smile.

"Felicity, you have *got* to be kidding me."

"This is just for the weekend, Mom!" I interjected. "I'm busy! I've got some big projects for school! So I'm not going to have the time to run back and forth and look after her. It'll easier if she just... hangs out with us! *And* I know the dogs will love her."

I craned my head so I could see past my mom and into the house (Gennie had trotted inside by now, oblivious to the chaos around her), and I could see her sniffing an unimpressed Sofia. Meanwhile, Henry was on the sofa growling, and the cats were backed up into a corner, hissing.

Fabulous.

My mom sighed. "Only this *one weekend*. Do you understand? It's a *Pitbull*. Do you know how aggressive they can be?"

"Mom, are you *serious*? She's five months old. Does she *look* aggressive?"

We both looked over at her at the same time. She was on her back, her legs wide open and tail wagging. The rest of the animals were giving her the side-eye, but she was blissfully oblivious, in her element.

That same night, when Tommy got home from work (he was in the process of shopping for a house for him and his soon-to-be wife), he absolutely melted when he saw Gennie. And I mean *melted*. "Who is *this*!" he exclaimed with the biggest, dopiest smile on his face.

"This is that puppy I was telling you about," I said, pridefully. "Her name is Gennie."

Tommy was on all fours and Gennie was hellbent on licking every inch of his face. "Her name is *Gennie*?" he said in between licks.

"I named her after *Forrest Gump*."

"Okay..." He continued cooing over her for a moment. "How old is she?"

"Five months old."

"Does she have a home?"

"No. We're having a hard time adopting her out. We just want to make sure we have the right person."

His eyes instantly lit up. "Well, Wheezy, if you can't find anybody, I'll take her."

"Tommy, you haven't found a home yet!" my mom burst out. "And she's *not* living here with us."

"That's okay, Mom," I responded. "She can stay at the clinic. I'm sure Dr. Nielson won't mind."

This wasn't the truth, obviously. Dr. Nielson wanted her to find a home sooner or later. Yet I knew I couldn't realistically force a dog on her, and she was right about Tommy: he *didn't* have a home yet, and after what Gennie had been through, I knew she needed stability and a solid home environment.

The following day, Dawn, Scott, and my nieces and nephews came over (we had somewhat of a tradition where most Saturdays, Dawn would come over with the kids and we'd make homemade pizzas and gab about anything and everything), and the second they all laid eyes on Gennie, there was a simultaneous gasp and exclamation of, "Who's *this*!"

"This is the puppy I was telling you about. Gennie. She's the one that needs a home. But Tommy's just said he's interested in her, so she can stay in the family forever now!"

I knew Mom was in earshot (I'd admittedly said this to provoke her), and she instantly shot back from the kitchen, "She's *not* staying here!"

Well, long story short, Scott fell head over heels for her (are you seeing a running theme with everyone who met her?), and within minutes, he was chilling on Mom's recliner with a cup of coffee in one hand and a big old puppy on his lap gazing up at him adoringly. This was the cutest image in the world, and it was made even cuter by the fact that Scott was a former powerlifter (so a pretty big dude) yet was just completely besotted with this puppy he'd met minutes before. And, of course, all of this was occurring in front of the kids, and so it didn't take long for the wheedling to begin. *"Mom, Dad, why don't we take Gennie home and keep her until Tommy finds a house?"*

I reckon that even before the kids asked this, the seed had already been well and truly planted the second they'd seen Gennie. Some discussions were had, and it was agreed among us that Dawn and Scott would care for Gennie until Tommy found a house.

Pretty much instantly, it was a done deal. I of course informed Dr. Nielson the following Monday, and he was beyond thrilled that Gennie was going to stay local with someone we knew would care for her how she deserved to be.

And that was how Gen-Gen entered our family unit. She proceeded to live a long, healthy life, and was adored by the whole family. At the end of her fourteen years on this earth, Tommy and Joan decided to euthanize her (she had reached a point of being really quite frail, not being able to control her bowels, and just generally having a lot of a lower quality of life), and so I arranged a friend to do this at home for us. Yet she still managed to be graceful and full of personality during her final moments. I adored that dog so very much, and even now, I can still see her sitting outside the reception window at Dr. Nielson's clinic, staring up at me.

The students and the atmosphere at Purdue were quite serious, but I handled myself well. I was growing academically.

Then again, not all what perfect.

Socially and emotionally, I really wasn't where a young twenty-something-year-old should be. I wasn't dating, and I had just one or two close girlfriends. Which, looking back now, definitely wasn't the worst of problems to have, but I definitely felt a keen sense of loneliness and FOMO.

As for work, the clinic was the more challenging of the two jobs. I enjoyed the grooming position and the family I worked for, and the money was good, but I was beginning to lose interest and steam with my decided college degree and was deeply needing a change of scene. I'd always been creative (I'd been designing on a dime *way* before HGTV made it popular), and one of the professional groomers I worked with went to an interior design school... which got me thinking.

After some careful consideration and reflection, I began to research interior design programs in the Chicago area, and came across two: Harrington College of Design in the city, and Joliet Junior College.

I chose JJC, and this time, this wasn't because of my mother's fears. The associate's program was honestly no different than that at Harrington, and it was half the cost.

With the decision made to begin at the JJC design school in the upcoming fall, I dropped the rest of my Purdue classes mid-term and began working full-time.

Looking back (even knowing how burnt out I was), this was perhaps not the brightest decision, but then again, I had no one guiding me and received only judgment and ridicule from my family once word got out.

Then, a receptionist position opened up at the vet clinic, and when I saw this, I immediately put in my notice with my other employer. I was craving the veterinary world, wanting to absorb anything and everything about it.

Little did I know that working full-time at Dr. Nielson's would make me grow tremendously and hold a special place in my heart for a lifetime.

Here, I learned how to foster good relationships between the doctor and his clients; how to calculate meds (yes, the girl who seriously sucks at math was able to calculate med dosages fast!); how to compensate for my shortfalls as a whole. I continued using cheat sheets of med calculations (everything and anything to back up my brain) and was interacting with representatives from all kinds of industries, from pharmaceuticals to pet food to lab, and I established a twenty-two-year friendship with some of them as I moved from clinic to clinic over the years. I even pondered crossing over to the other side and getting into sales.

Meanwhile, Denise was still teaching me everything I wanted to know. She loved to teach, and I soaked it all up. She often commented on my photographic memory (something I taught myself over the years during my college studies), and I also learned that I could handle emergencies really well, relishing the rush of adrenalin that accompanied them.

Multitasking also became my master skill or "trademark", if you will, and it was also while working in the clinic that I started to open my creative brain. Always thinking outside the box, I became a problem solver, and would much later down the road consult on the side for clinics that were struggling in certain areas. For now, to drum up business for Dr. Nielson's slowly dying practice, I got on the phone with inactive clients, touching base and trying to re-establish connections. My brain was on fire, offering solutions to a variety of problems, and while the vet tech was not always open to my ideas and often shut me down, the doc occasionally followed up on them, and this was encouragement enough.

One of my creative ideas was to redo the reception area, and Dr. Nielson gave me free rein. So, I spent a Thanksgiving weekend scrubbing down the entire area and patching holes in, sanding, and repainting the walls. It was when I had the job nearly complete that I was looking for nails to hang up pictures. I really didn't like bothering Doc in his living space on the weekends, but we needed to be ready to open back up in the morning, so I hesitantly knocked on his door and cracked it open.

"Dr. Nielson, do you have any more nails for me?"

"Felicity, can you come in here?" came the call from his bedroom.

Ugh. This creeped me out. His reputation as a ladies' man and the constant revolving door of lady friends during the weekends had me a bit uneasy as I approached his bedroom door.

At first glance, I just saw the older man stripped down to his underwear. *Fuck, really? Why me?*

Then, I realized he was soaking wet, with one of his feet turned around backwards.

Panic flooded my body.

"Dr. Nielson, what happened?" I gasped.

It turned out he'd been power washing the gutters when he fell off the roof and dragged himself into the building. He'd been lying there for about three hours. Thank God I'd needed to bother him for nails! I called 911, got him some shorts, and put his yellow lab, Chelsea, in the kennel.

And this was the beginning of the clinic's collapse.

The clinic proceeded to decline over the years, and as time went by in the clinic, it became clearer and clearer that I was going to soon be forced to make a very difficult decision. However, it seems serendipity was looking out for me again: a good client of ours happened to work in the visual design department of Marshall Field, and one day, she mentioned to me that they were looking to add additional designers for a multitude of stores. *Nice!* An opportunity was striking, and I was super-grateful.

Now, to weigh my options: did I work for Marshall Field and get my foot in the industry that I loved, or did I find a bigger clinic that offered benefits? I was nearing the age when I would be dropped from my father's insurance, so I had some major adult decision making to do. And I knew, deep down, what that decision needed to be.

Making the decision to leave Dr. Nielson's was hard. I loved him and the staff, and they'll always be family to me, but I needed that steady income, and I *really* needed some benefits. So, I made the practical decision to work for a four-to-five veterinarian practice down the other side of the street in a neighboring town—the place my mother used to take our pets to when I was little.

Working for four docs was challenging at first. Dr. Stockton had a hopping clinic and an even bigger team. I was fortunate enough to swoop right in and become friendly with all of my coworkers, however, and this is where I really maximized on my brilliant multitasking skills, juggling multiple phone calls with a variety of questions and needs while checking a rush of people with their animals in and out. Dr. Stockton's practical, humane, and ethical approach to medicine also met all my expectations, and his love and kindness to us employees led me to cherish this wonderful doctor, employer, and family man.

Dr. Stockton was the first employer I ever had who was truly invested in his employees. He wanted us to grow, and I do believe that he saw me as a bright, young, professional woman who was eager not to disappoint. He taught me all about his concierge approach, which I loved, and when I saw the white-glove service he desired, I took the ball and ran with it. I was full of suggestions on how to cater to our clients, and Dr. Stockton and his practice manager, Kerry, always approved my ideas and had me train the other receptionists.

One thing that I can say has *always* been a top skill of mine is dealing with people, and I only honed this skill further during my time working at Dr. Stockton's clinic. I was in my twenties, and was able to instantly build a rapport with clients with my big smile and high vibration. This definitely made my job immensely easier every single day. And when you're in a client-facing role (regardless of the industry), you learn how to deescalate tense situations with pissed off people *quick*. It's basically a job requirement if you're not going to fall flat on your face on day one on the job. There are a lot of people out there who are going to come to you already spoiling for a fight, after all, and that's not something I'll massively judge someone for: you could've just lost your job; a parent may be unwell; money may be tight... whatever. I get it. Even still, you better get your "diffusing hat" on if you're going to sit at the front desk for any company, because *whew*, some people can be difficult.

One good thing about the veterinary industry, however (and I learned this very fast), is that the people who are usually the hardest to deal with are usually just the people who care about their pets the most. They're the people whose pets are basically their children, and *this* is something I get completely. One such client had a dog who'd been unwell for a while, and so had regular appointments with one of the doctors in our clinic. This client was fantastic—a friendly guy, and clearly someone who utterly doted on their pet—though we suspected he was not one hundred percent mentally fit.

I was moments away from opening the clinic one morning (this will have been around 7:30AM) when, from where I was sitting, I suddenly heard an incessant pounding on the clinic door. My heart dropped to my ass—*What the fuck is going on?*—and I immediately sprang up to investigate. I hurried to the side door and looked through the peephole, and there was the client, in visible distress, crying hysterically.

I was instantly seized by both relief and wariness, relief because I now at least had a rough idea of what I'd be dealing with (fear of the unknown is more terrifying than any prospective situation I could've been faced with), wariness because this client was prone to such displays of emotion and I was alone in the clinic.

I opened the door and said, "Mr. Harrison! What's going on?"

Still sobbing, he screamed (yes, screamed), *"You killed her! You killed her!"*

I froze. *What the fuck...?*

Naturally, I was pretty caught off guard and intimidated by this guy at the doorstep who was screaming bloody murder (literally), but, emboldened with the knowledge the rest of my colleagues would be arriving in five to ten minutes, I propped the door open and entered emergency mode. "Let me help bring her in," I said briskly (he had the dog in question—the one I'd apparently murdered—with him), and we did exactly that. I'd brought a blanket from my childhood with me to the clinic that day (don't laugh), so I quickly fetched that, and we each took one end of the blanket and hauled the big, beautiful, and, yes, dead-looking, husky into the clinic. Once she was safely inside, I either texted or called the rest of the team (I can't remember which) with an SOS, asking for anyone who could be here fast to come immediately. I then put my phone down and immediately sat down with the client, who was still on a bit of a rampage. He was just repeating the words, *"You killed her! You killed her!"* over and over, rocking in place slightly.

One thing I'd learned by this point in my career was that when people were like this (i.e., hysterical and beside themselves with panic), they were just looking for empathy, solidarity, and to be listened to, and so that's exactly what I offered.

"Mr. Harrison, I am so sorry that this has happened. She was such a wonderful dog. I know your heart must be hurting, but trust me when I say that she's been in good hands the entire time she's been in our care, and that this was *not* done intentionally."

I paused. He gazed emptily at me, suddenly blank and silent.

"Mr. Harrison, the rest of the staff is going to be here in a matter of moments. For now, what can I do to help you?"

He just curled up on the corner bench and sobbed.

My heart broke a little in this moment, and I stood with him, silent and pensive, until I heard the door swing open. *I'm saved!* A bit harsh, maybe, but I hadn't exactly been expecting this the moment I'd arrived at the clinic at dawn.

One thing's for sure: my days spent working in Dr. Stockton's clinic and the lessons learned along the way really allowed me to tap into the cheerleader in me. I was a natural leader and automatically operated at a high vibration, and so I was efficient and brisk but personable in my approach. I loved nothing more than gearing the whole team up at the beginning of the day for an amazing shift, or opening team meetings and helping everyone get organized and maximize on their productivity, or helping everyone with their admin tasks and getting all their ducks in a row.

While times weren't always easy and there were of course always unexpected situations to deal with, the overall energy of the place was unbeatable. The goal was to put smiles on our clients' faces, meet everyone's (reasonable) wants and desires, and take care of every single animal that fell under our care to the very best of our ability. And they were definitely goals I could get on board with.

Looking back now, I can also see that my specific role within the practice (customer concierge) taught me more than any other role could have, and the growth that I underwent during that time formed the very roots of what it is that I do today. Within my role, I was taught (by Dr. Stockton) to deliver an unparalleled level of care to the patient that allowed me to build a real personal connection to them and their situation.

Of course, nothing was *perfect* within the clinic, myself included (it's a given that things are going to slip through the cracks sometimes), but overall, there was a culture of support within the team, and we didn't browbeat one another for sometimes dropping the ball. Instead, we always championed one another and worked as one collective unit, and would do whatever was necessary to stand by our colleagues. Yes, even if it wasn't in our job description. Because who gives a shit about something as arbitrary as a list of job expectations in your contract when there's an animal who's tapping out in the middle of emergency surgery, or when you suddenly need an urgent restock? Nah. You club together when the shit hits the fan, regardless of what that entails. End of.

This also meant that whenever I heard the words, "That's not in my job description," later on in my career, I'd circle back and be sure to make it a teaching moment. A team is only as strong as its weakest link, after all, and if you have someone who won't play ball in the midst of a cry for support, then they don't have a place here. Harsh? Maybe. Fair? I think so.

Importantly, I learned that *clients notice the behind-the-scenes shit*, good and bad. You might think that clients don't have a clue of what goes on in the background ninety-nine percent of the time, and in a literal sense, that's probably true (assuming you're doing your job well and maintaining a professional front), but clients still very much so pick up on the *vibe* of a cohesive, strong team, even if they can't put that vibe into words. If you work as a team and genuinely have your colleagues' backs, clients will not only come back time and time again, but they will also refer others to you. Facts.

Something else that really furthered my work skills at this time was the bonus incentive the clinic frequently ran, which definitely got us to push noticeably harder and get more clients coming to us. This was particularly the case during the spring and early summer, since in those months, it was custom for pharmaceutical companies to run incentives and thus for our schedules to be packed. These incentives were accordingly a *huge* morale-booster.

I was always on top of my game during these months (and during the rest of the year, of course, but this period especially was *super-*motivating), and one spring, the incentive we were running was around heartworm, flea, and tick prevention (that is, selling as much as possible to our existing clients). In one of our daily meetings, we decided we were going to track who was the top seller so we could really incentivize everyone.

Game on. You can really see my self-starter streak kicking in here!

One Thursday during this incentive, I had a client come in who was a regular and an all-round really nice guy. He had three or four (*very* big) dogs, and, naturally, the goal of the incentive was to ensure every client went home with everything they'd need to make sure their pet remained well taken care of (read: heartworm, flea, and tick prevention).

As it happened, we had just the day before received a bulky shipment of the stuff (a week's worth, to be specific), and so I was thrilled to be seeing this regular client here, since I knew he prioritized keeping his dogs up to date on all their vaccinations (including for heartworm). In other words, this was a prime opportunity to kick ass at our incentive. So, of course, I swooped *right* in there!

"Good morning, guys!" (He'd brought his wife to the appointment.) "How are you doing today?"

Meanwhile, the dogs were running around my feet, tails wagging and loving life.

"Hi, Felicity!" the wife responded. "They're all doing great! We're here for routine vaccines and a growth on one of our baby's legs…"

"Oh, boy, let's get that checked today too, then! When did you notice that? Has it increased in size?…"

You get the picture.

Fast forward to after this extremely riveting conversation about the dog's growth, and I was right in there. "By the way, all three pets are due for heartworm tests, and they're overdue for their heartworm, flea, and tick medication, too. The good news is, we happen to have this *awesome* promotion going on where if you purchase three boxes of the medication, you receive a hundred-dollar visa gift card to use anywhere. So, you'd *actually* save six hundred dollars if you bought a box of treatment for each pet today! You guys could use that for a nice dinner out, right?"

The wife giggled.

Fucking *bingo*.

"Absolutely, Felicity. Let's go ahead and get that while we're here, and we'll come back next week with Cooper"—the dog they'd left at home—"and get him up to date, too."

"That sounds terrific, ma'am. But to make it even easier for you, I can add Cooper's treatment to today's invoice for a bigger discount and just hold it until next week? How does that sound for you?"

"Sounds good to me, Felicity."

I was wasted in the veterinary industry. I could've been on fucking *Wall Street* at this rate.

"Perfect! I'll get all that sorted for you now. Dr. Dina will be in shortly. Would you like any coffee or water while you're waiting?"

Booyah.

The conclusion? I sold ten thousand dollars' worth of heartworm, flea, and tick prevention *just that day, and* I cleaned out all the inventory that we'd received just the day before in the process. It was a crazy amount of fun (yes, I'm serious). I *loved* the challenge, and, most importantly, I was building a deeper and more trusting relationship with our clients.

Later on in my career, still on a role, I went on to win the clinic prize *and* the pharmaceutical reps price, which is no small feat.

For this particular incentive, I'm pretty sure I won some sort of Alexa or Google Home, though clearly, it was the challenge and experience I valued the most in the end.

Basically, I was absolutely *thriving* in my workplace, and one of many of the *incredibly* important lessons I learned during this time was to *never* turn a client away if you wanted to maintain a positive relationship with them. This is Sales 101, and we followed this rule as though our very careers depended on it. It was a given that you'd do your utmost to immediately get them in, and if it wasn't an emergency, you'd get them in the following day. End of.

Obviously, it wasn't always easy to do this. It was, for example, a common occurrence for somebody to call up and insist their pet needed same-day treatment for, say, an ear infection, but when pressed further, they'd concede the pet had already been suffering from this for several weeks. So, do you turn them away, or book them in anyway and overload your staff? As luck would have it, it was always on days when we were beyond chock-full that we'd get calls like this (chock-full being when every appointment slot is taken, you've got a shitload of surgeries lined up, it's fifteen minutes until closing time, and you still have a waiting room full of patients to get to). Stressful, for sure, but there's still a right way (and a very wrong way) to handle this. In the moment, it seems fair to tell the client chewing your ear off at the other end of the line about Scrappy's horrible ear infection that you'll "get him in later this week, ma'am!" and it was always a big *yikes* moment whenever I overhead this. Remember that empathy and communication are chief in this industry, so no matter how sweetly you deliver this message, you'll ultimately be invalidating the owner's concern. A big nope.

The correct response? "Oh, Mrs. Johnson, I'm *so* sorry to hear that Scrappy has a horrible ear infection! Let me see what we can do. Now, we *do* have a waiting room full of people, so you're looking at maybe another hour before you get out, but of course we'd be happy to squeeze him in." (Let's be real, it's a quick ear swab and some medications. Is it technically an emergency? No. But is it *really* the end of the world to spend an extra five minutes overtime sticking a swab in the poor thing's ear for the peace of mind of his owner? Hell no. Pick your battles, people.) "How else is Scrappy feeling, Mrs. Johnson? Is there any diarrhea? Lethargy? How is Scrappy's appetite?" (If all this comes back normal, then press on with...) "That's great to hear, Mrs. Johnson! Let's go ahead and get him in for tomorrow morning. That way, you'll have the full amount of time to speak with the doctor and address anything else that comes up from now until tomorrow. If you would like, can we even keep Scrappy here for the day and give him a complementary bath?"

Do you see the difference here? Sure, we have some brown-nosing going on, but the bottom line is that you're getting the same result (not seeing the client immediately) *and* the client is leaving the conversation feeling *very* different. This open-ended approach to customer service is a winner every time, trust me. And I became a fucking *rockstar* at this—and, in a way, I came to really love it.

As I juggled a full-time clinic job and part-time design school for a substantial period, the designer in me began to flourish. I fell in love with my textiles class, and professors pulled me aside to compliment my talent and remark on how naturally creative I was. However, I struggled with the architectural ruler, and my kitchen and bath professor recognized my dyslexia immediately. She pulled a chair next to me every week to help me adjust my floor plans.

Who'd have thought dyslexia would also make reading a *ruler* a challenge?

I still suck at measurements, but I slowly started to map out a future in design. *Maybe this is my true calling?*

Whenever I came home full of excitement, my family responded, "Let's see how long this lasts." And maybe they were right: I have had a long history of inconsistent and bad decisions, but on the flipside, I'd also never received any guidance or support, and so I always did my best to make the right decisions with the limited support I had.

I don't wish to imply things were generally bad with my family at this time, though. On the contrary, we were at this point in the middle of a pretty long period (about six or seven years) where, oddly, I remember feeling as though we were suddenly a normal, functioning family. We were all young adults (as in, me and my siblings) and going about our "normal" lives: all of us were working (and I was balancing that with school), and Dawn was by this point married with two young children. Perhaps most strangely, my mom had transformed into the textbook grandmotherly matriarch who lived for her grandkids, which was a far cry from the mom I'd grown up with who'd had no problem with giving us a good slap if we "disrespected" her in some way.

I soaked up as much of this as possible while I noticed it was ongoing. Whenever we weren't working, we were with each other. As I've said, Dawn always came over on Saturday nights (when Scott was working) with the kids, and Sundays always involved a big family meal. I treasured these weekends massively, since it meant I got bonding time with my niece and nephew. It was during one of these weekends that I taught Heather how to ride a bike without training wheels, and on another Saturday, my nephew snuggled up with me while we watched scary movies and stayed there the whole night because he was too freaked out to go to bed alone. What's more, my mom would hand-design and -craft costumes for Dawn's kids (and trust me, they were *awesome* costumes), and whenever the kids were on school break and that break happened to coincide with my schedule, we'd all go to the beach, where me or Tommy would take the kids to the arcade, go-karting, or the mall— whatever we were feeling.

When I say we "all" used to go out and do these things, that doesn't include David. Truth be told, he was a grade-A dick during this time, and while *I* knew this was nothing out of the ordinary, it seemed that everyone else was only just realizing this. One time, Heather was riding her bike down Nan's super-long driveway, right near David's new BMW Z3 convertible, and long story short, she lost control of the bike at one point and fell against David's car, leaving a six-inch (ish) scratch in her wake.

A big inconvenience? Yes. The end of the world? No.

Even though she was only a little girl, Heather was *fully* aware of what David was like (kids see everything), and so she instantly knew she was in the shit.

And boy, did she panic.

Mom was meanwhile in the kitchen washing the dishes, and Heather, white as a ghost and trembling, ran inside and whispered to my mom what had happened, clearly already scared out of her wits at the thought of David finding out.

What happened next I'll never forget.

When David found out what had happened (I can't quite remember whether my mom told him or whether he just discovered it for himself), he went outside (to look at the scratch), came back in, and began *yelling* at Heather. And I mean yelling.

This was a seven-year-old little girl.

One good thing did come from this, however: David's girlfriend at the time, who watched this entire ordeal unfold, was so appalled that she punched him in the arm, *hard* (though maybe not as hard as he deserved), and called him as asshole.

I mean, yeah.

So, other than my brother's Davidisms, this was all round a pretty harmonious time for me in my life. This is a simple memory (and maybe a lot of people's "normal" during their young adulthood), but there was one time where I came home from work to find Nan cooking and feeding the animals with the Food Network on in the background. She asked how my day had gone and whether I wanted a cup of coffee, and from there, I slid my gym shoes off, curled up in my big chair, and drank my coffee with her while we caught up about anything and everything. This sounds so "nothingness", and maybe even a little silly to document or remember, but after the chaos that had been my upbringing, it was moments like these that really felt the most healing for me. I felt completely safe, heard, and at peace during evenings like this, and if I could have stretched those evenings into eternity, I would have. There's nothing more homely or comforting than walking in from work to smell something warm and delicious cooking and to be given the simple courtesy of being asked about your day. It's the little things that count.

What's more, this sense of comfort, normalcy, and peace carried right on into the holidays during these precious years. This felt like the biggest blessing in the world to me, since the Christmases of my childhood had largely felt pretty bleak and empty. It was as though this wholesome time of year just put a floodlight on how *not* wholesome and how *fractured* we actually were as a family unit. We always got lots of gifts thanks to Dad and his… *alternative* sources of income, but there was never that cohesive family vibe I now associate with the festive period.

Christmases (and Thanksgivings) during my young adulthood were a different story entirely. By my twenties, I had very much so tapped into my self-starter skills (as we have established), and so I was always raring to go to help my mom with prep. I'd head into the grocery store with my insanely long list and grab everything we could possibly need, and the night before Thanksgiving, I'd help my mom with food prep, including cooking one of two of our turkeys, pulling it apart, and popping it in a foil pan ready to be reheated with some extra turkey stock the following day. (We were a big-ass family with big-ass appetites, so yes, the two turkeys were a must.) On the day, my mom would make the pumpkin pie and stuffing (a job we all agreed only she could do. Nobody made pork stuffing like Momma did!) while the rest of us would be allocated our own individual jobs.

Again, this may sound simple, and maybe most people grew up as part of this kind of system, but to me, this was peak happiness: working as part of a team with my family. No tension; just working together to make a beautiful meal.

Throw in the fact that (as we have discussed) my mom was a ridiculously talented florist and so always decked the place with flowers, and the image is complete. She'd frame the front door, paned window, and French door with fresh greens, and she'd make the most astounding big velvet bows. We'd also wind fairy lights around the outside of the house and the bushes in our front yard. We also always had ten (yes, *ten*) Christmas trees (all of varying sizes), which meant once we sat back on Thanksgiving day, our stomachs bursting and a little tipsy, we'd look around us to find this beautiful festive wonderland of fairy lights and trees and flowers.

Pretty damn magical.

Mom and I would begin arranging all of this from right after Halloween, since there was so much to do in the few weeks before then and Thanksgiving, and it was always so, so worth it. The home would transform from something cramped and tired-looking to a true fantasy wilderness.

And, of course, this image was always made complete when Christmas day came around and there were mounds of presents beneath (one of) the tree(s). I'd always spoil my mom at Christmas. It was my way of showing my love and appreciation when I felt I couldn't do so through words. Maybe this was something I learned from my father! And, of course, the actual unwrapping was always great fun. I remember Tommy (who was probably about six foot one and two hundred and fifty pounds at the time) once opening a gift and holding it up for us all to see, and we all immediately fell into hysterics. It was a pair of tan, elastic-waist Alfred Dunner slacks.

"Gee, Mom, thanks!" he said feebly.

This made me laugh even harder. He didn't have the heart to say, "Eurgh! No way am I wearing these!" as (fairly or unfairly) I probably would have done.

I looked over at Mom, and she audibly gasped. "Oh, no, those are for Nan!" She burst out laughing. "*This* one's for you. I must have mis-tagged it. Sorry!"

You may be wondering if David at least joined in *these* festivities, but, fortunately (or unfortunately?), he didn't. During all these shenanigans, David would still be in bed, and for a significant portion of the day, he'd refuse to engage with us in any way, shape, or form as a family.

Not wanting him to miss out, Mom would lay his gifts next to his bed and leave him to it.

Not even this could dull the shine of our Christmases, however. I'm aware this is clichéd, but it truly is a magical time of year. It is a season that can make you feel so deeply comforted and *happy*, even if it's just for a short time. No feeling comes close to curling up on the sofa with a cup of eggnog and a Christmas film, the tree lit and the people you love around you.

With that said, for me personally, this feeling of peace and warmth and love was always inevitably interrupted by a firm knock back to reality via my job. Don't get me wrong, I *adored* everything (well, almost everything!) to do with my role in the veterinary industry, but one major drawback was definitely the fact that working the holidays was part and parcel of the role. And believe me when I say there's nothing more jarring than going from fairy-lit nights of Christmas movies and laughter to bleak, frosty, pitch-black Midwest winter mornings spent driving to the site of an endless slew of post-holiday emergencies: "Hi, it's Mr. Jenkins. Brutus just ate an entire pumpkin pie and has been vomiting non-stop... Can I get him in?"

Regardless of these (unwelcome but necessary) interruptions, I will always associate the holiday season of these years with a very real spiritual happiness and contentedness.

Basically, during these years, I was extremely busy with work and school, surrounded by people nearly every moment of the day, and I was oddly content with my family life. Yet I was lonely—something that will leave the most powerful, capable, and promising of people very vulnerable.

And it was then that I met Dan.

PART II
THE STRUGGLE

8

Hey, Baby

———

I WAS TWENTY-EIGHT WHEN I met Dan.

I'd wrapped up another long but fulfilling day at the vet practice, happy to have a fun night out booked into my calendar. It was early March, and a chilly but beautiful day in Chicago.

Dressed up in my favorite black cowl neck sweater, Gap jeans, and chunky-heeled, black, knee-high boots, I joined Tommy, his girlfriend, and one of his close friends at the comedy club. There, we laughed at the irreverent comedian's take on natural disasters, politics, religion, cannibalism, etc. (the full list of taboo topics) until our sides hurt... but the personal vibe was a little weird. Was this a double date? Or was it not? Would I even *want* to date my little brother's friend? He was fun and sweet and nice, and it was true that I was so lonely that I ached deep inside, but he was Tommy's *friend*.

After the show, Joan (Tommy's girlfriend) asked if I wanted to join them for drinks at Teaser's Pub. Apparently, a bunch of people were getting together to celebrate an old friend's birthday. Normally, I would have made my excuses and headed home. It was a Friday night, but every night was a work or school night for me due to my full-time employment at the clinic and part-time studies in the interior design program. Plus, as a twenty-eight-year-old still living at home, I was also worn down by my mother constantly keeping tabs on my companions: "Who are you going out with? I thought you were better than that." Maybe she was trying to protect me, but those kinds of comments generally burst my bubble and led to me just staying home. Which wasn't any huge loss to me. I'd had my fill of late nights as a wild teenager!

And yet to everyone's surprise on this chilly Friday evening (not least my own), I said, "Sure, why not?"

We were all kicking back a few, relaxed, loud, and joking around, when, in the middle of the boisterous gang, I noticed someone I'd never met before. He wasn't my type exactly. He had thick, bristly, curly hair that he kept super-short, a goatee, small blue eyes, glasses, a Tom Cruise nose, and broad shoulders, and he was tall. But *wow*, was he funny!

I leaned into Joan and asked, "Who *is* this guy?"

Apparently, he worked as an electrician and was neighbors with Jimmy, who worked with Scott and Tommy at the railroad. Neither Tommy nor Joan knew him very well, but he was buddies with our birthday friend, too.

I was intrigued, and so I directed many of my wisecracks at him... and he responded in kind. This back-and-forth continued over the next several hours. He was smart, sassy, witty... everything that I was. I had a blast hanging out with him, and finally rolled in back home at around four in the morning. I had to be at work at seven-thirty. I hadn't done this in *years*, but it didn't matter. I was giddy. I'd *met* somebody!

A mere few hours later, I was eagerly sharing all the juicy details with my girlfriends at work. I was all butterflies. Turned out this guy, Dan, had managed to get my number from my brother, and so I received a call from him the following Monday night. We chatted for hours, throwing one-liners back and forth to one another as we had done a few nights before, enquiring about one another's likes and dislikes.

It felt amazing.

And yet.

In among all the excitement and butterflies, the banter and back-and-forth, speaking to him felt... rushed. I could literally feel him pacing up and down his room through the phone, and something about our conversations felt harried, as though we were against a ticking time bomb. Eventually, I had to ask, "What are you doing? You sound like you keep pacing."

And he was. Turned out he paced for three hours that night.

Weird? I think so. But I was in the realm of butterflies, and couldn't have cared less that he physically paced back and forth for three solid hours. My head was in the clouds.

But I wasn't the only one with a certain gut feeling. Mark, one of my coworkers who was just a couple of years younger than me, pointedly said to me, "Don't settle. You look really excited, but you're beautiful. Don't settle." Right then, one of our regular clients came in—an attractive young professional just about my age. As he left, Mark said, "See! It's right in front of your face. If you were to ask him, he'd go out with you right now. Don't settle."

But it was too late. I was hooked like a drug addict. My fix was dopamine, and it felt *amazing*.

Very quickly, Dan and I went on our first date, which he had planned meticulously. He took me into the city on a Sunday and as we strolled through the museums, I gazed deeply into his eyes. *Who is this person?* I wondered. He seemed to have come out of nowhere.

We ended our first date with a hug in my driveway—a far cry from the girl who used to have sex with her boyfriend in that very same driveway!

Meanwhile, my family had assumed their usual posts. My mother and David took to judging, while Tommy stayed quiet. My family (with the exception of Tommy) were always flabbergasted if I spent time with newcomers, and they immediately set to judging. "Who is this loser?" they asked thornily.

Basically, Dan had no chance of survival in my family. We were brutal—and yes, I do mean *we*, because I was groomed into that role, too. Indeed, meeting Dan shone a spotlight on how obviously I played my part in the circus show my family performed each time someone new dared to enter our ring. Even still, I tried my best to "untrain" myself in this respect. I'd respond to their sneers with, "*I* thought he was nice. He was polite. He held the door open for me. He was considerate of my feelings. He made me laugh." True, he *did* drink an awful lot, but didn't all the guys I knew?

One date led to another, and then another... and my mom began to question me. "What's going on here, Felicity? What do you see in this kid, anyways?"

Dopamine. Dopamine, dopamine, dopamine.

A few weeks into our blossoming relationship, I went to the gynecologist for a regular checkup. I answered the routine questions as per usual: "Yes, I'm sexually active. Yes, I'm taking birth control. Yes, I've been on some antibiotics. Yes, I'll do a pregnancy test just to be certain."

When it came back negative, I didn't think about it again.

One thing about Chicago is that the weather in April seriously sucks. It's cold, rainy, and dreary. So it's not exactly uncommon to be a little depressed during this time of year, especially since April typically follows what feels like a very long winter.

It was in the April after Dan and I had met that I began to notice a dark, shadowy side to him that was quiet, withdrawn, and not up to doing much. I dismissed it as a small bout of depression characteristic for the time of year.

The truth is, I was oblivious to how far-reaching this side to Dan actually was. I was still riding on some of the aftereffects of dopamine at this point.

The truth is, I am a fixer—an empath—and we fixers naturally gravitate to every stray animal and person that needs fixing and love them passionately, when the reality is, we don't need to rescue everyone and everything around us. As a matter of fact, it's unhealthy for us to do so emotionally, physically, and spiritually.

In line with this train of thought, I often questioned my deeper intent with regards my gravitation towards Dan. Was it my loneliness? I mean, yeah. Did I deep down inside want to heal him? One hundred percent. I felt this from the get-go. Plus, the proof is in the pudding: when he was blue, I'd swoop right in trying to make him feel better.

What's even more unsettling about this is that at the time, I still really didn't know how to handle my super-spiritual powers (and yes, I do mean that literally. They're incredibly strong). Now, I can tap into someone's vibe and actively decide whether I want to heal or pull away, but back then, I was a sponge for all things breaking and broken, and people in need of healing were leeches sucking the life out of me.

So, naturally, at this point in my life, I became the conduit to everyone else's problems, which (surprise, surprise) ended up wrecking severe havoc on my nervous system and body later down the road.

What's more, as I got in deeper with Dan, I began to see more and more of the effects of his drinking. If his friends were over, they'd see him hit his sloppy drunk stage and quickly make their excuses and leave; he'd come home after a night out with our friends and pass right out; he'd drink until he was puking all over the bathroom or peeing in the corner of the bedroom.

Not subtle warning signs at all.

Of course, my girlfriends were like a broken record at this point: "You'd better think about this." "Get out while you can!" Yet I *didn't want to be alone,* and this meant I didn't want to walk away, even with all his messy, gross, drunken behaviors. I was just so excited to finally have somebody who loved me and who I could love back. Plus, sober Dan was *super*-kind and considerate. He just drank like my brothers and the guys I grew up with. Nothing out of the ordinary or to be worried about.

As the April days ticked by, the weather gradually perked up, and I noticed I kept getting cramps like I was going to cycle. I vividly remember complaining to my girlfriends at work about this. "I just wish my period would come already!"

But it didn't.

That following Sunday, I mentioned this to Dan, and to my surprise, he didn't seem even a little bit concerned. I, on the other hand, was shitting my pants at the *what-if*s. I kept trying to rationalize my symptoms in my head, trying and trying to come up with a logical explanation that negated the obvious conclusion. After all, hadn't I *just* had a negative pregnancy result three weeks before?

Clearly noticing my growing concern, Dan went out right away and purchased two pregnancy tests. I'd never done an at-home pregnancy test before, and as I took the boxes from him, my stomach was swimming with nausea and nerves. *What if I am?*

I shut his dirty bathroom door.

I peed on the stick.

I waited.

And the test read POSITIVE.

I was instantly seized by near-crippling fear. *I'm not prepared for this.*

When I finally emerged from the bathroom, Dan was standing there, curious.

My heart was pounding.

"It's positive. I'm pregnant."

I wanted to vomit as I spat out those words.

But Dan? Dan was literally unfazed. In fact, he was crazy-excited.

This was it. This was happening.

I'd finally found someone to love. I was in a good place with my education and my career. And now, I was pregnant.

So why did this feel so, so wrong?

On the car ride home that night, I called my best friend, Ginny, and shared the news.

She was speechless, and when she finally mustered the words to speak, she sputtered, "Oh, shit. What's your *mom* going to say?"

Never mind that. I knew I wasn't going to tackle that conversation just yet.

I called Joan next.

"Okay, well, babies aren't a bad thing. We'll get you through this!"

A pause.

"Your world is going to change, Felicity. You are keeping it, right?"

"Absolutely. Why wouldn't I?"

And it was true. I was keeping the baby. But that didn't mean that all I wanted wasn't to just curl up on my sofa and try to wrap my head around all of this; to breathe; to process.

But that had to wait. I had a busy Monday at the clinic ahead of me.

As I walked through the employee entrance, Ginny was there, and she instantly threw her arms around me. "Everything will be okay."

Suddenly, all this felt good and real. She was a single mom, so I felt supported.

When I told my boss, Kristi, her mouth dropped open. "Felicity, when I saw you the other day and we joked about you being preggo, I just

128 Pieces of Me

knew you actually were!"

These conversations might have been easy, but I knew the worst was yet to come. Eventually, I'd have to spill the beans to my parents.

I had some big talks ahead of me. The terrified little girl inside me squirmed with uncertainty.

I went back to my gynecologist that week, and, sure enough, he confirmed the pregnancy. "You knew! Instinctively, you knew you were pregnant when you were here earlier! It was just too soon to tell."

With this confirmation under my belt and time ticking, I knew I had to tell someone in my family. So, I called my sister Dawn on her birthday, April 25. After wishing her well, I said, "You're going to be an aunt!"

Silence.

"Wait, what? Felicity..."

Boy, I was two for two on these phone calls.

She resumed her silence on the other end before saying, "Well, babies aren't a mistake." There was a gleam of hope in her voice, which was somewhat encouraging.

I tackled the conversation with my dad next, and, to my immense relief, he responded with nothing but excitement. But my relief instantly dissipated with the words, "Did you tell Erin yet?"

Everybody knew that was going to be a rough one.

I even told my main boss, Dr. Stockton, before broaching the subject with my mom. And to be fair, his response helped to prepare me for my mother. He had invested so much into all of us employees that he probably felt like we were his very own flesh-and-blood children, and that he therefore had the right to react like a parent would.

At the end of a hectic day, I told him I was pregnant.

He stared at me. "Are you certain, Felicity?"

When I replied, "Yes," he hung his head, slumped his shoulders, and silently turned his back.

He was finished with me.

My heart broke, and to this day, it still hurts. He really believed in me and valued who I was, like a father with his daughter, and I was shaken to the core as he walked away. This felt like a whole new level of rejection. In fact, my inner child would ache for years over this, all the way until the point where I was ready to consciously do the repair work.

I have often wondered what he would think if we crossed paths today. Deep down inside, I know he would be proud of the woman that I eventually grew into. For now, though, I mourned my bond with Dr. Stockton. This was a really, really hard pill to swallow.

And there were still more people to tell.

Dan and I decided to break the news to his mom on Mother's Day with a *Happy Mother's Day, Grandma* card. Thankfully, Sherry was beyond thrilled at the news... or so it seemed. As soon as she got the chance to talk to me alone, she quite literally cornered me. "How's Dan handling this? How's his drinking?"

Baffled by her questions and refusing to admit (to her *and* to myself) that her son had a problem, I responded, "Oh, he's fine!" Sensing her uncertainty, I added, "Sherry, I wouldn't *be* here if his drinking was out of control."

Something of a half-truth. He wasn't fine, but his drinking wasn't out of *control*. Yet.

I was still living at home, but I somehow still delayed the conversation with my mother for as long as I possibly could. Our house had one bathroom with only a tub (no shower) and I obviously couldn't take baths while pregnant, which meant the only way I could now wash myself was by getting in, rinsing off at the faucet, and stepping right back out.

Of course, considering I'd always been partial to long soaks in the bath, my mom started noticing something was off pretty quickly. "Wow, that was fast," she'd comment, a slight frown on her face.

And then, the morning sickness arrived.

With the arrival of this impossible-to-mask symptom, I knew the time had come for the hardest talk.

My mom was lying on the sofa mid-week after work, and I took a spot in the big comfy chair next to her, pensively studying her.

She looked at me and said, "What do you have to tell me?"

My mouth was dry. "I'm pregnant."

She stared back at me.

"When are you moving out?"

My heart broke.

"Do you have anything else to say?"

Silence.

I got up and started packing.

9
Family?

I WAS PREGNANT, AND MY mom had kicked me out of the house. I was scared to death and isolated, and felt like I had no one to turn to except Dan.

It still feels like I'm interfering with an open wound whenever I think back to this time. I ended up feeling lonely and injured during the entire pregnancy, which was most definitely kickstarted by the moment when my mom kicked me out the house and turned her back on me. My mom had always done a great job of making me feel rejected, and this was no exception. As a matter of fact, this felt like the culmination of all her disappointment in me.

Whenever I thought about this too much, the pain felt almost debilitating. So, I tried not to.

And then there was Dan, who immediately took me in and said, "I want to ask you to marry me."

Textbook.

The pregnancy had happened so fast, my whole world was in freefall, my heart was hurting terribly, and I really had no clue if I wanted to marry

Dan or not.

My would-be sister-in-law reminded me, "You don't *have* to marry him," but then what else was I supposed to do?

I was vulnerable, afraid, and felt horribly alone. I didn't know what else to do.

And yet it *just didn't feel right.*

My mind was spinning, but, ever-so-graciously, Dan took the decision right out of my hands and went to my father to ask for my hand in marriage. Out of order, I fully realize, but I also know he was doing what he perceived to be the right thing.

My father said yes while the other half of my family judged silently, and, practically overnight, my fate was sealed. As though we were still living in the nineteenth century, or something.

This made me feel very, very uneasy, and this wasn't helped by the fact that with every passing day, I was seeing more and more of Drunk Dan. The truth was, I wasn't so sure that I wanted to be with him at all, never mind *marry* him. And yet my inner child was waiting my parents to guide me; to save me; to put me on their lap and tell me everything would be okay.

And did I get this at the time? No.

And I loved him. I still *do* love parts of him.

I was thoroughly, thoroughly confused, but I felt like I had nowhere to go. So, I accepted Dan's proposal. I put on a happy face, and we had an engagement party—which my mother, of course, boycotted. Another punch to the gut.

Suffice to say, this was a really rough start to the pregnancy.

The icing on the cake? Dan was one messy, messy man. He lived like a pig in filth. Of course, I swiftly came in and began nesting, trying to make his dirty little Cape Cod bachelor pad into some kind of home. *My* home. A home for our child. While he'd taken the news of my pregnancy very gracefully, Dan was accustomed to being on his own without a care in the world. Add to this the fact that he'd bought the home we were now living in when he was nineteen years old and fresh out of trade school, and he felt entirely validated in the opinion that dropping beer cans all around the house was not only acceptable, but his *right*.

Basically, I felt robbed of the joy that typically surrounds a woman having a baby, let alone her first, and my mother's harsh, narcissistic personality was the main culprit for this. She may have reacted in this way because she was terrified at the thought of having to relive her own hardships through me, and I can now find some understanding for that, but back then, the pain from the abandonment was real, and would continue to resurface much later down the road. For now, this was manifesting in the form of binge eating and trauma-based relationships.

As for my grandmother, she shamed me like I was her own daughter, embedding the deep roots of generational trauma that were already lying dormant within my soul's very map.

Thank God for Sherry, Dawn, and Joan, who all rallied around and helped me through my challenging pregnancy and preparation for the baby's arrival. Dawn constantly checked in on me, doing her best to mother me even as she tended to her own two young children. All through those long months, when a precious baby was growing inside of me and I couldn't share those moments with my mom, Dawn was there to selflessly wrap her arms around me (physically and psychologically). It also helped that her own little kids were impatiently waiting for their baby cousin's arrival. Their excitement made it feel like the special event that it was.

During my first trimester, Dan came down with what I assumed to be a stomach bug. I was maybe eight weeks pregnant. He was up all night with sickness and diarrhea, and in typical man fashion, he dragged his worn-out body to work regardless. Later that week, his symptoms were waxing and waning, and the doctors thought he must have experienced some food poisoning.

The following Friday night, he came home from work in an even worse condition but refused to go to the ER, so I gave him a bucket and slept on the sofa.

I was scheduled to work the next morning, so upon waking, I called his mother to come keep an eye on Dan.

Thank God I listened to my gut.

At around 10AM that morning, when at the clinic, I received a call from Sherry. She'd found Dan unresponsive, and he'd been rushed to the emergency room. Infectious specialists worked with him and performed a spinal tap, which revealed that he was suffering from non-infectious meningitis.

This was just the beginning of many trauma-based moments that, perhaps counterintuitively, kept the lifeline of our marriage lifeline going as our codependence grew.

This episode and my mom's behavior aside, my first trimester was overall pretty good, with nothing but a little bit of nausea. However, as my pregnancy progressed and I continued to work on my feet all day, I began to develop complications. This led to me being put on hydrochlorothiazide for gestational hypertension during my second trimester. High blood pressure is something I'm still trying to kick; maybe I'm wound too tightly!

Then, my pregnancy took an even more decided turn for the worse. During Labor Day weekend, my legs were completely swollen, and I went into the hospital. It looked like the onset of preeclampsia, and so I was instructed to keep my feet up as much as possible. All the scares!

On September 21, 2007, when I was around five months pregnant, Dan and I got married. This took the form of a small wedding ceremony witnessed by his mom, dad, sister, brother, and my father. My siblings joined us for a quiet dinner celebration that evening at a nice restaurant, and afterwards, Dan and I enjoyed a weekend of rest and relaxation in Galena, Illinois. All the glamor!

Meanwhile, I was still working at the clinic, but they were modifying my job to help me out. I went from being on my feet for thirteen to fourteen hours a day, five days a week, to sitting in a chair for that period of time. They rolled out the red carpet for this pregnant gal!

It was during this period that something particularly stressful occurred at work. We were just about to close the clinic when a client walked into the reception after having his appointment. I don't quite remember the client's pet. I want to say it was a cat, but I'm not entirely sure. What I remember most distinctly was that he *reeked* of alcohol.

Instantly alarmed, I called my supervising doctor (who'd just completed his appointment) and asked what was going on. Specifically, why had this stumbling, inebriated guy been allowed to just waltz into his appointment and not immediately been sent packing?

"I've had to call the cops," my supervisor said on the other end of the line. "He's obviously very intoxicated, and I don't feel comfortable at the thought of going home and leaving you with him." Gee, thanks! "If you can stall him so he doesn't leave before the cops come, I'd appreciate it."

Right. Mission: stall the drunkard careering around my workplace with his cat (or whatever it was). How hard could that be?

I put the phone down (obviously I'd kept my end of the dialogue discreet) and looked up at the client, who was standing at the desk waiting to check out. A little panicked, I began fiddling with the computer like an idiot and making far-fetched, random small talk. Obviously, I could see him beginning to grow impatient after a few minutes of this (understandable).

"What's going on? What's taking so long?" he demanded.

I could feel myself physically breaking into a sweat. "Oh, you know, technology! It's always... breaking," I said feebly. "I'm sorry for the inconvenience. The computer should be back up in a few minutes, sir."

Obviously, this did little to alleviate his frustration, and I could see him getting more and more het up with every second that went by.

I felt really quite uncomfortable at this point. I'd been left completely alone to deal with and hold captive a pissed-off and intoxicated man while heavily pregnant, not to mention the fact that I was basically boxed in by my desk. My only escape route was exactly where he was standing.

In other words, I'd be shit out of luck if he decided to try anything.

Around five minutes later (five long-ass minutes later), five or six officers suddenly burst through the entrance doors... and in that moment, the client's body language completely transformed. The officers escorted him out, talked to him outside, and drove him home, and, later, they informed us not to have his car (which was still in the parking lot) towed; that they would keep an eye on it.

These moments of extreme stress, both in and out of work, weren't exactly ideal during this stage in my pregnancy. On one Thursday night shortly after my wedding, one of the doctors there took one look at me standing at the clinic counter and said, "We're going to lose you."

Sure enough, I was put on bedrest that very night, and I was stuck lying on my left side for the next two months. This was pre-Netflix days, people, so I was stuck with cable TV. Oh, the horror! And this whole time, Dan continued to work all day before coming home to drink. Or going out to drink. Or going to the Sox game to drink. Or going to a bar to drink. All while I was home, lying in bed, lonely, heavily pregnant, and woozy.

And so my long charade of hiding how things truly were began in earnest. I was alone all day every day, and the loneliness was debilitating. I often called Dan on the phone, pleading, "Why don't you come home?" to which he'd say, "Oh, sure, after this round." That round would then last three hours, and he'd eventually stroll in at around 11PM, reeking of booze, kicking off his dirty work boots in the kitchen and dropping French fries on the floor as he staggered into the bedroom. His drunken night snacks always left a mess: a half-eaten burrito or McDonald's burger wrappers on the nightstand; fries on the floor by the bed. Basically, he gave zero shits, and I was so pregnant that I didn't even consider leaving him. The damsel in distress role eventually disappeared when I was ready to deal with all the literal and emotional garbage I'd accumulated, but at that moment in time, my entire mindset surrounding my current situation was "woe is me".

We somehow made it through an awkward holiday season, celebrating our first Christmas together with me bedridden and him passed out drunk after celebrating Christmas at his Uncle Pat's house.

What an absolute shitshow.

At least his family was excited about the impending birth. They were busy putting together the nursery, and they constantly monitored my progress—attentions I was grateful for. My doctor was also keeping a close eye on my health and the baby's progress. He really wanted those little lungs fully developed before the baby's entrance into the world.

I ended my pregnancy feeling a little more peaceful, albeit missing my mother's presence keenly. My body wasn't feeling too good, though, and because it was retaining a tremendous amount of fluid and my blood pressure was sitting insanely high, labor was induced on New Year's Day.

During those thirty hours, I could only have one person at a time in the room. I vividly remember nurses coming in and attaching padding to the bed bars to prevent any harm if I began to seize.

At around 7:30PM on January 3, after not much progress, Dan, Dawn, Tommy, and Joan decided to go and grab a bite to eat across the street while my dad claimed his post and sat with me.

They probably didn't even get a seat at the table before my father called them. It was time.

My sister perched herself in the far corner of the delivery room to film the birth, chuckling at my prayers: "Oh, dear God, please take this pain away."

And my prayers were heard.

After a few hours of labor, I delivered Evan—all six pounds, twelve ounces, and twenty-one inches of him—on January 3, 2008.

I was in shock and in bliss.

My dad was the first to swoop into the room and congratulate me, my legs still in the stirrups and all. *I can't believe this is the same man who once was strung out and abused his wife*, I thought.

He quickly asked a midwife, "Why is she shaking like that?"

It was all part of the normal endorphin release, but it was still comforting to see his concern.

My mother, meanwhile, did not once come to see the baby, never mind me.

My in-laws were nurse practitioners, and were aghast that my doctor had let me deliver vaginally. They believed he had put me at risk for clotting, and they weren't wrong: I had a pulmonary embolism eleven months later (but more on that later), and Evan had endured a hard, aggressive delivery. Even still, his Apgar score was good, and we were certain that he was a strong, determined little boy.

When the nurse first brought my little guy to me for feeding at around one-thirty in the morning, I was overcome with exhaustion and simply... couldn't do it. They also decided they didn't want me breastfeeding because I had so much magnesium and Pitocin in my system, so Dan tried to feed him, but the formula was just shooting out of Evan's nose and mouth like a firehose.

The nurses took Evan back to care for him, and Dan and I, grateful, closed our eyes.

When they brought him back to me the next morning, I still couldn't function. "Here's your baby!" they said jubilantly—but I felt beaten to hell. I had a nurse on either side of me, both gripping an arm, with the goal of getting me out of bed. One nurse had a look of horror on her face as she exclaimed, "She can't handle this baby!"

She wasn't wrong, but it was time to step up regardless. "No, bring him back in a bit," I said quickly.

When they obeyed later that morning, I was full of anxiety. *Do you remember how to change a diaper? What if he doesn't stop crying? What if he doesn't finish the full bottle?*

I was a new mom looking for reassurance.

Yet when they put Evan in my arms and our eyes locked, I knew in that very moment that this child of mine had been given to me for a deeper reason. *Could he and I have a soul contract?* He was hours old, but his eyes had hundreds of years of wisdom in them. He'd arrived strong and determined, and my intuition told me he'd be something amazing one day.

Thankfully, I started to get acclimated to his little old man face during the seven days I was hospitalized for. We struggled to adhere to a routine in the coming months with all the then-unknown health challenges that were on the horizon, but for those precious first days, I enjoyed my hospital routine with my beautiful baby boy.

But this period wasn't all post-birth, new-mom bliss. I was overjoyed to have this beautiful, intricately made little human that I was already connecting with so profoundly in my arms, yet this recovery period was anything but fun at times. I ended up having seven liters of fluid drained from me, and was just exhausted as a result of what I had endured. Obviously the latter was a very normal, natural reaction, yet looking back, I can't help but feel that this was possibly compounded by my sense of rejection and loneliness that had been triggered my mother (my new baby's *grandmother*) not coming to visit me (or him) once. They say it takes a tribe to raise a child, and I was feeling this lack of support from my mother big time.

When the time came to head home, I was terrified, but my mother-in-law volunteered right away to bring us dinner. *Thank God.*

Dan and I finally made it home at about 8PM, and I could hear Sherry bustling around the house and washing dishes. The wooden floors were covered in dirty slush from the snow outside, piles of clothes were heaped around the house, beer bottles were everywhere, the kitchen was littered with pizza boxes and fast-food garbage, the bathroom sink was thick with toothpaste and face shavings, the tub looked like a homeless person had bathed there for the first time in months, and the thermostat was set to sixty-five degrees.

What a warm, cozy welcome home.

This wasn't exactly the welcome any new mother would want. Even our bedsheets were caked in mud from the dog. The cold, sterile environment of the hospital had felt homelier than this. Even in the throes of my exhaustion, I felt my mind teetering toward sensory overload at the state of our home.

Sherry did all she could to put things in order while I hunkered down for the night—a long, long night. The baby was colicky and screaming, and he felt constipated. And to top it all off, he was vomiting every time I tried to feed him even a little bit. I knew something wasn't right, and I had no idea how to begin navigating caring for a poorly baby while I myself was so far beyond sapped. I felt like I had nothing left to give. I attempted to rock him and walk him up and down the hallway, but every time I fed him, he projectile vomited. We ended up in the recliner in the living room, just he and I rocking back and forth, both of us getting to know one another, listening to the January wind whistling through the bad window in the living room. This was one of many sleepless nights as a new mom,

Evan and I sat in the small hours, wrapped up in one another, with no clue how on earth we'd gotten here or where we were headed.

It was beautiful. It was exhausting and lonely. And it was absolutely fucking terrifying.

10

"Who Would Want You?"

———

I'D BEEN LOOKING FORWARD TO the "fresh start" that would surely come with the baby's arrival, but it seemed nothing was going to proceed smoothly.

Dan went right back to work after Evan's arrival following his involuntary hiatus prompted by the 2008 crash, and Evan continued to have mystery health problems—mysteries I was left alone to solve.

A couple of days after coming home, I called my dad to take us to the ER because Dan wouldn't come home from work. As a result of the continuous difficulties I was facing when trying to feed Evan, he was suffering from dehydration. He also ended up in the ER another time or two due to dehydration and, a few weeks later, an RSV. And, with Dan nowhere to be found, my father landed the role of ferrying us back and forth from these appointments. (I didn't feel like I could go alone; I needed a fellow adult's support while I was so exhausted and scared, not to mention still recouping from childbirth.) I vividly recall our doctor telling us the evening we found out about Evan's RSV how serious this was and how we absolutely had to keep two pairs of eyes on him at all times.

We came home and purchased a nebulizer, and I began nebulizing Evan every two hours, praying to God this would pass.

Turned out little Evan had gastroesophageal reflux disease, and the doctor's solution to this was to medicate him with Carafate thirty minutes before he ate to coat his intestine and keep him elevated thirty minutes before and after feeding him. He also advised that I feed him just one-and-a-half ounces of formula every two hours.

I was getting no rest in among all these worries and routines, and Dan wasn't helping in the least.

When I finally reached my breaking point, Sherry suggested adding a tiny bit of oatmeal to the baby formula. "Let's just see what happens," she suggested. And guess what? He kept it down. Sometimes old wives' tales are worth listening to!

Besides the GERD issue with Evan, he really was such a good baby, and so once we were on the road to resolving his feeding issues, I was ready to jump into action and spruce up the house. I'd been bedridden for so long that there was a severe backlog of household chores to be done, and I was ready to have these done and dusted and to finally craft some semblance of a home for me and my son. It felt so good to *move*; to run up and down the stairs. I am, and always have been, a doer, and so being confined to bed for so long had been tremendously difficult for me. This meant I was now fueled with a newfound vigor. I got each day started with cleaning the house, doing laundry, and organizing, Evan on hip or right next to me the whole time.

For that first month, I rode high on adrenaline. But my sleepless nights were stacking the deck against me. This meant that, maybe unsurprisingly, I was hit hard after just a few short weeks of this short period, and with this crash in energy, I could feel postpartum depression creeping in.

Even though I loved Evan, deep down inside, I desperately wished for my old life back. No Dan. No baby. Just me at home, doing my thing. I felt deeply horrible for this, and it took some good group therapy for me to realize that I was *far* from alone in feeling this way. For now, though, the guilt I felt was awful, so I did what I did best: buried the feelings so I could have a fighting chance at pushing through and embracing Evan through his many incredible stages of development.

Looking back now, I know this was symptomatic of me struggling to soothe the wounded inner child I still was inside. I'd been abandoned by my mother (who, by the way, still hadn't come to visit her newborn grandson once), and this only poked at still-open wounds from my childhood.

It was during this period, during Super Bowl weekend, that Dawn called me and said, "We want baby time. *You* get some rest."

I felt a combination of both insane relief and fear.

"Are you absolutely sure?" I asked. "Evan's feeding routine is pretty rigid still..."

But Dawn, the baby whisperer, swept him right up with an, "It's all okay!"

Rest I did—and, God help me, I just didn't want the baby back. Postpartum depression was here, and it was here with a vengeance. I dreaded the thought of picking Evan up that Sunday night. In the time he'd been gone, I'd slept—actually *slept!*—and it had felt amazing. I'd even showered and washed my hair. Who'd ever want to go back?

The truth is, I became very frantic and overwhelmed when I properly acknowledged this thought. I wanted the "old me" back, and I felt overwhelming, soul-crushing guilt for the fact that that thought had even crossed my mind when I'd been gifted with such a beautiful child. The cognitive dissonance I felt was real, and while I felt like some kind of horrible monster at the time for doing this back-and-forth in my own mind, this is just the reality of postpartum depression.

Of course, the dreaded evening arrived, but was softened by mine and Dan's plan to watch the Super Bowl at Tommy's with Dawn and Evan.

Upon walking through the door, Dawn took one look at me, and it was obvious that my feelings were written all over my face. She sighed and said, "Felicity, he's a high-maintenance baby, but he's *good*."

My fear and guilt seemed to crush my chest like a vice.

"Oh, I know. I'm just, well…"—I felt the emotion bubbling up—"I just don't know if I can *do* this." Tears began streaming down my face.

Dawn embraced me. "Then let us help you, Felicity."

So, it was decided that night that I would move in with her family for the next two weeks. Here came Dawn's sister with a baby in tow, crashing their tiny bungalow! Scott was working as a police officer at night and Dawn was working *and* had an eight- and ten-year-old at the time, so Dawn and I cared for Evan in shifts. I felt horrible for this—I felt I was adding a huge, unnecessary extra portion to her plate—but my niece and nephew loved having Evan and I over, and I know Dawn and Scott did, too. Coming together in moments of need is what family is about, right?

Dawn's kids were a dream with Evan. My nephew often asked to help dress him, and my niece, Heather, who was also a mini baby whisperer, rubbed Evan's head to soothe him through those tough moments.

Basically, Dawn and Joan were so incredibly supportive throughout this entire process. They validated my feelings, assuring me that it was okay to feel how I felt, and Dawn even fully opened up to me about her own postpartum depression. And, indeed, I could still recall this vividly: I'd spent the week with her to help her out when my niece was born, and remembered Dawn crying every night, whenever Scott went to work.

After a few weeks in Lowell, Indiana, Evan and I headed back home to the suburbs of Chicago. I was still suffering from depression, but I was hiding it a little better. It literally felt as though I was ten-year-old me again, pretending to sleep in my twin bed while a war was being waged in the neighboring room.

The truth was, my postpartum symptoms were devolving into more than just feeling blue or overwhelmed: I was experiencing vivid auditory and visual hallucinations. These moments were scary as shit. I can recall my first such experience, which was at my sister's: I was curled up on the sofa with Evan in his Boppy pillow next to me when suddenly, the image of me emptying a bottle of pills into my mouth flashed before my eyes.

And these intrusive self-harm hallucinations only intensified as time went on.

Thankfully, my in-laws found a reliable psychiatrist, and I was quickly diagnosed with postpartum psychosis. The doctor put me on medication and instructed, "You run five miles a day now."

My in-laws were also the ones to say to Dan when we came back home, "Dan, she needs sleep."

His response? "I need to work. And *I* need to sleep so I don't electrocute myself."

Priorities, right?

Dan was always a bit of a penny pincher and refused to hire someone to come in and help me during the day, so we needed to get creative to find a solution.

As a sort of compromise, I started to have baby breaks. Sherry or Dawn would take Evan for a weekend once a month, and sometimes, even newlywed Tommy and Joan would take Evan for a baby break.

These breaks saved my life, but they were also the start of Evan's own baggage—baggage derived from being tossed around like a football from an extremely young age.

By the time Evan was about four months old, my in-laws had divorced and my mother-in-law was wanting to purchase a place of her own. This meant that she and my college-aged brother-in-law needed to move in with us for a couple of months so that Sherry could save money, and this turned out to be a real blessing in disguise. During this time, Sherry and I were able to cook together, and she would occasionally spend the night watching Evan so that I could get some rest. Sometimes, when I was up feeding the baby in the middle of the night, my brother-in-law and I would sit and watch Adult Swim. It was good to have the company.

This period may or may not have formed the foundation for Evan and Sherry's extremely close relationship. During Evan's babyhood and throughout the rest of his life, Sherry was, and continues to be, by far the most amazing grandmother. And this period was only the beginning of her unconditional support when it came to Evan's wellbeing. Sherry and I admittedly didn't have the most comfortable of relationships, but she always did her best to make sure Evan was taken care of, and that is something I'll always be truly grateful for.

Basically, once I was able to fall into a routine with Evan and pull myself out of the fog of postpartum depression, my days were largely spent playing with Evan, cleaning, and cooking. One of my favorite periods as a new mom was when Evan was around eight to ten months old. At this stage, children's personalities really begin to shine, and I was so in love with my son and how he was developing. He had a big bald head, massive eyes, and an even bigger smile, but his personality topped the lot even at just ten months old. The foundations for the strong-willed, determined young man he was to become were being laid, and this was truly magical to watch.

Our routine became one I treasured. We would, weather permitting, go on walks twice a day, almost always in the late morning, after my chores were done. Our walks were one to two miles long, and once he was a little older, we began stopping at the park so he could have a go on the swings.

One thing that became evident about Evan pretty quickly was that he was never going to be a big napper. He had eyes that could see the whole world at once—a world he basked in with wonder—so napping was not on his radar. I was lucky if I got two hour-long breaks, which meant that with the exception of his trips to see Sherry or Dawn, one hundred percent of my time was spent with him—which worked for us. Evan always has been (and probably always will be) glued to my hip.

And Dan? Dan was never around. He'd work twelve-hour days, starting early in the morning, and when he came home, he'd go out to the garage and drink until it was time for him to pass out. He'd been excited at the *idea* of having a baby, but it was clear pretty much immediately that he was totally detached from the *reality* of parenting. He had no interest in creating family memories or rituals, and he was completely unreliable when it came to providing the slightest bit of help. Case in point: one time, I put on a big pot of spaghetti and asked Dan to watch Evan while I ran to Target to get some baby essentials, and when I came home, I found Evan sitting on the changing table just off the kitchen area, screaming, and Dan in the kitchen, cursing. It looked like one of the dogs had flipped the pot of spaghetti over.

In a nutshell, Dan wasn't cut out for any of this. It was easier for him to just go to work and check out as a father. It didn't take me long to realize that from a parental perspective, I was on my own with Evan.

In 2010, Emma Donoghue wrote *Room*, which was later adapted into an award-winning film with the same name. The central character, Joy, is abducted and has a child by her captor, and she and her young son live in a small, filthy shack. Her captor often visits and rapes Joy, but she lives to protect her son.

In principle, there was a lot of Joy in me for much of my married life.

Obviously, I'd entered this marriage of my own accord. Even though I didn't yet recognize my power nor wield any agency over my life, I always had the ability to forge my own path. That's undeniable. I *chose* to try to make a life with Dan. Yet it'd be remiss to not acknowledge the fact that once that choice was made, it was damn tough to leave, or to even imagine that I could muster the strength to do it all on my own. The bottom line was, I wanted to create a family atmosphere for the three of us, but Dan was clearly not up for facilitating that. Instead, he'd come home every afternoon with his eighteen- or thirty-pack of beer before going out to the garage, tinkering around, and drinking until he'd polished off the day's liquid supply and was ready to fall into a heavy slumber. Sitting down for dinner with us as a family was a rare occasion. It didn't fit into his routine of work, drink, pass out.

There was one stressful time when he lost his job and we were living on his unemployment benefits, but almost immediately, he found another gig that provided us with a good income *and* good benefits. It meant working him seven days a week, but he took this in his stride: work was something he knew he could do right. I was grateful for this, and he truly worked his ass off (in fact, there was a time when he was bringing home about twenty grand a month by working as an electrician), but this also meant he felt even more inaccessible. Everyone who knew him said money was his god, and this was never more obvious than during that first year of Evan's life.

I wasn't interested in wallowing anymore, though. So, designing on a dime, I set about making this bachelor pad into my home. I painted, washed the windows, and hung blinds and curtains, and I regularly walked through Target and TJ Maxx with an eagle eye, looking for great deals on decorative household items. However, that quickly came to a screeching halt. "You're spending way too much money," Dan told me one day, and took away my credit card.

Now, Dave Ramsey or Suze Orman would probably agree that ditching the credit card was a wise move, especially since I hadn't been taught to budget and manage money and I sucked at numbers. I *did* spend too much money, for sure. While I wasn't exactly blowing thousands, I didn't have a spending plan, either, and it showed. Even still, taking my credit card away entirely was bang out of order. We were supposed to be in a partnership, and he was treating me like a petulant, irresponsible child.

This was the first of many signs of financial abuse from Dan, and he always justified such decisions with, "I make the damn money. I say where the money goes. You can't be trusted with money."

I didn't quite realize the impact these words had on me at the time, but I can now say that, to this day, this last sentence (or anything along these lines) is a *massive* trigger for me. It makes me feel unworthy; incapable; spoken down to.

With that said, there were *some* benefits to this dynamic. When you're newly in a relationship, you each come with your set of baggage, skills, and faults. And as it happened, Dan was good with money and I was horrible with it. While his extreme control over our funds crept into financial abuse territory at times, one of the greatest gifts he gave me was guidance on how to handle money. He taught me to coupon, comparison shop, and budget. Dan would go to three different grocery stores to get the best prices, whereas I'd been set on shopping at my favorite grocery store for every item. He was the person to take me into an Aldi for the first time ever, which I stepped into with much trepidation—*Oh, my God, what is this? Everything is generic!*—and yet we loaded up the cart with so many more groceries than we would have ever have been able to at my preferred store that I couldn't deny that it made way more sense to go about it like this. He was breaking that brat in me just a little. We had $86.32 a week allotted for groceries (yes, that exact figure), and we used jars to set aside money for each household expense. I still use an envelope method to help myself budget, and to this day, I still go to three different grocery stores. Finances caused a lot of stress early on in our marriage, but as I became a better money manager, that smoothed out a bit.

However, I still wasn't allowed to have a credit card for the remainder of the marriage, and Dan gave me twenty-five dollars per week as my allowance. Dan wanted to nickel and dime everything. I had to give him a receipt for every single thing I bought, and he questioned me about every expense. "Where's the change from what you bought?"

Eventually, I got a part-time job on Saturdays just to get a little time out of the house and to have some pocket change, but I never really made enough to have a salary or feel like I could actually afford to escape.

On top of this, I was a bit of a wreck physically, too. Right after having Evan, I'd lost the baby weight and was briefly my tall, trim, one-hundred-and-twenty-five-pound self, but when the doctors put me on medication for postpartum psychosis, I ballooned up again and stayed between one hundred and ninety and two hundred and ten pounds for my whole marriage.

I just stopped taking care of myself.

This wasn't helped by the fact that Dan didn't allow me to spend money on myself—not for clothes, much less a pedicure or haircut—and so I lived in yoga pants and t-shirts. And with the weight gain came emotional abuse from Dan. "You're disgusting. Who would want you?"

Very quickly, I seemed to lose my ability to self-care entirely. In my younger years, I'd been the best at hair and makeup, but once I collided with Dan, it was like I could no longer figure out how to go about applying cosmetics of any kind.

This lack of confidence really wasn't helped by my physical health, too. Around November time, when Evan was about ten months old, I developed a pulmonary embolism and ended up in the hospital for a week. And to top it all off, Dan walked through the door at around four that very same afternoon with Evan, who was flush-faced. I was sure he was ill, but

Dan brushed off my concerns with a, "He's fine."

Dawn, on the other hand, took one look and backed me up. "Dan, he's sick," she said firmly.

This was pretty awful timing, since I myself had to be back at the doctor the very next day, and Evan's illness meant he needed to make a trip, too—all because Dan, as per usual, couldn't fucking take time off to care for his son. In the end, I had to call to make an appointment for the baby *and* write a note for the doctor authorizing Sherry to make care decisions. Meanwhile, Dawn drove an hour and ten minutes away from her house in Indiana to take me to the doctor. Once we arrived, my doctor lectured Dawn for the fact that I didn't have a coat. I was a very ill woman wearing just a sweatshirt in freezing cold weather because I hadn't been able to afford a new winter coat when I'd outgrown my old one.

My dad came over later that day, slammed one thousand dollars on the kitchen counter in front of Dan, and said, "Fucking take some time off work to care for my daughter. Money may be tight, but you're not that poor."

By this time, I'd been walking around for a full month with chest pain, coughing, and shortness of breath, and when I was finally diagnosed with my pulmonary embolism, I was immediately transported to the hospital, finally acquiring a room at around 6AM. I promptly fell asleep and woke around 8:30AM, and certainly did not fully understand the severity of a pulmonary embolism until the doctor came in, took one look at me, and said, "You're lucky to be alive."

I knew, right then, that I had some serious guardian angels.

He then went on to explain how fatal pulmonary embolisms can be, and said we needed to do a full head-to-toe exam to confirm nothing else was going on.

In the end, I stayed a full week in the hospital.

Thankfully, Dan, Sherry, and a babysitter managed to keep Evan alive while I was hospitalized, and yet when I walked through the door upon arriving back home, it was like déjà vu all over again: my sister was doing the dishes, baskets of laundry were piled in the living room, and the pigsty of a house was freezing cold. It was just like the first day we'd come home with Evan.

I'd also notably been prescribed a six-month course of coumadin, which led to another hard point in my life. Dan and I were advised to be extremely careful during sex while I was on this medication, since coumadin can cause serious (and maybe fatal) birth defects.

We didn't need telling twice.

Fast forward to April the following year (five months or so after my diagnosis and hospitalization) and I was feeling much better and was still regularly taking my blood thinner.

Only things weren't ever going to stay calm for long.

When Dan and I were intimate one evening, being totally impulsive and in the heat of the moment, I fell pregnant.

I was absolutely fucking staggered.

Now, I know certain medications can interfere with contraception, but Dan and I had assumed we were safe having sex during my period.

Yeah… turns out you most definitely *can* get pregnant when on your period.

So, there I was, not even eighteen months after giving birth to my son and not even six months after my near-fatal hospitalization, sat in the same gynecologist's office in the same scenario—only this time in a much more critical state.

Three different doctors ended up getting involved during this time. Two warned me that this pregnancy could kill me, though my original OB-GYN promised me he'd take care of me no matter what I chose to do. Essentially, the gist was this: while the high-risk pregnancy doctors certainly gave me options, it was far from guaranteed that I or the baby would survive this pregnancy.

Suffice to say, I was heartbroken—and faced with an impossible dilemma. But in the end, I had to go with the only option that actually felt feasible for me and my health. So, I terminated the pregnancy, a necessary decision I loathed making.

I struggled with this immensely. I don't judge anyone else for having abortions (I was, in fact, appalled at the Supreme Court's decision to overturn *Roe v. Wade* in 2022, but that's a whole different conversation), but never counted on it playing a part in my own life.

Yet here I was.

Making this decision didn't feel like murder or a sin because I knew deep down inside this baby wasn't meant for this world. And I knew I had to be there for Evan as fully as I could be. Madeleine, as beautiful as she would be today, was meant to be on the other side, in a state of peace and bliss with her grandparents.

I didn't tell Evan about this until much later in his life, simply because of my faith and how young he was—not to mention my own pain surrounding the topic.

I will meet our unborn daughter one day. But until then: sweet Maddie, may you twirl in the heavens, completely full of joy and bliss.

So, to summarize that first year and a bit of Evan's life, I was just going through the motions, trying not to sink. I tried going back to work at the clinic for a bit and was immediately attacked by a dog, my hand all torn up, and early one morning, I staggered up the stairs to pick up a crying Evan, and as I headed back down, I missed the first step and went flying headfirst with Evan in my arms. Thankfully, a soft-sided laundry basket full of towels at the bottom of the stairs protected Evan from the blow, but my head and arm went through the wall. Sherry talked me into a trip to the ER to have us both checked out, and while Evan was fine, I was severely concussed.

Shortly after that, I sprained my ankle on a hole in the backyard while taking out the trash. Onto crutches I went.

It's actually pretty wild to look back on this year. It was literally just one giant storm, with one horrible thing after another horrible thing after another horrible thing happening back to back to back, right after the other. No breaks. No opportunity to come up for air. Just go, go, go.

My unhappiness was especially obvious to me during the Christmas period. Dan really had a way of putting a real dampener on what was otherwise my favorite time of the year. He'd always get shitfaced drunk and end up passed out on the couch, unresponsive and certainly not down for an evening of food and movies and snuggles. Before long, I really started to dread Christmas Eve, since he *religiously* went through this cycle of getting absolutely obliterated and then spending Christmas day ill. This was a shame, since Sherry really went to the *n*th degree to make Christmas Eve as homely and happy as possible, yet this was near impossible with Dan around when he had a drink in hand or was on the floor (it was always one or the other). There were even some occasions over the years when Sherry cut the night short simply because Dan's behavior was so out of hand, and whenever this happened, it'd be down to me to drive us home and put Evan (and Dan) to bed. Then, I'd be sat alone in our living room, the Christmas tree lit and a festive movie playing, feeling hopelessly alone.

I knew I hated what my life had become, and yet a solution to change my life completely evaded me. I could barely work, and my inner child kept looking for someone to step in, take care of me, and fix my problems. *How can I do this all as a single mom? Who is my backup? Who will care for me?*

As crazy as it may seem now, Dan felt like my only answer.

11

Dear Diary…

———

I T WAS A SATURDAY AT about three in the afternoon, and I was coming home from work, carefree and unsuspecting. I'd barely set foot in the door when Dan wheeled like a bat out of hell—or, more accurately, staggered in. Alarmed by this, I immediately called Sherry.

"Why did you let him drive home?" I demanded. "Why did you let him drive with Evan?"

Equal parts infuriated and panicked, I went back outside to check on Dan, to find him sitting on the gate of the truck absent-mindedly burning himself with a cigarette. I'd noticed similar circular marks on his arms before, but he'd always made a barely plausible excuse about how he'd gotten them.

He only worsened as the night went on. At about eight o'clock, a mere five hours later, I found him in the garage, shooting up his legs with a BB gun. He was a bloody mess, and for the second time that day, I desperately called my in-laws for help. None of us could dial 911, but we did get him to the hospital, where he was admitted for a week and where the attending physician diagnosed him as an alcoholic and bipolar.

Surprising? No. Of course, the physician was especially concerned about my little son. He suspected Evan could also have mental illnesses and/or suffer from alcoholism in the future if he continued being exposed to Dan's behavior.

And this wasn't even the icing on the cake.

When Dan came home from the hospital, he said he didn't want to be married anymore. *"You're* the source of all this stress," was his explanation.

I didn't need telling twice. I immediately packed mine and Evan's things, and Tommy came and picked us up.

Because of the rollercoaster ride that was Dan's emotions, I often wound up on Tommy's doorstep. It may sound selfish to have put this on him to anyone who hasn't been through this, but I just couldn't see the exit for this ride, and, in all honesty, I still believe on a spiritual level that this just wasn't the right time to make such a huge decision.

Even still, Dan was rapidly worsening, and this took a tremendous toll on mine and Evan's peace of mind and overall health—and not just as a result of Dan's episodes themselves, but also as a result of all the house-hopping we had to do. But I still had a glimmer of hope for the family setup I'd always imagined, and so Dan and I began seeing a marriage therapist shortly after his own visit to the hospital. The therapy office was right across the street from our house, and, to his credit, Dan made time for therapy for a good couple of years (although I can't say that it had any effect on him at all). At one point, however, he just stopped going. I kept on for moral support, and when it became clear he wouldn't be resuming our sessions anytime soon, my friend Amy started going with me (she'd nap on the couch during my sessions).

I was sitting in the waiting room of this office one time when a man (maybe in his late fifties or early sixties, with really weathered skin and bad teeth and adorned in full drag) sat suggestively licking a lollipop, staring me down, clearly trying to rattle me. While this may not sound like a particularly big deal—just a creep being a creep—I do believe most of my unease here was due to my spiritual gifts trying to tell me something. Call me crazy, but I sensed demonic energy, loud and clear, and this scared me shitless.

For some reason, this stands out to me as a moment that was very representative of my marriage therapy experience!

Despite Dan's ultimate lack of commitment to the therapy sessions, he really tried to become sober and take his bipolar meds for a short period after Evan and I moved back home. He really wanted to turn his life around, and he wanted us back home, and so I obeyed, and promptly strove to find some semblance of normalcy. I was desperate to fulfil my role as a wife and do whatever I needed to do to create some sort of reasonable family life. But Dan's commitment to his mental health and sobriety proved short-lived, and the vicious cycle swiftly resumed—the cycle whereby I was kicked out of the house, Dan professed a change and asked us to come home, we experienced a brief honeymoon phase, and then there was another abusive incident. Over and over and over.

Turned out sober Dan was *really* uncomfortable with himself. He didn't know how to engage and felt like crawling out of his own skin when he wasn't intoxicated. This definitely explains why his period of sobriety and of treating his bipolar diagnosis was so brief. He was swiftly back to his old work-drink routine, usually after about a month of awkward, sober silence.

The older, wiser me shakes her head at this. Frankly, I can't believe I tolerated such abuse and considered this to be acceptable in a relationship. Clearly, I had so much growth left to do.

The whole cycle of our marriage was exhausting for everybody involved. I have no idea why a fellow adult didn't step in and say, "Okay, this isn't working. Time out. Let's get Felicity someplace safe." Then again, that may still be my inner child talking; the girl who just wants to be rescued and comforted.

I suppose the saving grace here was that unlike so many trapped women, I didn't suffer immense physical abuse. It was more on the mental and emotional side. Even still, the alcohol could undeniably lead Dan to an aggressive place. One night, after I had already taken my nighttime Depakote for my postpartum psychosis, he was getting aggressive enough that I felt endangered. I picked Evan up and headed straight to Tommy's, praying as I drove on the expressway. *God, please get me there.* Joan got Evan to bed as I sat at the kitchen table and just melted. *Thank God I made it.* The next day, Joan said they'd had to guide me to bed, I'd been so out of it.

There were so many occasions like that when I just had to flee and find another place to sleep. I even lived with my mother for a couple of months during one of those dark times, when Evan was in preschool.

Then, the abuse became a little more physical. Dan spat on me; cornered me; pinned me up against the wall. Sometimes, I suffered through sex just to deescalate a situation and avoid another fucking fight. Another time, Dan dragged me out of bed by my foot and hissed, "You're not worth having sex with."

I was riddled with panic and fear. *Dear God, when can I get out? When is the time?*

There was no question that I was stuck in a horrible cycle of abuse.

Or was I?

I was paralyzed with fear, *that* was for sure. The fear of doing this on my own. But was I *stuck*?

The bottom line is, I succumbed to the abuse because I didn't feel I deserved any better, and that was because ever since I had been little, my siblings had constantly drilled it into me that I was worthless.

Of course, my therapist couldn't tell me to leave my alcoholic, abusive husband, and even that aside, as crazy as this may sound, it wasn't my time to go. If I'd left my marriage sooner, I wouldn't be where I am today. I truly believe that it was God's plan for me to stay married during this time; that He took that time to prepare me for the ultimate divorce. This was, of course, hard on my body, but it ultimately made me stronger. Even now, it's like I can hear the Lord's words as he spoke to me: *I am going to free you in my time. It's going to be the hardest lesson, Felicity, but I am going to free you.*

And he did. But God, did the wait feel long.

> *Dear Diary,*
>
> *Hearing my beautiful boy say "Mama" warms my heart in a way nothing ever has before. I wonder if he will ever say "Dad"? Is it weird that he's just "Dan"? Maybe it makes sense. His dad is just that guy who wanders around our garage, tosses beer cans, and occasionally drives him to the grocery store.*

> *Dear Diary,*
>
> *For the sixth time, I had the meal I made thrown into the sink tonight. Will I ever learn to cook a meal that Dan thinks is good enough? I'm so discouraged.*

> *Dear Diary,*
>
> *It's nine o'clock on Christmas, and he's already drunker than a skunk. It's his day off work, and I guess that's the only other thing he knows how to do. He didn't care at all about watching Evan open his presents.*

> *Dear Diary,*
>
> *Dan says I'm too fat to have sex with. I feel so miserable. I don't know*

what to do to make it better. Would someone ever want me if I left?

Dear Diary,

What is a normal relationship? Is this normal? He peed in the sink. I guess that's better than on the floor. He's agitated and angry. We're packing up and going to my mom's house.

Dear Diary,

He looked at me this morning with some affection. He tried to kiss me on my mouth. I wanted to be sick.

Dear Diary,

We had a huge snowfall, but Dan was out of his mind today. "I want you out, you piece of shit. I want you out of my house." I can't believe this is my life. All my belongings were tossed over the deck in knee-deep snow.

Dear Diary,

Will I ever get out of this hell? The house is clean, the baby is cared for, and the dinner is ready, but Dan is angry again. How can I live this way? Dear God, is this what my existence is going to be for the rest of my days? Will I ever have a marriage where I'm unconditionally loved? Should I end it?

Dear Diary,

Will I ever experience true love? The kind that warms your heart when he enters the room? A man that makes you proud to stand next to? Will I ever be cherished as a woman, wife, and mother?

Dear Diary,

I nearly escaped another drunken, abusive night. This time, I learned that if I simply agree with him that I am a fat, lazy, worthless piece of shit, things will not escalate.

Dear Diary,
Maybe he's right. Maybe I am worthless and unable to live on my own. Maybe my life is meant to be this painful and empty.

Dear Diary,
No matter what I do, I can't break the two-hundreds weight bracket. I swear the weight that I carry feels like a shield of protection.

Dear Diary,
We had sex again last night. Dan was drunk and needed to get his rocks off, so once again, he had his way with me, and I did my best to hold back the vomit. Will I ever want to make love to a spouse and actually enjoy it?

Dear Diary,
I mustered up the courage and said no to another drunken Dan sexcapade, and this time, he pulled me out of our bed by my leg saying I must be a lesbian and that I don't deserve to sleep in a bed.

Dear Diary,
I FUCKING want to DIE! The feeling of worthlessness and hopelessness is so overwhelming. Please take me now!

By the time Evan was about three years old, we were undoubtedly in a prolonged miserable period, yet I often found myself caught up in the wonder and pride that came with Evan's development. He truly was becoming such an inquisitive, intelligent, beautiful-minded (albeit shy and quiet) boy.

I remember one time that Evan, always the problem solver, pulled his Little Tykes stool into our backyard so he could stand on it and lift the fence gate's lock. He also loved to grab one of Dan's belts, wrap it around the basement door handle and then his butt, and pull himself up and down, like a makeshift pulley system. His problem solving skills were astounding.

Evan's baseball career also began when he was extremely young: at the age of three, with tee ball. His natural talent was self-evident when you watched him play. Today, he is my southpaw pitcher and first baseman. He loves to be the hero in sports, and comes down hard on himself when he doesn't show up at his best. Basically, he's very competitive.

It was also around this time that I enrolled Evan in the local Catholic preschool, where he spent most of his days sitting on the teacher's lap. This teacher instantly fell in love with Evan, and could tell how quiet and withdrawn he was. Even back then, when he was very young (a time when children are usually pretty motormouthed and keen to be everyone's friend), it took a lot to get Evan to open up fully, even with his grandparents. I don't know if this was due to inbuilt trust issues or a lack of security during his formative years. Probably both.

The neighborhood he grew up in for the first five years of his life was a fun place for him. We lived on a block chock-full of kids his age, and they all had a blast playing with one another. And here is where I shined as a mother, too. I adored having a houseful of kids, making them peanut butter and jelly sandwiches and taking them for picnics. Perhaps I got this from my mother. I was also notorious for our backyard movies. We had a projector that we'd set up in the back yard during the summer nights, and

I'd bring out a long folding table, pop a white tablecloth on it, and set up a popcorn machine and an array of full-sized candy bars, water, and juices. All the kids would bring their favorite blanket or chair and curl up outside to watch whatever fun movie I'd picked while us adults sat around the firepit kicking back a glass or two of wine.

Evan and I also loved to bum around during his younger years, always out and about, whether at the zoo or the children's museum. No matter where we were or life's circumstances, we always found an adventure for the day.

Basically, Evan was crazy-bright and fun, and it was him that kept me grounded and sane.

Yet I was walking on eggshells all the time, trying to keep the peace; to keep Dan from exploding. And I was finally at my first breaking point. I was so done. So exhausted. So broken. I tried my best to protect Evan from the rages Dan would go through, making some lame-ass excuse along the lines of, "Dad is tired. We should go outside to play!" but considering Evan's ridiculously advanced social intelligence, I'm almost certain he picked up on most (if not all) of it. This manifested in Evan beginning to express disdain toward his father when he was around five— only little comments here or there, but enough to set alarm bells ringing in my mind. I'd attempt to play this down with something like, "Oh, Evan, it's your dad. He loves you." Not a lie, but Evan still didn't exactly appreciate how Dan showed up as a husband and father, and I'm sure my feeble excuses for Dan's behavior only complicated his feelings further.

Little did I know that this growing sense of injustice and hostility within Evan would catalyze a whole chain reaction of unexpected events later on in his life.

While I won't deny the fact that the impact of this time on Evan will overall have been a negative one, as my and Dan's relationship continued to wax and wane, Evan grew stronger with me. It was almost as though his little five-year-old self felt the need to step up as my protector.

But this didn't mean I could allow this cycle to continue.

I knew what I needed to do. Imagining actually *doing* it felt bone-chillingly terrifying, but I had a responsibility in my son, and this just couldn't go on. So, with a girlfriend in tow, I mustered the courage, codependent and fearful as I was, to visit an attorney to determine my legal options. This was an absolutely gigantic step for me, and so, encouraged, I finally opened up to my parents about how bad things really were—and my dad, not thinking twice, cut me a check for two and a half grand. "That attorney you spoke to—here's her retainer. You don't need that shit in your life, Felicity."

I returned to the attorney and asked her to just hold the check for the moment. I then talked to my parents about moving out, and my mom agreed that Evan and I could come home, to her place. "But this is temporary," she said firmly. "Get your shit together."

"Yes," I agreed. "Yes, I'm ready. I must do this now."

Of course, deep down inside, I *wasn't* ready. I was still clinging onto the hope of us working things out. Plus, I was deeply afraid. The mere thought of doing this on my own was enough to paralyze me. Most nights, Dan tortured me with his drunken-mouthed affirmations, and these lowered my confidence even further: "You're going to fall on your face if you leave me. You'll amount to nothing, Felicity." And why *shouldn't* I have believed him? After all, these were old, familiar ideas that had been pounded into me throughout my life. It couldn't be a coincidence that I kept being told the same thing by different people. Right? This was just further evidence of the veracity of these opinions.

A few nights later, I went over to Sherry's house for dinner with Evan. I was looking for solace, and I guess that I thought she'd see my pain and, as a mom herself, reach out to her son to try to encourage him to get help; to save his marriage.

"You know, Sherry, things aren't going well," I ventured. "I don't want to have to consider divorce, but I don't know what else to do. I'm afraid."

In that moment, I thought my meaning and intention had been understood, but, to the contrary, Sherry, instead of encouraging Dan (like I assumed most parents would), called her son and instructed him to get a good attorney. "She's filing for divorce and will make it hard for you to see Evan!"

Now, of *course* that wasn't what I'd said, but that was the message that was relayed. And so, of course, Dan came home drunk and fuming just as a furious Chicago snowstorm was starting. "I want your shit out of here."

He began chucking my clothes over the back deck, out into the snow. It was abundantly clear I should be leaving, but I didn't want to have to drive in the middle of a blizzard in my little red Saturn Ion. My only option was to triage another potentially nasty situation—and ASAP.

I tried to pacify him while Evan clung to me, his father in a full rage. I said whatever I had to until he passed out, and then set about reassuring Evan that "Dad just struggles with controlling his emotions" and "we're safe".

What a load of bullshit.

We left when the weather meant I could safely drive away, when Dan was passed out and the snow was slowing down into ghostly drifts. Once again, there I was with my son, a laundry tote of our belongings and me white-knuckling the snow-covered expressway on the way to my mom's.

My dad promised to help me file for divorce, and while living at my mom's house, I worked part-time at the veterinary clinic near Dan and I's home. I made this work by dropping Evan off at preschool, working for a few hours, and then picking him back up.

Obviously, my mom's neighbors immediately started asking what was going on, and whenever I was approached by them, I hid the true situation, instead delivering a vague story about construction on the house that I didn't want to be living in the middle of.

About a week after our move, Dan began the usual routine. "Babe, when are you guys coming home? I'm sorry. You know how I get at times. I really miss you. I need you." While I stood firm with my decision, I promised him that I wouldn't file for divorce quite yet. He responded to this by making promises again, pledging he'd do whatever he had to in order to get sober. Presumably to prove his dedication, he threw himself into Alcoholics Anonymous and began visiting me and Evan on a weekly basis at my mother's home.

I was confused over what was best to do. He certainly *seemed* to be putting in the effort to make real, tangible changes in his life. Then again, I could see my mom wasn't looking at all well: every so often, I found her sleeping the whole day away, and this was happening more and more frequently. Looking back now, I strongly suspect she was experiencing active depression. So, for the sake of Evan and my mother, I decided to stay with her, at least for the time being.

During this time, my father came over regularly, and he made no secret of the fact that he'd spotted my mother's sudden lethargy, too. "Erin, come on. Why are you sleeping so much?"

This was touching to me. I could see that finally, he really had made amends. He was actively and selflessly taking care of her and checking in. What this also meant, however, was that I wasn't in my head and that my dad could see it, too: Mom wasn't in a good way. In fact, it felt as though she was deteriorating out of nowhere. Things at 302 Brownell just didn't feel right.

Meanwhile, Dan's visits were becoming more and more frequent, to the point where soon enough, he was coming over every night, sitting in the burgundy wingback chair, sipping on his coffee, and chatting about politics with my mom. I didn't miss the fact that he often snuck in questions pertaining to what he needed to do to get me back. The whole thing made me uncomfortable: the separation; living at my mom's; this man I was married to. Everything just felt off; discordant.

If a genie in a bottle had presented itself to me at the time and I'd had three wishes, they would have been to make the pain go away, for Evan and me to have an easy life, and to find true, authentic love and a stable family life for Evan. But, of course, such a phenomenon did not present itself, so over the next few months, Dan made promises to all my family members, and on the surface, they all seemed supportive. My dad asked me, "Are you sure you guys can't figure this out?" and once shrugged, "Evan needs stability."

Successfully coerced, I eventually brought Evan and I back home for a family night, and it wasn't too bad. Dan had cleaned all the alcohol out of the house, and we were once again falling back into the inevitable happy honeymoon phase.

My family watched silently. God knows what was said behind closed doors. I almost wonder if they thought it was easier for me to just be with him, too. Either way, they definitely played a role in stealing every ounce of confidence and courage from me over the years—not to mention the low blows they made in my presence.

It was as a result of this lack of support and guidance that I was conditioned into the "victim role" I embodied for so many years. And it was this "victim role" that meant I, inevitably, gravitated back to Dan.

Within three months, Evan and I were back home, and the divorce idea was shelved.

12

No Rest for the Wicked

———

IT WAS SPRINGTIME, AND WE had given a second chance at our relationship. Well, more like second chance number five hundred and fifty, but still, Dan wasn't drinking, and things were generally going well. We were in a good spot.

During one of these pleasant spring evenings, I sat outside with a couple of my neighbors, relaxing in the red Adirondack chairs I'd had painted a few days prior. We were watching the kids run back and forth as they played, and at around five in the afternoon, one of the neighbors cracked open a bottle of wine. As I've mentioned, I've never really been a big drinker, but it was a lovely afternoon, and I was enjoying the company and the kids' burning off their energy. So, I indulged.

The conversation and wine were well and truly flowing when Dan got home from work. He pulled up, walked over, took one look at me and the neighbors, and went inside, storm-faced.

I had dinner ready, so I called Evan in and fed the family, and throughout the whole meal, I could feel Dan's vibe was off and withdrawn. I tried to subtly poke around to see if it was his day or the atmosphere outside that was the culprit, my heart hammering at the all-too-familiar feeling of impending doom. But he wouldn't answer me, and I knew deep down that the right thing to do was stay inside and focus on his sobriety.

And yet I just wanted to have one evening that was fun and carefree in the company of other adults.

So, we wrapped up dinner and I went back outside for round two. I had a full glass of wine, and the guys were conversing with cold beers in their hands. It was then that Dan flung open the front door and came down the four porch stairs, walked up to the group, and cracked one open.

He thought he could handle it, but that was the beginning of the next decline.

This may sound like a small catalyst, but it was enough, and slowly but surely, he went back to having at least a couple of beers a night... and then we were swiftly in the midst of another downturn in the abuse cycle.

And then ensued another year of shit together.

In hindsight, I obviously should have supported his sobriety and encouraged an alternative to family time that evening. I get it: I fueled that relapse. Regardless, rightly or wrongly, I was at the point where I was over babysitting him, and I didn't understand the complexity of substance abuse in the same way that I do now.

And things weren't only taking a downturn in my relationship. In the midst of my marital freefall, my dad's hep C turned into a cancer diagnosis, and he declined dramatically as we entered the fall of 2012. Most days, he wandered around higher than a kite on opioids prescribed for an old injury. This was when the doctors were handing them out like candy—the prelude to the crisis. We kids joked and called him Ozzy Osbourne, but it was still troubling to watch him like this. He constantly muttered to himself and staggered around the house, his head totally in the clouds.

He entered hospice the following year, having put up a tough fight for the past ten years while holistically treating his hep C. It was time.

The worst part? In late January 2013 (around the same time as my dad's admittance to hospice), I got a phone call from Dawn. Nan had been rushed to the ER. She'd gone over to my mother's house, slipped, and face-planted a cast-iron stove, splitting her face open in the process. She'd managed to call 911, and our neighbor, Donna, had rushed over when she'd seen the paramedics arriving. She was able to let us know that they were taking my grandmother to St. James Hospital in Chicago Heights.

I'd just picked up Evan from school, and was thankfully able to leave him with my neighbor until Dan came home from work.

When we all arrived at the hospital, the diagnosis was most likely a brain bleed, so the next step was transferring her to John H. Stroger, Jr. Hospital of Cook County.

Oh, Lord. County hospital?

They reassured us that she'd be in good hands; that it had one of the best neuro departments in Chicago. But Stroger was a county hospital with a notoriously scary reputation. It's what the TV series *ER* was based on. Gang bangers regularly rolled up and threw injured people out of the door in front of the ER and drove away. Still, faced with no other option, we decided a carpool caravan was best, and once we pulled into the parking garage, we greatly feared for our safety and my Nan's health.

The place was massive. It sat on what we called "circle campus", a conglomerate of teaching hospitals next to one another. The security immediately warned me, Dawn, and Mom to stay together in a group and to go to the bathroom in pairs; to stand outside each other's bathroom stalls and keep our purses close to our bodies. People were often doing drugs in the bathroom.

The hospital waiting room was packed like sardines. In one corner, Channel 7 News was live reporting on something. It was a madhouse.

On our first trip to the bathroom, my sister-in-law, Rachelle (David's wife) and I went together, swiftly taking in the drama as a Mexican kid came flying through the front doors of the waiting room. He was cradling the left side of his face, wailing, "I've been shot!"

Half his face had been blown off. I shit you not. God's honest truth. Try wrapping your head around that gory horror—something most people will only experience while watching a movie—while your grandmother has a suspected bleed on the brain.

It was both terrifying and exhilarating. If I had to do my life over, I'd be an ER doc in a heartbeat.

As we were walking down the hall to see Nan, Dawn and I noticed my mother was huffing and puffing just trying to keep up with us. She *really* wasn't in a good way, but our focus had to be on Nan for now.

The doctors established that Nan didn't have a brain bleed, but they kept her in overnight for observation anyway. Once we knew that she was in good hands, we went home, my little brother heading back the next day to pick her up. Once he arrived, Nan told him that the Mexican boy had died. She'd heard the family wailing all through the night. She also said she'd received the absolute best care from the young interns who were working there. Nan then recuperated at my mom's house, and just as I thought I could take a moment to come up for air, the universe decided it had other plans for me and my family: not even a week went by before Nan called me to say something was wrong with my mom.

What the fuck is going on?

In a panic on that sunny day in early February, I wrangled up Evan and dropped him at my girlfriend's house, who lived close to my mom's.

I wasn't sure what to expect. Nan had been vague over the phone.

As I carefully navigated the morning traffic, I noticed a tightness in my chest. I was physically struggling to get enough air. *No, this can't be a panic attack. Deep breaths in and out. You got this, girl.*

Nan greeted me at the door in her housecoat, visibly shaken. My mother was sitting on the sofa, evidently struggling to breathe and with terrible edema in her legs. I immediately knew she must have congestive heart failure: she was showing the classic symptoms that I saw in animals, and I assumed these were typical for people with heart failure, too. I told her we needed to call an ambulance.

"I'm done," said my mom—a phrase she said quite often.

"Erin, you're not done. You have us and grandchildren. Let's go!"

What a stubborn old bird she was. Watching her gasp for air, I knew we couldn't sit there and go back and forth on this topic, so I chose the best, quickest alternative, and drove her across state lines to the ER at a little hospital in Dyer, Indiana, myself.

I called Dan to let him know where I was before calling my father's family. His mom and sister lived in the condo just across the hall from him, so they were able to check in on him when hospice caretakers weren't there.

Once in the ER of St. Margaret's, I once again found myself making the unwelcome phone call to the rest of my siblings. You know that feeling that comes with being unprepared for a big test? The anxiety and adrenaline that you feel? Amplify that by ten, and that's how I felt. *What in God's name did we ever do to deserve the fucking shitshow of a life we've all had?* I ruminated. As I sat in another ER wondering what my mom's prognosis was going to be, I could only think, *Can things get any uglier?*

Dawn finally arrived at around one o'clock to relieve me. There wasn't a concrete diagnosis yet, but we could all feel something heavy looming.

By that evening, the doctors diagnosed my mother with stage 4 lung cancer and congestive heart failure. She would go home once stable.

Mom has cancer and heart failure, Dad is in hospice with advanced cancer, and my grandmother is injured and unable to care for herself. What the hell is going on here?

Weirdly enough, this was actually a positive moment for me and Dan. He managed to rise to the occasion, and told me to bring Nan to our house. So, I went back to my mom's, packed up my grandmother and her little Shih Tzu, Sophie, and moved the two of them in with me and Dan. The neighbor could feed my mom's cat for the time being, but Sophie needed extra care. The poor old thing was in just terrible shape.

The following working day, I brought Sophie to work with me and said, "Fix her." After a round of high-dose antibiotics, a switch to a hypoallergenic diet, and daily medicated baths from me, she was, indeed, "fixed".

Meanwhile, my grandmother was recuperating well, and was soon well enough to return to my mother's house, who she wanted to help. My mother was sixty-four years old and didn't want to treat anything, however. She was hooked up to her oxygen tank, smoking like a chimney, and facing her own mortality.

The following week, I took her to the pulmonologist, and upon our arrival, I found the waiting room was filled with people much older than her—men and women well into their seventies. What intrigued me was the number of Anniversary belts these men were wearing—indicators that they were former employees of the steel mills in northwest Indiana, notorious for causing lung cancer. Proudly, these grumpy, beaten-up men displayed their buckles, while the ladies bore smoke rings in their silver-white bouffant hair, a sign of way too much nicotine in their environment.

The culprit for my mom's turn for the worse in the health department was evident.

We were shown into the exam room. I sat in the chair, my mom on the table in her bra. I could see the fear in her eyes. I tried to reassure her—"Everything is going to be fine, Mom"—but she just gave a disbelieving, "Mm hm."

At one point, the doctor had to exit the room to take a phone call and didn't fully shut the door. We could hear him speaking around the corner, and we listened with dismay as he said, "I've got one in the room right now. I give it a month."

What a dick. He didn't even have the common decency to shut his office door or speak with a little more compassion.

My mother immediately asked, wide-eyed, "Is he talking about me?"

I lied through my teeth. "No, Mom."

Two Fridays later, we had to proceed with arranging hospice for my father. No rest for the wicked. He was rapidly declining. To put it bluntly, he was near death. There was no room for denial. It was time.

Life felt numb at this point. I was just going through the motions of helping whoever happened to be in need at the time. Old images of my father, young and dashing and elusive, began to flood my heart. He was handsome, with a mouth on him and a "don't fuck with me" persona—a personality trait that I carried in my adulthood—and even though he'd done wrong on so many levels, he'd made the absolute most of his second chance and done his best to make things right. The absent father that I'd grown up with was now attending his grandchildren's soccer games, going to church, and playing with his little grandbabies. He was thoroughly living a joyful life, and was soaking in as much good as possible.

Basically, this was going to be difficult.

The family gathered at his house that afternoon. We surrounded our father with love and compassion during his final hours. No grudges or hurt feelings. Just simple compassion for a man who'd done his best to do good after his past mistakes.

We reached out to my mom a few times asking if she wanted to come and sit with him, just to be there with all of us, but she declined our requests. We all knew it was because she couldn't bear to see him like this. She loved him, as screwy as their relationship was, and yet the walls she'd put up to protect her heart wouldn't let her say "farewell", "go fuck yourself", or "I love you". Even Nan, who still to this day speaks in aggravation of my father, came to say goodbye, but it was just too much for Mom. There was far too much water under the bridge.

The next seventy-two hours proved intense and exhausting. I had a hard time wrapping my head around the fact that I was already at death's bedside for the second time, watching another family member pass on. *Why does God keep choosing me for this job?*

This is something I still ponder.

Many friends and family of my father came to his bedside to pay their respects during these few days, and while we probably should have been distracted by this, what we all noticed most was the new abundant spiritual activity around us—and by that, I mean all the *what-the-fuck-did-I-just-see?* moments. While I've always been rather spiritually gifted, my siblings and niece don't appear to share this gift (at least not to the same extent that I do), so when we began to see a stream of dark shadows filtering into his room, it spooked everyone, big time. I knew that there wasn't any need for me to be fearful, however. We called upon Christ and Archangel Michael to clear and protect us, and Dawn and I prayed throughout the night. If I'd had a sage bundle with me, I would have lit that bad boy up and cleansed his room, but there was a part of me that knew deep down inside that he had to pay the piper. His soul wasn't going to be at rest until acts of forgiveness were requested.

And that's where we came in.

We prayed hard, requesting forgiveness for him; for whatever blood was on his hands to be washed away.

At one point, Dawn, my niece (Heather) and I stood over him, praying to the Divine Mercy Chaplet. *May God forgive this foolish man and put his soul to rest.*

Even though the front door was closed, my father's house alarm system kept going off in response to these prayers. We all giggled at this, but eventually, Dan asked if he could disconnect it. He was clearly spooked by it.

We sat around, taking shifts to check on Dad and sharing stories. He couldn't really speak, and we didn't know how long he might need care for. Hospice was coming once a day to check on his vitals. My grandfather had passed in about twelve hours, but my dad was having a rough time.

The second day, the hospice workers decided to come in every twelve hours, but as the day wore on, it became clear that the family was exhausted. Tommy suggested we hire a nurse. Rachelle balked at this and said she didn't want to spend the money, but Dawn and I were especially tired and in need of a break. Dan himself could see how worn out I was. "We'll take care of it," he said.

It was during moments like this—moment of crisis—that the logical, sensible, good person that was in him came shining through.

A beautiful young nurse came to relieve us at about seven o'clock the following Sunday evening. She cleaned my dad up, freshened his bedding, and snuggled him in a nest of pillows for the evening. My father had a rocking chair glider that we'd moved to his bedside for her to settle herself into, and her presence was both comforting and a relief.

Into the night, one by one, we peeked in and checked on them both, and she was always sitting in the rocking chair reading the Bible, my father muttering something—I think to family members who must have been at his side.

Early the next morning, before 7AM, I popped my head in the doorway and asked how the night had gone. Her response only confirmed what we'd all experienced for the past seventy-two hours. "You know, I've done this a lot, and I am a Christian woman, but ma'am, there's a lot of activity in here. I could feel the cold presence of other things enter periodically throughout the night. I just kept reading my Bible."

That following Monday morning in mid-February, the sun was shining dazzlingly, peeking its yellowish-orange glow over the frost-coated roofs, and my dad was much more at peace. His breaths were longer and stronger—the opposite of active death, which is characterized by short, shallow breaths.

At around 7:10AM, on February 13, 2013, my father, Richard, passed away peacefully, surrounded by his four amazing, strong children. A sense of relief swept my body. His struggle was over.

We struggled. We grieved. We cried. And we called my mom.

"Hello, Mom. Dad passed away."

"Okay, you guys. I'm coming over."

13

You Were a Good Mom

———

I FEEL WE ARE ALL born with a purpose. I'm not saying that this means life will always be bliss—maybe your pain is your purpose, or a certain lesson you need to learn—but I do feel that my father's life experience left me with the understanding that God *does* give people second chances, and my father's lesson happened to be redemption.

What beauty to see in his passing.

After his death, we buried my father, and at the end of February, we began to pack up his home. Unfortunately, we found that a lot of the jewelry and money he owned had been stolen, so Dawn and I spent as much time as we could at my dad's, sorting through the rest of his belongings, donating clothes and furniture, and determining who in the family might want various items.

Throughout all of this, I was still trying to mother a toddler and maintain some kind of home life. I couldn't get my head above water.

We also sorted our father's finances, got things transferred into my mother's name, and put his house on the market.

Meanwhile, my mother was continuing to stare her own mortality in the face. She spent the following three to four months wrapping up both her and my dad's estates and making sure everything was paid off, which turned out to be a blessing in among all the devastation.

This was also (counterintuitively) proving to be a very calming period for my mom in her life. For the first time, she was comfortable and free of financial worry. Because she and my father had remarried, he'd left her with a nice pension and investments, which meant after all the years she'd spent scraping for groceries and taxes, the constant money struggles were gone. She was finally able to kick her feet up and retire, if she wanted. If she wanted to sell the little dump on Brownell and move to northwest Indiana and buy herself something cute and small, she could.

Finally, the freedom to breathe had graced her world.

My mom turned sixty-five on June 7 of that year, and we four kids celebrated with her. A week later, Nan called Dawn to say my mother didn't want to eat. Nan had been cooking for her every night and she'd had a decent appetite, but one night, my mother just told her, "You know, Mom, I'm done."

We'd had hospice workers at the house the day before, and my mother, with a cup of coffee and a cigarette in hand, had refused the care with a dismissive, "I'm fine."

The next day, my mother called Dawn to say that she was dying—a message Dawn conveyed onto me first, since I was the closest one to the house. And so once again, there I was, white-knuckled on the expressway, Evan strapped in tight, this time on the phone with the hospice lady who'd been at my mom's the day before, who was speaking to me urgently down the line. "Felicity, listen to me. Do not call nine-one-one when you get there. Your mother doesn't want to be resuscitated."

I was scared to death at this point. I had no fucking idea what I was about to walk into. All I knew was that I was emotionally and mentally exhausted from life.

We pulled into my mom's driveway, and I snatched Evan out of his car seat, informing him we were going to check in on Grandma. "I need you to sit here on the porch, okay, buddy?"

I didn't want him walking into the living room and seeing my mom in God knows what state.

He nodded and plonked himself down, cross-legged. I blinked back tears and unlocked the front door.

The house hadn't changed from the night before. There was still the thick smell of stale smoke, dirty dishes in the sink, and the stack of mail by the sofa she had called bed for the past eight years or so. It was on the corner of this sofa that she was perched.

Her hair and makeup was done. She was a deep shade of purple in the face, and she had her oxygen on. She couldn't speak; only mutter. She felt most comfortable being hunched over.

This is a very painful part of my life for me to reflect on. My heart broke seeing her in the throes of such blatant, naked suffering.

I called Dawn back and told her that hospice was on the way.

"Dawn," I added, "what's the status of mom's estate? Did she finalize everything?"

"No."

"Fuck *me!*" I paused for a second to breathe. "Okay, we need to call her attorney and get them here, stat. She needs to sign off on this."

I was afraid to stand by my mother, she was in such a bad state. It was obvious she couldn't sit up. "Do you need to use the bathroom?" I asked her.

I got an affirmative response and cautiously lifted her up, helping her to walk to the bathroom. It was while she was sitting there that, for the first time in my whole life, I said, "I love you. You were a good mom."

Fuck all the bullshit and emotional neglect that we'd been through. At that moment, it was all irrelevant. This woman had been deserving of so much more than what her lot in life had been. She'd been completely robbed of so many of the experiences people treasured when on their deathbeds.

I got her back to the sofa, propped her up a bit to help with her breathing, and called all my siblings one more time. They, the attorney, and hospice were all on the way. It was when the hospice workers were signing off on her paperwork that her attorney walked through the door. As we liaised with the attorney, I noticed the attorney's husband seat himself on the burgundy club chair that my mother loved. I'd given it to her years ago for Mother's Day, and it was where she could often be found sipping on coffee with her feet kicked up back in the day. The gool old days before the depression and the empty house.

Tommy walked in and looked over at the man in the chair. "Mr. Hagel, how the hell are you?"

"Tommy. It's good to see you."

It finally dawned on me that this guy had been our history teacher in high school. He took a look around the mess of a house and my purple-faced mother signing her will. "This is heartbreaking for you kids."

The attorneys left shortly after, but the hospice workers stayed behind, waiting on a hospital bed that ultimately arrived at about four o'clock in the afternoon. They set this up where the club chair that my mother loved had been, and then left.

Suddenly, we were left in silence.

There my mom lay, in the great room where she had raised us four kids.

Dawn busied herself by taking out the garbage and doing some dishes. She couldn't handle being close to my mother while she was in this state. Still perched next to Mom, I let Dan know that I was unsure if I'd be coming home that night, and one by one, my siblings told me they were leaving. They couldn't emotionally handle being there. We stood outside to discuss who would stay with Mom, and everyone made excuses about why they couldn't stay, suggesting that I did instead. My heart sank at this. *I don't want to.* I didn't feel strong enough. *Why me? Why can't one of them do this?*

Joan, clearly recognizing the fear in my eyes, said she'd stay with me. God bless her for rising to the occasion!

Everyone else took this as an invitation to slowly walk away, hearts heavy with the inevitable.

Meanwhile, Dan was, weirdly, being really supportive. "Babe, you do what you have to do," he said when I told him the new plan.

Joan and I proceeded to make ourselves as comfortable as we could, getting the coffee going and checking my mother's vitals. As the night deepened, one by one, the family united once again to be with my mom. Heather. David and Rachelle. Tommy had to stay with his son (and honestly, Dawn and I thought he just couldn't do it, anyway), but David went and slept in his childhood bed while Rachelle sat in the great room and talked with me, Joan, and Heather. It was quiet and peaceful, and eventually, Rachelle and Heather fell asleep on the plaid sofa my father and I had bought for Mom years ago, leaving me and Joan to talk quietly and keep checking on my mom.

It was pushing midnight when Sophie started pacing and whining. I looked over at Joan, crept out, and swept Sophie up in my arms, placing her on the hospital bed beside my mom. Her tail wagged as her little Shih Tzu nose guided her to my mom's face. She licked her before nesting by her feet.

And just like that, my mother took her last breath.

I tried feeling for a pulse, but there was nothing.

After about twelve hours of active death, my mother was gone.

It was peaceful. Very different to my father's passing.

Sophie had instantly known. She could sense it. And so could I. Just like that, the rope that had been connecting Mom and I all those years, fraught with tension but still hanging on, had been severed. The world felt impossibly large and gaping and empty. I was officially an orphan.

My heart felt like it was caving in on itself. I was in so much pain. *Why has God taken everything I've ever known away from me and my family?* It would take years for me to understand all of this. For now, I didn't cry. I couldn't. I was just fucking numb and exhausted, and prayed for my own hole to crawl into.

First, though, there was admin to do.

I called Dawn and Joan called Tommy, and then I made the calls to the crematorium and hospice. Rachelle and Heather popped their heads up with the commotion. "Is she gone?" asked Heather, crying. Heather adored her grandmother, and my mom loved her grandkids perhaps even more. Grandma, as Heather called her, had always been loving and nurturing to her and Jack, something we kids had never seen or experienced as children.

Dawn came and brought Nan, who started crying, "I've lost my best friend," as she kissed her forehead and held her daughter's hand.

I'm awed by the strength my Nan displayed in that moment. She'd buried both her husband and child. God knows how she didn't completely shut down there and then.

Dawn was crying, too, but she went straight back to the dishes and started cleaning and organizing, throwing herself right back into her maternal/caregiver role; her tried-and-tested coping mechanism.

In this moment, I also felt a little heartbroken for my aunt (my mother's sister) because she never once came over when my mom was sick to see her. She was nowhere. Then again, this had also been the case during my grandpa's passing. She really wasn't around for that, either; not until the very end. I almost wonder if she struggles with death/loss in general and pushing it from her mind is her coping skill.

Anyhow, I digress.

Rachelle woke David up, who couldn't even look at my mom. He was sobbing, and still was when they went home.

Dawn asked me to wait until hospice arrived, and so I left as soon as they did, which meant I hit the road at around 3:30AM. The expressway was empty, and I didn't even have the radio on as I drove. Just dead silence all the way home.

When I got home, Dan asked if I was okay, and it all came pouring out. "My mom died," I sobbed as I crawled into my bed.

A few hours later, six-thirty rolled around, and Dan got up to go to work. I forced my eyes open. "Don't go," I begged. "I need you." I was heartbroken and weeping.

"Look, I love you, but I've gotta go."

"But Dan, my mom just died!"

All I heard in response was the slam of the back door and his dirty work boots clunking down the deck stairs. I woke up perhaps an hour later to Evan cheerfully saying, "Hi, Mom!" with his little smile and big brown eyes, happy to see me.

I started to sob again, crying out, "My mom died." I was struggling to think straight, and I called Dan and said, "*Please* come home. I need you."

Of course, he wouldn't budge. He had his job to do. I sent text after text begging him, but he was unresponsive.

Evan wanted to play with the kids next door, so out we went. I did my best to keep my composure until I saw my neighbor, and then I just broke down, telling him that my mother had died.

"I'm sorry, sweetie," was all he could say.

I plopped down in my Adirondack chair, sobbing as he brought me mug after mug of coffee, consoling me and calling Dan himself.

Later that day, when Dan eventually got home, we went back to my mom's house to pick up Sophie and Chessie (my mom's cat) that I would now re-inherit (if there's such a thing as that). I felt very overwhelmed upon entering the house with Evan, Dawn, and Nan. It was filled to the brim with her and my dad's furniture, all cramped into this less-than-one-thousand-square-foot home. It was suffocating, as an understatement. I think we were all pretty overwhelmed, not only because of the weight of all we had recently endured, but just from being in that space. It felt as though the room was bursting with memories and feelings and energy that was all too heavy to process.

Evan was sitting in Grandma's favorite red chair that he'd always loved when he began to express, panicked, that he couldn't breathe. In that split second, my emotions ranged from disbelieving to confused to very, very scared. It was only a few moments later that he sank into a full-blown panic attack. Leaping into action, Dawn and I took him outside, sitting with him until he calmed down.

Once he'd managed to calm down a little, it became clear to me we needed to head home. As other parents of children with mental health issues will understand, it shattered my heart (as an understatement) to see my son in that much distress, and I truly realized in that moment how much emotional weight he was carrying. It was no wonder he was so overwhelmed.

That was the first physical manifestation of his struggle with his mental health.

My mind racing, Evan and I headed straight home. At one point, I turned to look at Evan in his seat in the car, and was shocked: it looked as though all his energy and lifeforce had been utterly depleted.

And that was how I spent my first parentless day.

And the worst part was, life was only going to get more difficult for Evan to deal with.

Three days after my mom's passing, Joan, Tommy and I took the kids to see *Monsters University* to get our minds off things. Sherry came to pick up Evan a day or so later, and got very angry when she learned of this. She said it was something *she* had planned to do with Evan. "Next time you want to ruin family time, give me some notice," she snapped.

I asked her for a little grace. "My mom just died. I'm busy going through all her paperwork. I just didn't remember that you'd wanted to take him."

No deal. Soon after, she moved to Arizona for a job, and about a month and a half later, she had her own mental health crisis, and it was then that it finally hit Dan how much I'd needed his support when my mother had passed.

This move impacted Evan hard. What many didn't seem to consider was that this move meant he'd ultimately lost all his grandparents mere months apart. It probably felt as though the earth had fallen out from under his feet. While he'd certainly already been conditioned to adapt to radical changes in his life, this was probably a little too much for him to handle. Really, I think this would be too much for *anyone* to handle, never mind a young boy who was used to having a stable support network.

I tried to support him through this as much as I could, but at the end of the day, he was battling tremendous loss, and I hurt as I watched him hurt, powerless.

Perhaps unsurprisingly, it didn't take long for our family dynamic to shift. As deeply narcissistic as my mother was, she'd been the glue that had held our family together, and upon her passing, Dawn was ready to step in and be the mother figure; the controller. So, the four of us tried going out for Sunday breakfast together, but that didn't last long. David and I couldn't communicate at all. We just sat looking at each other with nothing to say.

It was then that I realized that I had no one to turn to anymore and that I needed a plan for safety.

And I needed to heal. Badly.

I started looking around for ways to get my life on track and build a better future for me and my son. I voiced to Dan the fact that I had dreams of going to graduate school in psychology, but he shut that down in a hurry. There was no way he was footing *that* bill. So, I searched for a compromise, and found a one thousand nine-hundred-dollar course to become a certified life coach, and *that* was a plan and cost I could sell to him.

I pressed through that certification and got to work trying to run and build a coaching practice. I created a dinky website using the few dollars I'd managed to sock away and put my business out there.

Little did I know that this would form the advent of a long, transformative, utterly life-changing journey.

I was doing small speaking engagements at places such as local libraries, and with every available moment that came my way, I was working at this new idea of a business, the end goal being me becoming self-sufficient and successful… whatever that looked like.

At one point, I teamed up with a fellow coach in the area, and we worked on creating some workshops and seminars together. We also did a piece on the local radio to plug a seminar about a women's day retreat we were hosting, and the radio managers loved our energy so much that they asked if we'd consider doing our own little weekly radio show.

I was on Cloud Nine, and so when Dan came home that night, I excitedly told him my news.

His response?

"Fuck you. No. It's not going to happen."

That was when I truly realized that I was married to someone who had the goal of keeping me down. Every time I thought I was making headway, I'd come crashing into him—the ever-present brick wall in my life saying no. Whenever I got a client, my feelings of utter ecstasy were extinguished with a wary, "As long as it doesn't interfere with my work schedule or take you away from Evan," from Dan.

He energetically cut the cord on any progress that I made, and my coach friend was quick to tell me so. "You're only going to get so far until you let him go," she told me. "He's the biggest obstacle in your life right now."

While trying to build a coaching business and negotiate this cycle of me constantly butting my head against the Dan Wall, I visited a healing center near me. The healer there guided me through meditations and walked me through Reiki sessions.

I also began journaling. Every time I was alone, I wrote to myself and encouraged myself. *I can do this. I am the creator.*

I hid affirmations all around my house—little notes to myself in an attempt to keep my spirit and energy elevated throughout the day.

This was only the beginning of the first of the many phases I underwent to prepare myself to "get strong".

14

A Taste of Freedom

———

" IT'S A FORECLOSURE. THEY can't afford it."

I was visiting Tommy in Indiana, and had seen that the house across the street from him was for sale. I'd noticed it had been on the market for a while, and so asked Tommy what was going on with it.

Dan, Evan and I were currently upside down in our Illinois home, and the housing market had crashed. Meanwhile, this cute little house with a full basement and big yard was going for one hundred and twenty-four grand—*definitely* affordable for us—not to mention the fact that it was across the street from a safe house for me. This ideal prospect left only one question: *How do I paint this picture for Dan?*

That night, I had cocktails flowing and Dan's favorite dinner prepared, and I did my best to put him in a happy state of mind before broaching the subject.

"Look, Dan, nothing's here for us," I said slowly. "Our neighbor is selling drugs out of his house." (This was the absolute truth. I'd literally recently had a DEA agent pull up in my driveway, hand me his card, and inform me the neighbors were dealing drugs.) "We don't know what they're going to bring here or what might happen. It's not safe."

I paused.

"I went to Tommy's today, and you know, that house across the street is for sale. They only want a hundred and twenty-four for it. I could get a job out there, and I'd have Tommy to babysit." Silence. "Just something to think about."

Turned out I needn't have worried. Dan's interest was sufficiently piqued, and the wheels started turning. Relatively quickly, he began to actually entertain the idea of putting in an offer for under one hundred and twenty grand. He liked the idea of being able to pay off the mortgage in three to four years and then being able to start saving.

Well, we soon did just that. Dan called the bank, our offer was accepted, and before I knew it, we were moving.

We decided to redo the new house before moving, which was ideal, as Dan was a great project guy. From that point, we packed up Evan and went to work on the new house every weekend. We painted, redid the floors and kitchen, bought new appliances, added new trim, waterproofed the basement... just made sure that everything was tip-top. I loved that house, and with a five-hundred-dollar mortgage payment, I knew it was something I could even afford on my own, if need be. I was hopeful it wouldn't come to that, though: Dan and I were in another honeymoon phase, and in all fairness, there was, in fact, lots of healing going on. We started having Sunday dinners at our house once again; my brother, his wife, my niece, and maybe some friends often came over so we could all enjoy the day together.

Finally, there was a moment of peace in my life, and it felt *really* good. I began to think that we were meant to be together after all.

Predictably, however, the peace passed. We were floating two mortgages, and our attorney in Illinois said, "I can't advise you to do this, but if you were my mother, I would tell you to stop paying the mortgage in Illinois."

So, we did. We knew this meant our credit score would take a hit for a few years, so we traded in my car and got something practical for the family, leaving Dan with my little Saturn to drive to work. Then, we stopped paying our original fifteen-hundred-a-month mortgage. This was financially not a bad decision to make, but the house was in Dan's name (he'd bought it as a young man, and he took pride in having it), so it was hard for him to do. He took pride in his credit; in his finances. The foreclosure process was heavy on him.

And he dealt with stress with alcohol.

Often, he wasn't around for family dinners; he'd still be working when dinnertime rolled around, and so Evan and I would eat together. Then, when Dan got home, he'd immediately go to the basement or garage to work on projects and drink, and at about eleven, he'd say, "I'm just going to order Jimmy John's."

He was slipping back into his old self-destructive cycle, and with this, the old abusive behaviors returned. Many nights, when Dan was angry and drunk, I'd call Tommy, who would take me and Evan in for the night. "C'mon, Evan, we're going for a sleepover at Uncle Tommy's," I'd trill, trying to mask over my upset with near-hysterical, forced joy.

Now, however, there was an extra measure of pain: one of our neighbors was a single mom—a nurse with three kids—and I'd welcomed her into my home, fed her kids, and sat outside in my Adirondack chairs visiting with her. I trusted her. As things deteriorated within our home and the abuse and drinking increased in frequency, however, Dan and the neighbor started to get buddy-buddy, and one evening, I came home to find her with Dan in my kitchen while the kids were playing... and the vibe was off. There were definitely some boundaries being crossed.

And as if that wasn't enough, we were back to where we used to be on the verbal abuse front, with Dan calling me "fat", "ugly scumbag", "useless", "lesbian"... anything and everything he could think of. We were right back in the horrific cycle of "get out", "stay", "I can't stand you", and "I can't live without you", and I was fleeing to my brother's between each of these stages.

It was now undeniable. I needed out.

Seeking something warm and familiar, I went back to the clinic I'd started working at in my early twenties and had thrived in. I was fully open with them about what was going on in my life, and, to my utter joy, Dr. Nielson welcomed me back. I was still very cognizant of the fact that this had taken me right off my "self-sufficient and successful track" and landed me right back where I'd started, however, with cleaning kennels at night—except now, I was in my mid-thirties and had my son with me.

Evan was able to do his homework while I cared for the animals, cleaned, and restocked supplies, and I suppose the silver lining was that I was at least making *some* money, putting away a few dollars every so often towards my eventual escape.

Or so I thought.

When Dan found out about this money, he just said, "Well, then, you can make your car payment," and so the five hundred dollars I might have saved became two hundred.

Back to square one.

The money that I was granted access to was in the closet and designated for various purposes. For this, Dan lined up labeled cups with exact, consistent amounts: $86.32 for groceries; forty dollars for pet food; $22.50 for entertainment; twenty dollars for my weekly allowance. He took care of all our other expenses, such as the mortgage, through the checkbook.

In my desperation to save some money on my own, I tried pocketing a little money from another cup and saying I went over my budget at the grocery store, but Dan caught on to this really quick and made me return any item that pushed the grocery tab over the limit.

Dan had always had a safe full of cash from working side jobs, and when we'd lived in Illinois, he'd never trusted me enough to give me the combination to the safe. Once we moved to Indiana, however, he shared the combination but counted the cash on a weekly basis. When he was drunk enough during counting, however, his math wasn't as good, and he'd more often than not work out the sum wrong, and once I noticed this, I sometimes went into the safe after he'd counted while drunk on a Sunday night, grabbed as much as two hundred dollars, and stashed it in an envelope that I'd hidden in another room. For me, this was an emergency stash; a little something in case I needed to run and pay for a hotel, or something along those lines.

Dan knew I was only saving between two hundred and two hundred and fifty dollars a month working for Dr. Nielson, and started to get suspicious about his figures often being off after his Sunday counting. Quickly, I started feeling guilty and feared that I might get my ass kicked if I was caught, so I took my emergency envelope, put it in the safe, and said, "You know, Dan, you have a separate envelope here in the back of the safe." It contained about one thousand five hundred dollars, which soothed Dan and calmed my moral compass. *I'm just going to make it good again. I'll figure it out*, I assured myself. But I was still back to square one. Again.

This was a really low point for me. This wasn't helped by the fact that I still wasn't caring for myself physically. I didn't brush my hair, and I weighed about two hundred and twenty pounds. I was hopeless. *The only way I'll leave this marriage is by death, either by my own hand or his.* It felt as though there was no way out. It was hard to function.

Soon enough, I got into the routine of dropping Evan off at school before plopping down on my beautiful L-shaped sectional sofa and dreaming of ways to commit suicide.

My family, meanwhile, was telling me that I needed to get out. I did lots and lots of praying and was going to church, doing everything I could to pull myself out of this pit of hopelessness. The depression was coming in waves. *Please God, make the pain go away.*

Of course, God answered my pleas with a different plan.

A couple of things happened. For one, I googled Reiki classes near me. I was finally listening to my intuition and being guided down the path that I'm on today—the path of a healer—and a Reiki practice popped up with a name that rang a bell: Linda Rosenthal. I knew this name was very familiar, but I couldn't quite figure out where I'd heard it.

It was when I walked into the class to be attuned and I looked over that I clicked: there was Dr. Harth, one of the veterinarians I'd worked for at the big clinic. He was married to Linda.

"It's me! Felicity!" I called over, although I knew I was unrecognizable from my former self.

This familiarity gave me the security to completely throw myself into Reiki.

Reiki opened my eyes to my deeper gifts as a healer and the fact that we hold the power to heal ourselves. Over time, a lot of spiritual leaders told me, "You are resilient. You have had mountains crash on you, and then a bigger mountain, but you got through it."

That has been my life lesson ever since then. My mantra.

For now, though, I was in a cycle where I always got through a trial and felt really good for it... and then that powerful negativity from Dan (or whatever negative force was surrounding me at that time) would pull the rug out from under me.

I've learned since then how important mindset is, and I began to really pay attention on mine during this time. Due to my PTSD, mindset continues to be a daily area of focus for me, and it was Dr. Harth and

Linda that directed my attention to this. People certainly come into your life for a reason.

I love him them both dearly.

The second thing was this: after dropping Evan off one day, a girlfriend called to say one of the other clinics had an opening. Inspired, I went and talked to them, stating upfront the hours I could work, and, to my surprise, they were eager to make it work.

I know for a fact, as clear as day, that this was God answering my prayers. When my girlfriend had called, I'd been in floods of tears, at a loss with my income and how to make ends meet, and now not only was an opening here (something that had apparated from thin air), but a clinic receptionist had messaged me on Facebook asking if I was looking for work.

The "how" behind God's work may remain a mystery, but there's no denying when it's at play. I had, quite literally, been blessed.

I was now able to work a shift while Evan was at school, and then my brother said Evan could come over to his house after school, which meant I could work afternoon shifts after dropping off Evan with his cousin, Matthew, until Dan came home.

My mental energy was skyrocketing as a result of this new routine and the additional money I had coming into my pocket. I could see a little more light ahead.

Of course, Dan soon realized I was making more than I had been before, and said I could pay my own cell phone bill as a result—most definitely a power move. I was always happy to pay my own expenses, obviously, but we'd previously agreed Dan would shoulder my phone bill due to the imbalance in our affluence, and now here he was, removing more and more of my agency.

It was no secret at this point that our relationship was declining quickly... again. He started to go out with his friends and not come home, and I'd often find myself without a babysitter on a Saturday morning, when I was supposed to be heading to the clinic. I'd also gone from sleeping in our bed to sleeping on the sofa with Evan because it just wasn't safe. I was afraid Dan was going to strangle me in my sleep. And my concerns hadn't come out of nowhere: I often woke up in the middle of the night to find Dan hovering over me, a disturbing, unsettled look in his eyes.

"Dan, what do you need? Go to bed," I'd say, more than a little spooked.

"Why won't you sleep with me?"

"Go to bed. I'll be there in a minute."

I was out at lunch with a friend from the clinic, Susan, when she mentioned that her husband, Tim, had held onto a little starter house in Munster, Indiana, a cute little Cape Cod with a full basement and small backyard. Her mom had lived there for a while and they'd also rented it out for a bit, but now, it was sitting empty, so she said I could take it if I needed.

I told her I couldn't afford it.

"Then tell me what you *can* afford," she insisted, "and let's try to meet in the middle."

I laid out for her what debt I had left and how much I was making, and we agreed on eight hundred and fifty dollars a month.

Deal.

I probably don't need to point out the fact that this was clearly God at work again. Looking at the technicalities alone (my lack of income being the chief one), finding a new place to live should *never* have been that easy, and yet here we were. It felt like the universe was putting everything in place to allow me to leave Dan for good.

That was in August, and from then, I started socking away between twenty and thirty dollars every pay cycle to begin preparing for the move. With that money, I bought four sets of silverware, four bowls, four plates, four sets of sheets, a coffee maker, kitchen utensils, kitchen canisters, and so forth. The main reason I was able to pull this off was Susan giving me the keys to the house before we'd even officially moved in so I could store everything there. Dawn also had one of her kids' childhood bedframes going spare, so I bought a mattress and, hey presto, Evan had a safe place to sleep.

I then began saving up for my own mattress. My friends already had a dining table, washer, and dryer at the house that I was able to use, and Susan's mom had some lace valances that I loved that they let me keep up, too. The wallpaper in the bathroom was the same small, beautiful rose pattern that had been in my mother's bathroom.

"This is like Grandma's house," my niece said when she saw it.

The clinic was within walking distance of what was about to be my new home, and I started busying myself with making it feel like home whenever I had a spare moment. I painted the walls a neutral gray and had the rugs cleaned; I painted the door red (the color of power); I bought blinds and Tim helped install them. He and Susan were angels throughout the entire process.

Sometimes, I spent my lunch break at my new house, just so I could get mentally prepared for the change I was about to undergo.

Meanwhile, most of my family and the ladies at work knew my plan, but not Dan or Evan.

I saved up about three hundred and fifty dollars for movers to come get a few pieces of furniture that belonged to me, which they were scheduled to do the week before Thanksgiving. Dan was working twelve hours a day every day that week, which was lucky. I didn't want him around when we left, and I certainly didn't want him to know where we were going.

I was anxious in the leadup, and Dan started to sense something was up. "You're acting odd," he commented at one point, frowning. I brushed his suspicious remarks off, trying my hardest to keep a poker face so I could throw him off the scent.

My first month's rent was already paid, the Wi-Fi was installed, and I had arranged for Evan to spend the night at Dawn's house that Friday night. Everything was ready.

Well. Almost everything.

Turned out there was an ice storm scheduled that Friday night, and as I watched the weather turn from bad to worse, my fear surrounding the prospect of the move not happening grew. As luck would have it, though, three guys showed up on the Saturday and said, "We're here to move some stuff." They were a little confused about what the job really entailed, and were clarifying what needed shifting—"So we're going to take this sofa, this giraffe ornament..."—when I sort of broke down.

"I'm scared. I'm leaving my husband. I don't know if I can do this on my own."

This was the scariest moment of my life, but we still managed to get the stuff packed up and transferred to the Munster house. Weather-induced delay aside, it went without a hitch, and this was mostly thanks to the incredible movers I had. Upon arrival, we found that the L-shaped couch that I'd purchased years before was just too big, and the movers volunteered to go back, free of charge, and swap it out for a loveseat that was in our home office.

Before leaving, one of the movers said, "I don't know you, but I think a year from now, you're going to feel different. From what I know, your life is about to change."

What a beautiful soul.

Dawn came over that night and brought Evan, who was full of

questions. "What's going on, Mom? Why is our furniture here?"

Up until this point, Evan had been glued to my hip, usually sleeping on the sofa with me at night, and so this was probably a whole lot of change to take on at once.

"We're living here now, Evan," I told him gently. "I think it's the safest thing for us to do."

He took it right in his stride. "I couldn't agree more, Mom." His relief was palpable. "This'll be really fun," he added. "No more screaming from Dad!"

I'd deal with his emotional baggage later, but I shit you not, that was his reaction. Thank God.

With everything in place, I texted Dan.

> WE HAVE MOVED. WE ARE LOCAL. YOU DON'T NEED TO KNOW WHERE WE ARE, BUT WE ARE CLOSE AND WE ARE SAFE. I WANT A DIVORCE. I WILL DROP EVAN OFF AT MY BROTHER'S FOR YOU TO SEE HIM.

As for Dawn, I don't think I was prepared for her reaction to our new place. I can vividly recall her silence; how her eyes darted around the room and then seemed to stare into space, as though she was having a hard time acknowledging what she was seeing, before she briefly sat on our small sofa. She didn't stay for long; she dropped off the promised bucket of chicken and mashed potatoes before leaving with my niece. She wasn't celebrating our safety at all. I think there may have been some jealousy here. That, and/or fear of the unknown. Regardless, with our little spread, Evan and I hooked up the TV and streamed some Netflix before going to sleep in our own beds.

This was the first feeling of peace I'd had in a long time. I was ecstatic. I had my space, my son, and my freedom. It was amazing.

I was finally living my best life.

On Dan's end, however, I feel it's safe to assume there was no peace.

While I still managed to find the headspace to bask in my newfound liberation, I also had to dedicate much of my energy to filtering out the pages worth of text messages he was constantly sending me. He had clearly lost control, and in response to each of these notifications, I just told him to respect my space.

Things were about to get a lot more complicated, however. Thanksgiving was fast approaching, and, not wanting to keep Evan away from Dan during this holiday, I informed Dan that Evan would be at Tommy's, and that he could come over to see him, if he wanted to. Of course, he took me up on this offer, and my God, did he look horrible when he walked through that door. At some point during the celebrations, Tommy asked Dan if he wanted to stay, to which Dan responded with a curt, "No."

Later that day, after Dan had left, Tommy told me he was concerned over how Dan looked, and that he thought I should check in on him.

"No," I said firmly. "I'm *not* going over there."

"Well, *I* can't. I have people here."

Seeing his point, I begrudgingly went across the street and knocked on the door.

No answer.

I rang the doorbell.

No answer.

I still had a key, so I opened the door, and was immediately hit with a pungent smell.

I greeted the dog and went into the kitchen, perplexed.

The oven door was open, and the gas was on.

My body completely seized with panic.

I started scrambling to open all the windows, to find the house had been locked up tight.

When I succeeded, I went down the hall to find Dan lying down in the bedroom.

"Dan, what are you *doing*?"

"Just leave me alone."

I grew desperate. "You can't do this. You have a *son* to take care of."

While this event may sound shocking, moments like this are typical in the abuse cycle. The abuser often drops off into a melancholic *I-don't-have-anything-to-live-for* phase in an attempt to draw the partner back in. So, as I reasoned with him on the bedroom floor, I avoided the subject of the divorce entirely, focusing instead on pointing out the fact that we needed space in order to get to a point where we could healthily co-parent.

In the end, he came back to Tommy's and celebrated Thanksgiving with my family, but I still felt as though I was treading water, trying to keep things on an even keel.

I reached out to Sherry shortly after Thanksgiving to let her know that she might want to check up on her son, and clearly, this checkup was needed: I looked up one night to find Dan standing outside my bay picture window, demanding, "I gotta see my kid." I had to call Tim over so he could warn him off—"I don't want to have to call the cops. Come on, buddy. You have to go"—but Dan continued texting me all the while, saying he wanted me back. This time, however, I knew for sure I wasn't going back. I was loving my newfound sense of safety and peace a little too much.

Within a month, I lost twenty pounds, to the surprise of my family members, and while it's true that I was walking and exercising, I also believe that we hold onto literal excess baggage as part of our protection when we're in constant fight-or-flight. So, it was probably that protective baggage that I lost. Not only that, but (despite the backend comments from Dan and my family) I was successfully taking care of Evan and had rent paid up to four months in advance, and Dan was giving me two hundred and seventy-seven dollars every week for child support (which I kept throwing toward rent to keep my future secure).

And it wasn't just me who was thriving: Evan seemed to have been given a whole new source of energy. He was a bouncing ball of light, totally in his element. Clearly, the sudden lack of fear and tension in our lives was doing wonders for him, too.

After that disastrous first Thanksgiving apart, I tried to urge Dan to respect our space at Christmas, but, of course, this was too much to ask. It had already been planned that Dan would have Evan on Christmas Day, but Dan decided last-minute that he wanted to see his son on Christmas Eve, and so turned up at the house. And because he was still able to push my boundaries, I let him in.

It was immediately clear that Dan had a hard time with seeing us in our new home. He barely lifted his eyes from the floor. "This is very nice," he conceded. "Nicer than I thought."

I wonder if he was struggling with how nice it was or with the fact that I was clearly dedicated to leaping into my own. Either way, his physical discomfort didn't stop him from pulling some tricks, and so Dan spent that Christmas Eve with me and Evan, infiltrating my safe living area. When Evan went to bed, Dan continued to try to push my boundaries, like he always did. Historically, he'd always gotten his way, and I truly believe that he thought he would this time, too.

"Babe, I need you," he wheedled. "I need you both to come back home."

Here we go again.

What scared me was what would happen when Dan didn't get his way. That was a potentially dangerous, ugly situation. *What do I say to soften the blow?* I wondered, more than a little panicked. *I let him in here. He's under my roof.*

It took me saying insistently and repeatedly, "Dan, you have to go," to get him out the door. I was holding firm, but I was also scared to death at how this could potentially blow up. That time, however, I won, his head hanging down as I shut and deadbolted the door behind him.

The rest of my family didn't exactly alleviate my stress during this time. What I considered to be the healthiest decision I'd ever made my family perceived as an opportunity to resist my growth. From the moment I walked out on Dan, I began to see a change in my family. Did they have Evan's best interests at heart? One hundred percent. Did they deep down want to see me fail? Fuck yes! I didn't quite get that message yet, however, and so I was still seeking validation and approval. And each time, I got slammed mentally or emotionally by them.

My stress wasn't helped by the fact that Dan, clearly not taking this time to self-reflect and heal, kept making his little trademark stunts.

One day, Dan's father dropped me a message to ask if he could see Evan, so I went to drop him off, totally unsuspecting. When I arrived, he said, "I don't know what's going on. My son isn't in a good place." He sighed. "Anyway, how are you doing?"

"Good," I responded. "I just want peace in my life."

And at that moment, like a bad omen, Dan came walking out of the bedroom, glaring at me. Obviously, I'd had no idea he was there, but his dad had apparently just picked him up from the bar. On a Sunday afternoon. He'd been at the bar the full night before, drinking himself into a stupor. Dan demanded to know why we couldn't get back together, to which I responded, "Throw yourself on Match, get on Tinder, go have sex with someone else, *something*. I don't care."

I'd already said this to him by this point, but this time, it seemed he listened to my advice a little *too* closely. Two months after I'd moved out, in the January, I went back to the house to pick up some of my belongings, and as soon as I walked in, I knew the vibe was off. It was when I looked by the garbage can in the kitchen that I saw some small Adidas slides.

Dan came sauntering out of the bedroom.

"I'm just here for the rest of my stuff," I said hesitantly.

"That's fine," he shrugged.

I went into the bedroom and saw beer bottles all over his nightstand, what used to be my bedside table (on "my" side of the bed), and the floor. When I examined the floor further, I spotted at least three used condoms. *Yuck.*

Dan smiled at me, smug. "I'm in love."

I grabbed my stuff and filed for a divorce the very next day.

Technically, Dan and I still owned the home in Indiana, but he had since moved in with the woman he was seeing, Stacy. This new development meant my attorney had to write up a different type of child support agreement stating that Stacy was to vacate the premises while Evan was there for any parenting time with his father. I tried to reason with Dan and explain that while he may be infatuated with this woman, that didn't mean he truly knew her. "And I don't know this woman, either," I reminded him. "There's no way my son is going to be around her."

At this point, I'd already known he'd been seeing somebody, but given the very limited time we'd been separated for, I would have realistically expected this to have been a one-night stand, if that. Yet here we were, Dan proclaiming his love for another woman two months after our separation. He obviously struggled with being alone and clung for dear life to the first thing that gave him attention—a rocky foundation to build any life upon.

I will be honest, a part of me was hurt at his moving on so quickly. How did he go from "I want you back" to being "in love" with someone else that fast? In retrospect, he will have known exactly what he was doing. He had taken to saying things like, "She's tiny and beautiful and has big breasts, and *you* are trash, and *you* are going to fall on your face and want to come back to me, and *I'm* not going to take you back, because I love her." I had to constantly check myself, reminding myself that Dan knew exactly how to make me self-doubt. *Did I do the wrong thing? Am I going to fall on my face?*

So, yes, it was initially difficult for me to wrap my head around Dan's new relationship, given the very short timespan that elapsed between our separation and his getting with Stacy. Now, though, I feel like this was God trying to give Dan a second chance at building a good life. I believe we all get a second chance, just like my dad did, though whether we make the most of it or not is in our hands. Do I believe Dan made the most of this second chance? Honestly, not really, but besides looking out for Evan, Dan's life is frankly none of my business anymore.

Stacy did try to get a little controlling during the divorce, which led to my attorney having to put Dan in his place and tell him that Stacy couldn't change the locks on the house, etc. while I was still a co-owner and had belongings there.

It was while all this was going on that Dan and I also set up a meeting to arrange parenting time. While I was sitting on my couch waiting for him to drop by, I saw him drive past out the window. Confused, I called him, and upon picking up, he said we couldn't get together that night anymore.

"We just need thirty minutes to figure out this parenting stuff," I insisted.

Turned out that he'd had Stacy in the car and she was in the process of moving all her belongings in.

When he came back to the house, Stacy got out and said, snidely, "This is my time. This is my house."

Clearly, she thought she was going to push me around.

"No," I corrected her, "you're moving into my *husband's* home that *I* still own. If you ever look at my son wrong, touch him, or harm him, I will fucking kill you."

This obviously meant it was then my turn to get into trouble. My attorney had warned me not to physically threaten anyone, as is standard, and I'd clearly crossed that line.

On that awkward note, we went into the house, Tommy by my side. All the while, Stacy was cajoling, "This is *my* house now."

"Oh, fuck," Tommy muttered.

He knew me a little too well.

Successfully riled, I turned and said, "C'mon, Stacy. Let's have some woman-to-woman time! Let's go to the other room."

While this was clearly a rocky start for my and Stacy's relationship, in the end (as is often the case with current and/or ex partners of someone abusive), we ended up somewhat looking out for each other, both possessing the grim, mutual understanding of the risks of being around someone of Dan's temperament. The thing is, it's extremely difficult to navigate an ex-husband who has such severe mental issues, and it seems that situation brought out the worst in us at the advent of her and Dan's relationship.

Dan continued to linger outside my bay window whenever he dropped Evan off. It was like he wanted me dead and was trying to figure out how to make that happen. Stacy would meanwhile yell at Dan from the driver's seat, "Get in the car! Let's go!" Dan was clearly still feeling very angry. And vengeful. The situation was so stressful that my landlord, well-aware of all that was going on, started leaving his pickup in the driveway and his dirty work boots by the door to make it look like a man lived there.

I attempted to file an order of protection on more than one occasion, but always encountered one major obstacle after another that prevented me from carrying it through.

Basically, this period was a struggle, but these horrible events were blessings in disguise. Little did I know that they were paving my path to freedom and success.

And God, was that success going to be worth it.

PART III
THE REBIRTH

15

Exploration

———

I WAS IN THE PROCESS of building my own empire.

Amidst Dan's tantrums, I was still living my best life with my son in our cute, cozy two-bedroom house with its full basement and garage.

It was undeniable that new energy was manifesting itself *really* hard. And I was so ready to get on board that new wavelength. I set up a vision board and regularly added to it, affirming my goals and dreams. I practiced daily meditation and prayer. While these practices weren't new to me, I really started to focus on those daily activities on my journey to rediscovering who I really was.

It was also a given that a path to greater earnings had to be part of the vision I was crafting. I was still working at the clinic down the street making nine-fifty an hour, and this just wasn't conducive to me fulfilling my goals. Sitting on the built-in bookshelves at home was a ceramic cookie jar I had given to my mom years before, and my goal was to keep that cookie jar filled to its little roof with funds to take care of me and my son.

Propelled by this need for self-sufficiency, I considered opening my home to Reiki clients, and, realizing that I felt comfortable enough in my own space to do so, I bought a massage bed and a set of white sheets. My sister-in-law had a photographer friend who agreed to do me a favor by taking some marketing shots for me, so I set up my Reiki workstation with my crystals. The friend took some nice photos in exchange for a thank-you barbecue dinner at the joint next door, and using these photographs, I set up a Google business page for my Reiki business. And so my business was born.

Amazingly, clients began to find me. So, my new routine involved dropping Evan off at school in the next town over before working around the house for a bit and then going to work at the clinic (mostly in the afternoons). For about ten hours a week, Evan and I also went to another clinic, where I did the nighttime cleaning and restocking. This meant it was only Saturdays that I could squeeze in a few Reiki clients. Dan, however, was cooperating with childcare at this time, and so started picking Evan up after school. Dawn also helped out as much as she could, often watching Evan while I saw Reiki clients or picked up a shift at one of the emergency clinics for extra cash. And this gave Evan and I the breathing space to create something of a regular routine: bike rides on the trail by our home; nightly basketball games in the driveway; weekend runs (or I should say *I* would run) in Wicker Memorial Park in Highland, Indiana, as he biked or skateboarded next to me.

Then again, not all with Dawn was sunshine and rainbows, and my first real slap in the face from her occurred around this time. I'd arrived to pick Evan up after a shift at the clinic one Saturday when she handed me a one-hundred-dollar Aldi gift card. Grateful, I exclaimed, "Jeez! Thanks, Dawn!" She knew money had been tight and food a bit scarce, so I was massively grateful.

Her response in front of Evan? "Just make sure you don't sell it for money. Feed your kid."

What?

This caught me completely off guard. It wasn't like I was some kind of methhead. The implications of her statement were insane, and couldn't have been further from my reality. I was stung, confused, and thoroughly pissed.

This strange dig aside, Evan and I were owning our new space and life, and I cannot convey quite how nice it was to be able to just *relax*. My inner child did the talking sometimes, and she reveled in the fact that I could have a bag of chips, sit on the couch, and watch TV without a single care in the world. Evan and I could have ice cream for dinner, if we wanted. There was such a sense of freedom and relief, and I was finally learning to love myself. I made it my mission to reintroduce myself to me. *Who am I? Oh, this is what doing your hair feels like! This is what doing your makeup feels like!*

I had a niece who was in hairdressing school, and one time, when she was practicing on my hair (which was long and thick), she gave me a weird sort of short layer in a fit of boyfriend-related rage, and the only fix was to chop off the whole mess so it was boy-short. I was upset at the time, but I'm realizing now that there was a bigger reason for this. Sometimes, we need a physical "cutting away" to let go of all the old emotional baggage.

I began getting myself together in the morning, grooming myself, putting in contacts, and thinking about my clothes a little more. Even though my wardrobe was as minimal as could be and I was broke, I would still daydream about the perfect outfit for this or that.

I also joined a local gym for ten bucks a month and slowly started to recover my fitness. My health journey would be put to the test years later from all the impact of the stress I'd dealt with, but for now, I was moving in the right direction. In the beginning, I did nothing but walk on a treadmill, but I slowly started to add in some strength and resistance training. I was reintroducing myself to the gym world like an old lover. It was something I used to do and love in pre-Dan days, and throwing myself back into it felt insanely liberating.

The long and short of it was that I began to put myself first and take care of myself. I was making huge strides in reclaiming myself and my life. I was working toward making myself strong again, both physically and mentally, and beginning to truly discover who I was.

My sex drive also began to reawaken at this time, and I had a *whole* lot of newfound curiosity in that area. Near the end of my marriage, Dan's attitude toward intimacy and sex had been, "I own you and I'm having sex with you now," and he was always drunk during sex, so it was, to put it bluntly, really gross. This meant that with time, I just learned to disassociate myself from it. I found myself in the most unusual places in my head during sex. Now, though, I was eager as hell (and scared to death!) to explore. My body didn't look like it did pre-baby, but still, Stella needed to get her groove back! I just needed to make sure it was with someone I felt safe with. So, around two or three months after the move, I racked my brains for who that special person could be; someone who I trusted enough to not hurt me.

I immediately thought of an old family friend. Steven had been Tommy's best friend (the one who'd accidentally knocked him out when Tommy was about ten!), and the two of us had hung out a lot in my teens and our twenties. We'd had fun back in the day, and at one point in our youth, we'd had sex, but it had never become anything more than that.

I gave him a call, and it turned out that he'd heard I was getting divorced. He was divorced himself, and, as luck would have it, we had even more than that in common. Steven was a good guy, and he began to coach me on what to expect from men, really reminding me of what I deserved. He loved me as a friend, and I can say to this day that even though we lost touch, I still love him dearly, too.

We started getting together for sexual exploration when my son wasn't home. This was my number one rule: no males in the house when Evan was home. I just couldn't fathom doing that and having Evan experience the revolving door of men I knew other kids had. Evan was struggling enough with the transition as it was. He didn't need anything else adding to the mix.

After being with Dan for ten or eleven years, I was incredibly nervous about the idea of having sex with a different man, and was still kind of disassociating. It ended up taking some intense therapy for me to realize that this long-term issue would take quite a few steps to repair itself, but what's important is that despite this uncertainty, I *did* begin to explore my sexuality, and I could feel that drive returning.

One good friend in his fifties, who was in an open marriage, also filled that need for me at one point. His wife knew me, and I was comfortable in this situation, but I also knew that I wanted more from my sex life (specifically, more intimacy), and I wanted it right away. I just didn't realize how many steps I'd have to take before reaching the substantial relationship I desired.

I was working two jobs, trying to raise my son, and keeping my Reiki practice going when Dan and I officially filed for divorce in the January (after I'd discovered his relationship with Stacy). My little cookie jar was full, but it was still a crazy juggling act to keep the funds coming in *while* trying to carve out time here and there for myself. I was literally one financial crisis away from bankruptcy, and this happened at the same time as me needing to take some trips to the ER for a diverticulitis flare-up.

January as a whole was pretty damn rough. We celebrated Evan's eighth birthday on the third by going to see Blue Man Group and having dinner in the city with Susan and Tim (a beautiful gift they gave him), but then that night, I came down with food poisoning. Two days later, I woke up struggling to breathe. This didn't seem to be anything unusual at first: ever since my pulmonary embolism, common colds had always hit my chest bad. My lungs will forever be compromised. So, unconcerned, I dropped Evan off at school and called in sick at work... only to have Dr. Sam tell me I couldn't take the day off unless I had a doctor's note advising as such, and to come in if I could make it.

I drove myself to the ER and was diagnosed with pneumonia.

To top this off, about a month after the divorce was finalized, I was working an afternoon shift at the vet clinic when Dr. Sam and her husband, Tony, walked in. Tony was an imposing six-foot five-inch retired Chicago cop.

"Come here, Felicity," Dr. Sam called when she saw me. We all filed into her office, Tony shutting the door behind him.

That's a little weird, I thought.

"What's up?"

"Do you remember that one day you took petty cash?" Dr. Sam said suddenly. "It was a couple of months ago."

We frequently took petty cash to run errands for the doc, and one Saturday in January, she'd said, "Why don't you get money out of petty cash and go get us some donuts?" And I'd done just that, placing the receipt and change in the box when I returned.

I asked her to cut to the chase. "What are you trying to say to me?"

The vet proceeded to say that I had shorted the petty cash of six dollars on that day.

I told her, truthfully, that I didn't think that I'd walked away with any money, and suggested that she check the end-of-day deposits, since this easily could be where the discrepancy was.

"If you get the ledgers, I can help you figure it out," I added. "I can't make sense of anything without looking at the books, and I can't really remember any specific details from that day."

To my shock, Dr. Sam was hearing none of it. "You stole from me, and we need to let you go."

I was struck dumb. "Sam, I didn't steal from you," I said firmly, panicked. "This is either an honest mistake, or the deposit is over. Why didn't you come to me when this happened? I *need* this job."

To my horror, her tone was cold and detached. "I don't care. You stole from me."

"I've been doing this a *long* time," I pressed on, undeterred. "You *know* this is all I know, and I have a good reputation in this industry. Why would I jeopardize all that for six dollars?"

"I don't know, but you have to go."

My heart pounding and my cheeks aflame, I gave her the keys, walked out, wrote a check for six dollars to the animal clinic, and left it on the counter. The only time I'd ever been fired from a job was at the age of twelve, when I couldn't bus tables fast enough.

The worst part? A few days later, an employee messaged me to tell me that the deposit had, indeed, been over. The evidence that I hadn't stolen a penny had been right there all along.

I was completely stunned, and yet looking back on this whole strange experience, Dr. Sam's office had clearly been dysfunctional from the get-go. I'd known that when walking in—I could feel it—but I'd still desperately needed the job, and still did when she wrongfully let me go. Then again, spiritually speaking, everything happens for a reason, and while it was ugly and hurtful at that moment to be fired from something at which I had always strove for excellence in, I still always respected Dr. Sam and her staff moving forward. I knew I'd end up interacting with them again at some point and that bad blood would be on her hands, but that didn't mean it needed to be on mine. I could choose to simply exit gracefully.

This didn't mean that deep down inside, I wasn't scared shitless at my sudden uncertainty regarding what my future would look like. Everything was now totally up in the air, and with a young son to take care of, this was terrifying.

Once I walked out of those clinic doors, I called my girlfriend who lived down the street, in shock. It was tough just letting it sink in. I cried and cried, and then went to pick up Evan. My rent was already paid for the next six or seven months, but I was stressed about how I would now make ends meet after that time was up. *Which sofa will Wheezy land on with her son?* was a constant fear that lingered throughout my post-divorce life. What's more, I could feel hate from the people in my life, or maybe even envy. It felt like everyone was constantly waiting for me to fail. This wasn't helped by the divorce debt and hospital bills that were also overwhelming me. I simply did not see how I could possibly meet all my financial commitments *and* keep me and Evan afloat at the same time.

As a last resort, I went to Dawn, the trustee of our parents' inheritance, but she wouldn't let me have any of it. I would "only blow the money", according to her.

Lovely.

At least I had the support of my Reiki circle. After informing her of my current situation, another Reiki practitioner said to me, "This is when we have to trust in God."

Amen.

I ended up being out of work for four months, but during those months, my Reiki and coaching practice, graciously, opened up like crazy. I was seeing clients left and right, and we didn't go without food, heat, or electricity once. (Well, maybe electricity one time, when I screwed up on the budget bill and the company shut me off during a snowstorm. That was a crappy mistake!) I'd drop Evan off at school and then have my home open for business, seeing three to seven clients a day, and I was working out daily. It was amazing, and that cookie jar was fucking *full*. Evan and I were living the dream. I was supporting us *and* not sleeping on one of my siblings' sofas or begging Dan to take me back.

I was doing it alone.

When we entered this new era of calm, I started to ponder what I really wanted in a man again. I told my friend I was looking for someone to go out to dinner with; someone who was successful and operating at a slightly higher level. I really wanted to grow myself into a successful person. One thing I'd known when I'd left Dan was that I wanted a second chance at the life I knew I was meant to lead.

After listening carefully, my friend said, "I know the perfect man. Tom is a high-powered attorney going through a divorce, and he's also looking for a no-strings-attached woman he could take out to dinner with clients."

Hmmm, no strings attached and an occasional dinner date for me? Why the fuck not? Sure, I can do this!

So, my friend gave Tom my number, and we began to chat casually. Tom was asking all the right questions, so this was a breeze. "Did you go to college?" "How well do you hold up in uncomfortable situations?" I replied honestly to everything he asked, and was moved to the next level of the game: a coffee date.

Now look, I realized that I was about to enter an arena that would open my eyes to the devil's playground where there's power and money, deceit, and greed... but oh, boy, did I witness some serious shit!

The day we met for coffee, I dropped Evan off for school and got myself ready. Tom knew that I was going through a divorce, and I assumed he'd pieced together the stereotype he was expecting before he'd even met me: single mother, minimum-wage job, minimal education.

I don't think he realized that I wouldn't fit into that box for much longer.

I managed to pull together a business-casual outfit: a pair of pencil jeans from Gap, a white blouse, a navy blazer from Nordstrom Rack, and a pair of nude heels. Design on a dime. And I loved what I saw in the mirror! I looked so polished and sophisticated. My hair had grown out into a classic bob, and I was really mastering some natural makeup skills. I was crushing it.

When I walked into the coffee shop, I was swept by nerves. I couldn't see anyone who resembled what he'd said he looked like.

I grabbed a cup of black coffee and made myself comfortable. I'd seen a man who was working in his car eyeballing me a few moments before, and sure enough, a few minutes later, he entered the coffee shop. He was wearing a custom navy suit and had brownish hair with lots of silver. My heart fluttered. This was everything I desired to be and to be with. *Holy shit. Could this potentially work out?* He flashed his expensive smile as he glided into his seat. "Wow, you're very pretty," he told me.

I melted even more. There was a magnetic spark between us.

He'd grown up poor, like I had, but had really done well in his career. He was confident, very smart, and smelled of power. In other words, he was everything I was manifesting for myself, and I was amazed by the world he commanded. He opened my eyes to the world of success. Through him, I met a lot of high-powered, high-profile people, and at these swanky dinners, I sat and observed everything. Unfortunately, however, I also saw and heard things that I thought corrupt and illegal; a world that lacked a moral compass and reeked of deceit, evil, sex, and drugs.

One night at dinner in the city, the mood shifted and became relaxed, and people pulled out a ton of drugs and booze. This made my Uncomfortable Radar flare immediately, and thankfully, Tom could see that and politely got a car for me to go home.

Tom played the character I needed when we got together for dinner dates. He was charming and down-to-earth, but at his core was a heaviness that I didn't like. I was also picking up on a few mind games he'd attempted to pull me into.

In the end, I found I didn't want what came with Tom's territory, and so I broke off the relationship. I was so eager to find the one (a little *too* eager, when I look back now), and so it seemed patience was to be my lesson this time around.

I was back to square one, which was okay. I was about to be consumed with Evan's baseball season—something that will always fill my heart with joy. I thanked the universe for bringing this man into my life, and got a little more specific with my manifesting: *Okay, the man I'm looking for is a businessman, but who has a moral code.*

In all areas of my life, I was now trusting in God and manifesting abundance. Meanwhile, Evan was having another stellar baseball season and people were still finding my Google business page for Reiki and coaching, which was amazing. This didn't mean I'd called off the job search, however. Financially, we were skating on thin ice due to the aforementioned divorce debt and hospital bills, so I couldn't afford to have the Reiki business be my solo gig. I needed another source of income, and fast.

After almost four months of searching, a couple of job options opened up. One clinic was offering a really nice benefits package, but the drive was about an hour and ten minutes away. The other would only start me at twelve dollars an hour, but the goal was to move me into a management position, and it was only ten minutes away from my house.

Evan was mentally struggling and in therapy during this time, so the choice essentially was: take a job opportunity that would only pull me further away from Evan but could help us out of our sticky financial predicament, or take the no-benefits job that would make me a little more available for Evan.

Talk about being stuck between a rock and a hard place.

In the end, I chose the job that was close by with no benefits. It would mean I could drop off Evan at school and then hop on the expressway for a very short commute. However, I just wasn't prepared for the fact that, no matter how hard I worked, I was going to be hit hard financially. I traded in my car because the lease was almost up and I had an overwhelming amount of divorce debt piling up, and there was not much income.

Though I continued to be optimistic, the reality of it was that I was experiencing one of the scariest financial crises I would ever go through. My divorce was nearly over when I had to fire my attorney and hire a new one. The state of Indiana fucking sucks when it comes to divorce and women. I was also trying to get dental work done before my previous insurance ran out. Basically, I was in survivor mode, and my body and health would pay the price later on.

Meanwhile, Dawn was still firm in denying me any inheritance. "Felicity, everything is wrapped up in stocks. We still have so much to get through."

Fuck 'em all, with their snide comments. My eyes were wide open, and I knew it was Evan and me against the world.

I'd given up a bunch of the Reiki time to take on the full-time stable clinic job, so even though I had a job at the clinic and was making good money from the Reiki sessions, I was hanging on by the skin of my teeth to cover the car payment, insurance, gas, rent, and food.

These times were not the easiest, and yet I had a newfound hope; a vision for my and Evan's future. While my circumstances remained trying, I'd experienced a fundamental mindset shift, and it was this that led me to see these circumstances (and the ones that were about to befall me) as what they were: lessons, opportunities for growth, and preparation for the future. A future that I knew would be glorious.

16

John

———

I HAD MY NOSE TO the grindstone, doing my thing, taking care of my son, and fitting in Reiki clients when I could. As I'd hoped, I was promoted to a small management position at my clinic job in 2016, and I also had a full-time hospital manager position in the works.

As part of my managerial role, I worked the floor on Thursday as an assistant to the doctors and vet techs. I treasured this time *immensely* because it was the part of my role in which I could spend some one-on-one time with our clients and really connect with *people*.

On one such Thursday, I headed into a room housing an elderly cat who'd been brought in for numerous symptoms of kidney failure (increased thirst and urination, rapid weight loss... the works). I was manning this appointment, and upon entering the room, I found a beautiful older woman—probably in her sixties, with long, glossy blond hair—with what I presumed to be her granddaughter (I guessed seven to nine years old). Now, Veterinary Practice 101 is when you introduce yourself to the owner, you also make a point of introducing yourself to the animal. As you probably could have guessed, this is more for the benefit of the owner than the pet; it immediately sets a precedent of good, attentive care. So, as the little girl danced around us (as kids do), I cooed to the cat and asked the woman the standard questions: how long had the cat been exhibiting the reported symptoms? Any new symptoms? Any vomiting? Diarrhea?

The little girl continued dancing around us as I pressed on with the questions, and in my peripheral, I could see her moving what some might call a little... erratically, even for a young kid. She was sort of limping around and randomly grabbing my scrubs and arm. I looked down at her occasionally and smiled, a little weirded out by her behavior.

Once the appointment was done and I'd put the cat back in her carrier, the little girl grabbed both of my hands and, finally, made eye contact with me.

This was when shit got a little weird.

In those moments, her hands clasped in my hands and her eyes searching mine, she told me everything. She didn't *speak*—she remained completely silent—yet I heard and understood, clear as day, what she was trying to say. I truly wish I could describe this better, but all I can really say is that the moment our hands joined and our eyes met, I got a crystal clear message flash in my mind. That's it. It was as clear and obvious as if she'd spoken the words aloud. The message was that she was happy and at peace whenever she was playing with her doll.

I still get chills when I look back on this.

Baffled, I turned to the woman and said, "Ma'am, she's telling me something. I don't know how else to say this, but I have a message for you. Your granddaughter wants you to know she's most peaceful and happy when she's playing with her doll, and that her doll has long brown hair."

The woman stared back at me, her eyes so wide I could see the whites all around, and her mouth (literally, as if in a cartoon) fell open.

"I... know this might sound strange, but I'm... gifted, of sorts," I said slowly. "I don't typically share that with people in my work environment, but your granddaughter insisted that you know this."

The woman began to cry silently.

"My daughter overdosed six months ago and passed away," she finally said, shakily, "so I stepped in to care for her daughter. My granddaughter. She's mute."

As she spoke, though she was (understandably) shaken, it was as though I could physically *hear* a weight being lifted from her chest. From her soul.

"Can I speak to you in private about this?" she asked as she was about to leave.

"Of course." I fumbled for one of my business cards. "If you like, you can come to my place when I'm off from work, and we can go into some more detail about this."

This may sound like an unusual story, and don't get me wrong, it most definitely is, but this type of experience actually isn't an especially rare occurrence when you have spiritual gifts and, specifically, a knack for "downloading" messages. And yes, this can be a little draining at times. There are days when it is especially taxing on my body and spirit, and I find myself wishing I could just block out the noise around me. But when it comes down to it, I know God has given me this gift for a reason, and I would never seriously dream of giving it up. Plus, how could you ever wish away the ability to give people like that grandmother—self-sacrificing, doting people who've had a tough-ass ride—the gift of "downloaded" messages from their loved ones? I'd be out of my mind to want to be rid of that, even if it can be a little overwhelming and burdensome at times.

In the end, she took me up on my offer of an at-home consultation, and we ended up completing a couple of Reiki sessions. Turned out, like so many people, she just needed to take a moment to acknowledge and consciously let go of all the emotional trauma and baggage she'd been unknowingly carrying around. She'd recently dealt with the passing of her daughter, *and* she was currently dealing with her son's own drug addiction, and so she'd had the weight of the world on her shoulders before we began working together. Yet within just a couple of months of work, we managed to alleviate some of that pain, frustration, and worry.

Basically, this woman was just a kindly, hard-working soul who'd become bogged down by a prevalent issue in the area: substance abuse.

Clearly, this role opened me up to some unforgettable experiences and interactions. Yet there was still a part of my life that felt really quite empty: my romantic life. After my little dating stint, I'd decided to put romance on the backburner and focus on my little family instead, largely because I knew Evan needed my attention. He was beginning to have meltdowns as a result of him being bounced around so much so I could work during his younger years. So, I knew were my focus needed to be... but my girlfriends knew my hesitance to start dating again was less to do with my bigger goals and more to do with the fact that I was holding myself back. And because of this, my one best friend at the time kept pushing me to get out there.

Whether she'd stolen a selfie with Evan and cropped it or discretely snapped a pic of me I didn't know, but all of a sudden, I started getting notices from Match.com. I hadn't signed up for this dating service, but, sure enough, my credit card statement reflected it.

My friend fessed up. Unbeknownst to me, during one of our pizza and movie nights at my house, she'd taken a picture of me and created and paid for a Match.com profile. When she'd previously encouraged me to go out and explore, my response had just been a closed-off, "There's no one out here in northwest Indiana that fits my criteria." While I'm not trying to attract in hate mail, it cannot be denied that northwest Indiana contained slim pickings of white-collar single men. Undeterred, however, she branched out on my behalf, and I started talking to some nice guys through Match—and, funnily enough, I didn't experience *anything* comparable to the online dating horror stories I'd heard before. Every single northwest Indiana guy I spoke to was super-polite and respectful. These region boys weren't bad at all! In fact, there was one who had every quality I was looking for. His name was Vince. He was a few years older than me and funnier than a whip. Vince had a great career and a good work ethic, but what won me over was that he was raising his ex-wife's kids even though he wasn't the birth father. How selfless of him!

Vince was running strong, but deep down, I could feel that even though he met all my criteria, he wouldn't push me into being the woman that I was meant to be. I was hardcore manifesting this strong powerhouse woman I knew I was inside, and with Vince, I could feel two things: either we would get too comfortable and both end up fat and happy (which I didn't want for myself), or my overbearing personality would scare the shit out of him.

Not what I was looking for.

Once I ended things, I of course missed his sense of humor and Green Bay Packers smack talk (yes, I am a Packers fan), and the million-dollar question still remained unanswered: when would the man I had been praying for arrive?

Hi, how ya doing? I know Munster.

This message sent to me in July 2016 proclaimed to be from someone called John. After some social media stalking, I found out he was seventeen years older than I was (my age range was mid-fifties), so I ignored the first couple of *Hello, sweetheart* messages, reasoning he was probably some old creeper, and kept scrolling.

I don't know what prompted me to finally respond, but what I do know is that when we did connect, we chatted online a little and I quickly realized that I'd maybe been a little quick to judge. He seemed like a nice man.

After a few go-arounds, he asked if he could call.

What the heck, why not? I mean, it wasn't like it was going to *go* anywhere. He was just a nice older man who was fun to talk to. So, I agreed to a call. And he was a fucking riot. He was *so* transparent. In his scraggly, deep Chicago voice, he spilt everything and told me so much about himself. I could hear him puffing away on his cigarette between breaths of conversation. He'd been divorced for six years, and he had adult kids. "You gotta be careful. I've dated some women who just want to take you for a ride," he remarked at one point.

Okay...

We talked a little about what we both did, and it turned out he'd grown up around quite a bit of wealth and had had the "hard work" mindset drilled into him from a very young age. So, he was financially secure, independent, and hard-working. Tick, tick, tick.

Despite his anything-but-modest origins, he sounded super-down-to-earth and straightforward. And he wanted to meet up for dinner.

I didn't have much hope pinned on this in terms of a relationship. I really thought it would just be dinner with a nice older man. And dinner would be fun, right?

We met at a nice Italian restaurant. He was my height (shorter than me when I was wearing heels) and a little stout, but he was handsome, and, importantly, had an overwhelming energy. His presence was boisterous, and he was saturated in Creed cologne. (I assumed he wore too much to cover up the chain-smoking habit he had.)

As we knocked back our drinks, he smiled, and I thought, *Wow,* that's *an expensive smile.*

We had the best time. All he did was talk about himself (not in a bad way, but about his childhood, his first marriage, and dating), and I just sat there trying to filter through the information and read him. As an empath, I find that people frequently feel comfortable just spilling their stories out to me, and I was trying to really dig deep and get to know the spirit of this guy who'd suddenly entered my life.

Then, in the middle of the restaurant, he planted a kiss on me. I wasn't prepared for that, and the bashful side of me took over.

We finished dinner and went our separate ways. "It was nice to meet you," I said, and didn't expect anything more.

Now, as we know, I'd been praying for God to send me the man who was meant for me. I wanted to settle down and create a stable family where my son and I could have a good chance at a second life. And I'd already found that I liked the grounding energy of men in their fifties (a little older than I). They tended to be past the BS, without anything to prove. So, I was praying for an older, more mature man; someone in business; someone successful.

Perhaps I should have been more specific about how *much* older. Nevertheless, age is just a number, right?

As it turned out, this lovely, funny man who was seventeen years my elder texted me the next day. And the next day. And the next day. He called me and poured his guts out to me about his family; about growing up on a horse ranch and going to boarding school; about fond family memories of piling into the car with his four siblings, dog, and duck (yes, duck) and going to the lake house, where his mom cooked up a huge batch of pork chops. He had great stories and even greater memories. I envied his childhood.

I still only listened, sharing very small and select pieces of my history here and there. At this point in my life, I was beginning to fully understand the depth of the dysfunction that prevailed in my family, and so didn't feel comfortable with sharing stories of food scarcity or my dad's seedy side-hustle. Regardless, I agreed to a second date—dinner at a place near me. Then a third date—a visit to my house. After working fifty hours a week, I was exhausted and really not up to stressing over a night out, and I also wanted to see what John's reaction would be to my place; to a normal little lifestyle. I wanted to feel his vibe toward my setup.

He came over and made himself right at home. He'd been brought up with much more opportunity and seemed pretty well off, yet he exhibited no sense of entitlement or surprise when he entered my space. He just lit up a cigarette in my kitchen, just like he was at home.

"No, you have to go outside to smoke," I said firmly.

He was cool with that.

I made a lasagna, and we had a great, relaxed evening. He had good, grounding energy, and brought me a sense of peace. He was so normal and comforting and good. Basically, he made it past that first test, so the next test was in the bedroom! I was still looking at this as nothing more than a fling, and so in my eyes, this was just some casual sex… and an opportunity to fulfil my curiosity. *What would it be like to have sex with someone much older than myself?*

Let's just say it didn't disappoint. But I still didn't know how much further we were going to take this relationship. Obviously, I was still in this juggling act of being a single mom while trying to stay financially afloat, but I was also trying to be the best version of myself, and dreamed of eventually growing into a successful businesswoman. I impressed on him the fact that I needed to work on Saturdays, to which he responded, "That's okay. We could just hang out at your house. I like it there. It's quiet." And when he next came over, he brought me some chicken salad and put it in the fridge. It was a sweet gesture: he realized how little extra time I had for cooking.

I threw in some laundry, and we just sat and talked. In my head, I was trying to figure out what stage of the game he was in. I told him that I could feel the presence of a lot of women around him, and again, he was an open book with me. "I wasn't a good first husband. I did a lot of cocaine and cheated on my ex-wife a lot."

"Where are you now?"

"I went into rehab a couple of years ago."

"What about the women?"

"Well, I want to find the right one. So, you have to date a lot."

So, the jury was out on where we were going. I could see that his inner child and history with addiction meant he sought validation through women, but how far this went I couldn't foresee. Not until much later in the relationship. All I knew was that John was undeniably very patient, and we truly had the best time growing this relationship. Very, very *slowly* growing this relationship. He told me how all the other women he'd dated had just wanted the money, and how he knew I wasn't like that. He told me, "I can feel you're The One, sweetheart. I just know you are."

All I thought in response to these proclamations was, *Okay, old man, slow down.* He was being forward for sure, but I couldn't deny that I loved his presence. Whenever I could skate away for a weekend to his house, we puttered around gardening, painting, or doing other projects, and the domestic peace that settled around me during these days was blissful after a lifetime of fight-or-flight and scarcity.

The first time I went to his house, it felt so peaceful and quiet, and yet I could feel an overwhelming energy saying, "Don't get too comfortable." *Where is that coming from?* I wondered. Was this my empath-psychic skills kicking in again? It took a few visits before I was able to connect the dots concerning this protective, stern energy. I was feeling stern male energy: strong, quiet, and tall. I looked around the house and then up to the second-floor threshold, where I saw an image of a tall, quiet, balding man staring down. He was wearing a cowboy belt buckle and cowboy boots.

I later found out this was John's father, who had passed away sixty years before. And he was looking down on us.

I truly believe his dad was trying to protect him.

I met his eyes and told him, "I'm not going to hurt your son, don't worry. I'm not going to take advantage."

Over time, while his father's presence remained, the protective, dominant energy did not. I could see, at the core of everything, that John needed to be taken care of, and I truly believe that I was brought into John's life to help him to heal. A soul contract, of sorts.

I brought him acceptance and growth, and he brought me normalcy and peace.

He did move in a different world, though. One night, when we were going up to his house, he said, "Bring a bag. We'll go out to dinner." I've always been a bargain shopper, managing stylish looks on a dime, and I brought a classic little black designer dress. "Wow, you're going to fit in well here!" he said when he saw me.

What does that mean?

When we went to dinner, I walked into Phony Land—beautiful, beautiful phonies, with fake teeth, fake boobs, fake hair, and fake personalities. *Holy fuck. How am I supposed to compete with these women?* I was having to overcome myself; to avoid reverting to the mindset of the little girl who'd never felt good or pretty enough. And the truth is that, for a good four to five years of my and John's relationship, I *didn't* feel good enough in his world was full of women who threw their cleavage in the face of any man wearing a Rolex or driving a high-end car. I watched these women, with their glossy hair extensions and perfected manicures, with a deep, deep bitterness and, beneath that, unworthiness. The feelings they produced within me said much more about me than about them, of course, but for now, judgment settled into my gut, thick and syrupy and toxic. I was clearly still in a place of pretty low self-esteem, and my (strong) reaction was a sure sign that I needed to do some more inner healing work.

After we dated for about four months, I wanted John to meet Evan. I needed John to truly evaluate whether he wanted to do this again, considering his kids were grown. So, the three of us went to a Mexican restaurant, and when John excused himself to go to the restroom, my spiritually gifted son looked at me and said, "He's a very kind man."

"Yes, Evan, he is."

While this meal appeared to have been a success, I was bracing for John not wanting to continue our relationship.

Turned out I needn't have worried.

"He's a cute kid," John said. "He's quiet, like you."

"But do you want to keep seeing each other?"

I was trying to give him an out.

"Yeah, I don't care."

On we go, then.

While John was cool with everything, Evan would soon display much uncertainty and displeasure surrounding the relationship. This was, of course, understandable, considering I was his only stable parent and he thus likely felt the need to keep me close.

It was also around this time I started to really notice Evan begin to decline, little by little.

Evan had always been a rather private, quiet child, and it was largely because of this that I didn't learn until much later down the road the full extent of quite how impacted he had been from being bounced from house to house so I could work. This is a harsh reality many single parents that are just scraping by have to face at some point. There's now a bit of an epidemic of "backpack kids", thanks to the rise in single parenthood. I'd be seriously interested to see some stats on their mental health and wellbeing, because if Evan is anything to go off, this type of upbringing often has much more far-reaching impacts than we think. Don't get me wrong, I have friends that had to do the same whose kids just go with the flow, but Evan was the complete opposite, and it was around this point that he began having mini meltdowns of, "I don't want to go to Aunt Dawn's house, Mom!" and, "Why can't we just stay home?"

It hurt to hear this, but I *had* to work. I had literally no other option if I was going to keep supporting the two of us. So, all I could do was reassure him. "Evan, I understand, but Mom has to work."

It was when Evan was in third grade that I saw the biggest shift. At this point, he'd been seeing the sweetest therapist for around a year or so, but we weren't making too much headway. Dan would pop in on these sessions occasion, and I can recall the starting signs of his attempts to manipulate, control, and hyperfocus.

Do keep in mind that at this point, it had been two years since I'd left Dan, so in the grand scheme of Evan's short life (and his tender age and temperament), it was kind of a given Evan was going to struggle with quite so many life-altering changes occurring so close together.

In retrospect, do I regret moving so fast knowing what I do now? Absolutely. I fully own the part I played in making Evan's world an uncertain one. But I knew I needed to work hard, and fast, or I'd end up living the life my mother did, and there was no way in hell I would have survived by working part-time, like Evan kept requesting. If I'd done this, we would have certainly ended up back with Dan or one of my family members. It was clear from the get-go that if I didn't hustle, and hustle *fast*, we'd sink.

So, that's what I did.

Naturally, though, Evan continued to reject the changes that popped up out of nowhere in his life, and who could blame him? We were clearly both in survivor mode. Sure, we were thriving compared to how we'd felt when living with Dan, but that didn't take away from the fact that if I didn't work my ass off and seize every opportunity that came my way, Evan and I would wind up on the breadline and/or back in a toxic household.

I didn't want that for us. It was a lose-lose.

Even still, while I knew Evan was extremely resistant to change, I could already see the joy, peace, and stable family unit we could develop with John, and so I hoped, desperately, that Evan's wariness would change with trust and time. My and John first year of dating was just heaps of fun as we got to know one another, and I wanted Evan to feel just as on board as I was. While this may sound cheesy, I honestly felt like a kid again, and John felt the same.

Not too long after we started dating, John and I decided to conquer our health together, and both began to lose weight. His highest weight was two hundred and ninety-three when we started, and as I write, he is now one hundred and ninety. It was around this time in our relationship that he earnestly expressed that he felt like he was going through a rebirth of sorts, and he was. We both were.

Basically, the contrast between how I felt about myself when with Dan vs John was like night and day. I'd felt as if I'd had no agency around Dan and was a victim of my circumstances, but around John, I felt empowered, capable, and sexy. I slowly opened up to John about my spiritual practices and world, and the first time I did a reading on him, I told him how I was getting the message that he felt like the outcast in his family and like he'd never been heard, and that his siblings had tried to keep him in line.

He was shocked at all this, as well as the other stuff that came up that he'd never shared with me before.

One thing was for sure: we were *good* for each other. Loving him wasn't hard or self-destructive. I wasn't constantly picking between my happiness or his. Instead, everything was *easy*, natural, and uncomplicated. We helped each other to grow in leaps and bounds into the people we were always meant to be. We reveled in seeing each other thrive, and this permission to live out loud fully allowed me—allowed *both* of us—to flourish.

Clearly, we'd found something truly beautiful.

While all of this was going on, I was still working through the divorce proceedings, and when we were getting close to finalizing the divorce, John said, "Why don't we go somewhere to celebrate? I'll make the arrangements."

I agreed, and thought maybe we'd travel to Wisconsin or somewhere similar, but in November, John told me we were going to Mexico.

"I can't pay for that," I protested.

"This is my treat," he said. "You work really hard. Let me just give you this."

I was dumbfounded.

"Thank you. I appreciate that," I said quietly.

I applied for the passport and got ready to board an airplane for the very first time in my life the following January. In the meantime, considering we were planning a vacation together, I thought he should probably meet my family. So, I invited him and his daughter, Morgan, to join us (as in, myself and my family) for Thanksgiving. Leaving Dan had been excruciatingly stressful and difficult, and after making that leap and enduring all of the abuse, I hoped my family would be happy for me.

When we all arrived for Thanksgiving, I headed toward the kitchen and happened to overhear my brother and sister talking. "Oh, yeah, she's only taking him for the money. She's a fucking user."

David's voice.

My blood instantly boiled. "I heard that," I called over. "Why would you say that?"

"Stop eavesdropping. That's all you ever do," he said, unbothered.

Why can't you be happy for me?

My family were more than a little two-faced when it came to things like this. They warmly welcomed John and Morgan in their usual way, yet the passive aggression towards me was real. My sister angrily hissed at one point, "Felicity, button your top up! Your tits are showing."

I mean, what the fuck?

Despite the lack of (authentic) warmth or support from my family, I continued to grow with John. We kept doing our little projects. He had a lot of loneliness in his life, and I helped to heal him from that.

We spent our first Christmas together, and then we had an amazing vacation in Mexico—the Grand Velas Resorts in Riviera Maya, a time that felt like spring break for the both of us. The cocktails and food came in strong for seven days, and we had so much fun—way more than I had anticipated.

It was then that I knew he was The One. This fact was cemented as I drove home after flying back to Chicago and staying at his for a night. It was snowing, and I just started crying.

I missed him already.

I was in deep.

17
Mrs. B

———

OUR RELATIONSHIP CONTINUED TO EVOLVE over the course of the next couple of years. John was now coming over more (even on weekends, when I had Evan), and while we had taken things slowly, things were very clearly progressing, and so it was time to talk about the next step.

I don't know if this is because I was self-sabotaging, but I always gave John an out. So, when we started talking about the next step and marriage, I vocalized the idea of me and Evan staying put and John and I simply being partners who lived separately. Why blend a family, finances, etc.? I realized that marriage and cohabitation would involve a prenup, trusts, and a potential battle down the road, so did I even want to venture down this avenue?

After very long discussions and a sincere evaluation of where we both wanted to be long-term, marriage it was! I would eventually be Mrs. B. The thought made my heart pitter-patter. I loved everything about this humble, kind man, and he felt the same about me.

For Evan, however, this was a different story. Evan and John had their moments, and Evan once expressed, in the midst of a heated meltdown, "I thought it would be Mom and me forever." John was always so compassionate and understanding, constantly giving Evan the opportunity to express himself, but he also knew Evan needed a strong male role model, and wanted to be there for him.

But Evan just wasn't sold.

He had his own stuff going on, too. He was slipping in school, just skating by, and was experiencing some underlying social and emotional issues. Later testing would also lead us to understand that Evan had a handful of learning challenges, like me. Academically, Evan had always struggled, even since being a toddler, because school was what he called "boring". Whenever he said this, it was as though I can *see* his old soul coming out; as though deep down inside, his old soul was like, "I've been there and done that, and now I want to seek adventure." It wasn't intellect he lacked: if he applied himself, he cruised by easily, but most of the time, he could only bring himself to do the bare minimum. And now, it wasn't only academic stress he needed to contend with, but the prospect of his home life drastically changing.

Perhaps these apprehensions from Evan had some merit. After all, I can remember telling John early on in our relationship that I didn't think he'd been destined to come into our lives until much later. His response to this was, "God knew you needed me sooner." And to be honest, I think John was correct with this. John was that grounding, strong, down-to-earth masculine energy that I'd needed, since I have a tendency to operate at a mile a minute with my head in the clouds.

Bottom line: we instantly got along like two old kindred souls, and this only confirmed to me my suspicion that this wasn't the first time we'd been partners.

That's not to say our relationship was always perfectly easy. No relationship is. The biggest life lesson I learned through my relationship with John was how to love someone with detachment. That is, how to accept the fact that they will operate in whatever way that feels most natural to them, and how to understand that this is not a reflection of who I am. Basically, not everything everyone in a relationship with you (romantic, spiritual, or platonic) does is personal to you. Everyone is dealing with their own shit and deals with everything differently. Sounds obvious, but I think this is a truth a lot of us struggle to wrap our heads around.

A key example of this was how John showed support. He was *always* supportive and encouraging to me, but he was still very flippant about progress. I think he struggled with voicing when he felt proud of his loved ones, and this meant that if I was rocking my life and producing great work, he struggled to give me credit where credit's due. Our weight/fitness journey is a great example of this: when we first got together, I struggled to shed any weight, big time. It was only when I learned that my body was actually insulin resistant as a result of PCOS that I realized I could lose weight by fasting, only eating one meal a day four out of seven days a week. Once I started doing this, I lost a tremendous amount of weight, my bloodwork fell into alignment, and I felt an incredible amount of relief and pride over the fact I'd finally overcome this hugely difficult journey.

John's response? "Yeah, not bad. You're getting there."

A killer, right?

It took me a good couple of years to recognize the fact that John's brain just worked very differently to mine, and that the reactions that I often interpreted as cold or uncaring were actually anything but. The truth of the matter was that his world was one of no accountability, unhealthy habits, and deep insecurity. Yet he was by far the most patient person I'd ever met. Regardless of how bleak and hopeless my life looked at times, he just sat there and reassured me that all would turn out okay. And this was often all I needed to hear. For all his faults (and mine!), John was my biggest cheerleader.

In among all of this, John and I were planning on going on another vacation to Mexico the following winter, during which time Dawn agreed to watch Evan for me. What I didn't know was that John was planning on popping the question on this trip. He and Morgan had gone ring shopping a few times before making the final decision. Interestingly, however, his son remained unaware of the engagement until after the fact. My feeling was that his son was a bit apprehensive regarding the whole relationship. Later down the road, he would express how much gratitude he had for me for helping to turn Morgan into the independent lady she is today, but for now, he was a little wary, which was understandable.

We had another five days of our holiday left and were preparing for a dinner out when I whined about putting a dress on again. "Why can't we just order room service?"

Before I knew it and amid my mini temper tantrum, I noticed John was trying to get on one knee.

"John, are you okay? What's wrong with your knee?" I asked, alarmed. Clearly, it didn't cross my mind that he could be proposing.

Until he asked the question.

I felt like I'd won the lottery! The man I admired and loved and who made me proud to be his partner had just asked me to marry him. So, of course, my answer was a resounding, "Yes!" I slapped a dress on my sunburnt, exhausted body, and we celebrated. I snapped a pic and sent it to my family.

Crickets followed.

There was not much genuine enthusiasm. The only conversation I had with them was with Dawn. I told her I wanted to tell Evan about the engagement when we got home, and she agreed this was the right thing to do.

When we were done with our trip and had headed back to Dawn's to collect Evan, I noticed Dawn was actively holding herself together with a tough, stern exterior. Ignoring her less-than-amused facial expression, I came bopping through her front door and noticed Evan watching TV in her bedroom. I then bopped right back over to her and shoved my left hand in her face in excitement. "Isn't it beautiful?!"

No response.

"Dawn, really, aren't you excited?"

She finally said, "What about Evan?"

I understood her concern. John and I had already spoken with Evan's therapist about how to deliver the news. "I'll speak to him," I responded.

This ended up being the first of many more moments of abandonment in my life.

When I did speak to Evan, he was upset, and tried hard to resist the change. In the long run, Evan and John would create a friendship of two kindred souls, and Evan would even ask John for his forgiveness for how he initially treated him and the relationship— "Please accept my apology for me always taking my anger from my dad never showing up like you do, out on you"—but for now, things were a little tough going.

The truth is, while I was thrilled with the new connection I'd found and with where I could ultimately see my future going, blending a family is *hard*, and John and I knew this. His kids were grown by this time and pretty much off on their own, living life independently, and so you might have thought that only Evan would have required some time to process the new relationship, but this wasn't the case; it *definitely* took some time and graft to gain John's children's trust, too. Well, perhaps just his son's. Morgan (his daughter) liked me right off the bat. She told me I "wasn't like the rest of them" and that I was "real".

I mean, I didn't disagree with her.

John's son, on the other hand, has always lived out west, so I think it took some time for him to see that my intentions were pure and that I had no ulterior motives behind marrying a much older man (well, besides wanting to be with someone who was actually mature and had their shit together).

This work was nothing compared to what John had to do to get Evan's approval, however. It seemed we were just going to have to sit and wait for Evan's trust to build.

And it wasn't just these people who had a very... lackluster response to our engagement. Shortly after our return from Mexico, John and I were invited to a member of John's family's wedding. This was to be a three- to four-day celebration (one night being about cocktails, another about a dinner, another about the actual wedding and reception... you get the gist)... and it was this event that ultimately told me everything I needed to know about exactly how I was going to be viewed in John's family.

Of course, I was very enthusiastic about this entire event. I knew it meant a lot to John, and it would (hopefully) present a golden opportunity for me to really get to know his extended family and form some bonds with them. So, once that first night rolled around, I got all dolled up in our hotel room, excited for a night of drinks and conversations with the people my husband-to-be loved.

Well, that dream was very quickly dashed.

Pretty much from the moment we walked into that room, it was evident from the atmosphere and everyone's body language that I wasn't exactly going to be welcomed into John's side of the family. My heart plummeted to my feet as reams and reams of people came up to me to say, with a glint of judgment in their eye, "So, this is Felicity," followed by a quick side-eye to John. No, "Oh my God, I'm so happy to finally meet you!" No, "I've heard so much about you." Instead, the whole exchange felt laced with passive aggression and *falseness*. Call me paranoid, but I had somewhat of a sixth sense for cattiness and insincerity. And these people were meeting *all* the criteria for the people I'd met before who'd be really forthcoming to your face and then be giving you the "up-and-down" to their friends the second you looked away.

Not something I was in the habit of entertaining. It reeked of insecurity and grossness. But, of course, this was John's family. Must be on best behavior.

To make matters worse, I could tell during that night that John was messaging another woman. Call me paranoid, but to me, the signs were clear as day. He was constantly checking his phone and flushing and giggling and tapping like crazy whenever he saw he'd received a notification.

So, yes. Not exactly the evening I'd anticipated as I'd gotten myself ready in that hotel room. But the show must go on.

The family member's wedding day was very quickly upon us, and, to put all modesty aside for a moment, I looked fucking incredible. This was my first "black tie" wedding, and I pulled out *all* the stops: a breathtaking emerald green velvet dress, adorned with sparkles that glimmered every time they hit the light, beautiful shimmering earrings to match, and Louis Vuitton shoes. This felt like my Cinderella moment. I felt like a goddess, and I was excited to forget the subtle slights of the days before, let my hair down, and celebrate this union with the people John loved.

Of course, the behavior didn't change ("frosty" is the word that comes to mind), but I pushed through.

Looking back on this now and truly processing the fact that not only did *I* allow myself to be this mistreated (albeit covertly), but *John* also allowed it, is equal parts baffling and disappointing to me. While I had begun my healing journey at that point, I wasn't far along enough to know any better, and there was so much work left for me to do. Plastering on a fake smile for those women knowing that the moment they turned around they'd have nothing but shit to say about me? Being told by a member of John's family to remove my Louis Vuitton's (why? Because I wasn't good enough for them?)? Watching John parade on the dancefloor with woman after woman (and no, I'm not talking aunts or cousins, I'm talking attractive family friends I could tell he'd taken a shine to)? All of these memories now whir through my mind like a videotape, and I can't help but wish I could talk to Felicity Of The Past and tell her she didn't have to put up with this and that "her person" wouldn't subject her to this. That sitting on these problems would only breed more resentment, heartache, and damage for everyone involved later on down the line.

After this trip, my brain was a complicated place. Yet when it came down to it, I *did* feel happy, so the wedding planning went into full gear. While Dan and I had basically had a shotgun wedding, I kept my second wedding simply elegant but impressive, an intimate celebration with only family and a few close friends.

I was thrilled. I'd never experienced the full affair like many younger women have—the whole tradition of mother and bride dress shopping, picking out flowers, and crafting invitations. So, I built up this expectation that I would do all this with my family—but, as it turned out, the first go-round of dress shopping was the biggest dud. My sister and family had zero interest, to the point where it made me uncomfortable.

Since we don't address this type of stuff in my family, however, we continued to sweep it under the rug.

I didn't let this halt my plans, though, and in spring 2019, Evan and I moved in with John and I left my clinic job to take a position at a clinic closer to our new home.

Evan transitioned well at first, and our wedding details were seamless and perfect for a June wedding. I was happier than a clam! However, while this wedding-planning bliss stuck around for some time, Evan started to struggle with this change in location. It wasn't until our move (when Evan entered the fourth grade) that I began to really see his depression creeping in. Fourth grade was "the angry year" for him, and why shouldn't it have been? New town, new friends, new therapist... and all right before COVID hit.

The area we'd moved to was very affluent, which meant it was full of super-entitled kids. "The kids are dicks here, Mom," he flat out said to me once, and I couldn't disagree with him. I think he really struggled to connect with anyone and feel like he had a place there, and I get that, because, in all honestly, I myself felt like that for a while. Up until this point, I'd always lived in a "blue collar" middle-class community... and when I met John and learned that he lived in one of the wealthier suburbs of Chicago, I was a little taken aback. I'd been there before and always thought it looked insanely beautiful, yet I knew, when imagining myself living there, that it was going to be a hell of an adjustment and a lot to take in. It was one thing to *imagine* living there—to people-watch its residents and fantasize about what their lives might be like—but it was another matter entirely to actually make such a huge move up the (meaningless but ever-present) social ladder. I managed to get little snippets of what our lifestyle could feasibly look like there whenever I went to visit him while we were dating, and was a little overwhelmed by what I saw. So, as a sort of coping mechanism, I approached the whole thing as though I was a tourist for a long period after we moved. It wasn't that I felt like an outsider per se. It just didn't feel real. How was little Wheezy *here*, in all this luxury? Surely there had been some mistake?

Indeed, it turned out, like all things, this luxury came with a price.

One thing that I learned quickly about John upon moving in with him was that he placed a *lot* of value on the superficial things in life. Case in point: whenever we went out somewhere and he ran into someone he knew, he always primarily associated them with how much they made and how big their boat was. Of course, this kind of shit not only meant absolutely nothing to me, but actually clashed with my core beliefs about what makes a person valuable. So, naturally, I made it my mission to slowly start working with John in such a way where I could (hopefully) open his eyes to the fact that surface-based relationships don't hold any value in the true human experience, and that how much a person makes has no correlation whatsoever to the kind of person they are.

Now, I don't want my message to get lost in translation here. I'm not saying that I *dislike* people who place value on such things or base their relationships around them. What I *am* saying is that this whole attitude definitely carried quite a low vibration, and I quickly tired of these conversations about wealth and objects. I struggled to put on a phony smile and pretend to like someone just because they had a certain number of dollars coming into their bank account each month, or because they had a bunch of properties on an island somewhere. As friendly and outgoing as some of them were, I could sense a sort of disapproval and judgment beneath the surface from them toward me (and my and John's relationship), and this was draining to constantly be around… especially when my "role" was to be giggly and agreeable. This just didn't gel with me. Hence why I really wanted John to do the work and see where I was coming from with it.

This wasn't the attitude I took on straight away, however. Us humans all just want to be loved and to fit in as our "default" mode, and I was no exception to this. So, in those earlier days, I pulled myself back and kind of went "into" myself, smiling and laughing when needed but ultimately allowing myself to feel "less than" for my lack of riches and material abundance. And I think Evan was experiencing that same kind of cognitive dissonance.

Then again, I couldn't deny that the meltdowns were becoming more frequent and he was starting to use manipulation so he could maintain some control. I love being a boy mom, and I feel like I fell into the role really quite naturally when I had Evan, but in the fact of these tantrums and meltdowns, I started to feel some anxiety surrounding Evan's behavior and my role as his parent. I really do feel like parenting has become a whole new feat in recent years, and with the rise of cancel culture, I was wary that if these meltdowns ever occurred outside of our family unit, he could make a mistake that he'd be penalized for in the future.

I don't mean to imply here that people shouldn't be held accountable for their actions. I am also most definitely not excusing acts of prejudice or irresponsibility. Kids *and* adults should be taught consequences, period. What I *do* mean is that there's something very backwards about continuing to punish someone over something they did or said many moons ago, before their brain was even fully developed. We learn by making mistakes, so how the fuck does it make sense that grown-ass adults are still being put through the ringer for the *necessary* mistakes they made literal decades ago?

As luck would have it, I ended up having to face this fear head-on shortly after our move to John's place.

Evan was in fourth grade and new to the school, and was absolutely loving his time there so far (he hadn't yet become disillusioned by his peers' superficiality), even if he wasn't the happiest at home. So, imagine our surprise on one Sunday night (at 9:30PM, to be specific) when we received a call from a concerned father at the school. I could immediately tell by the tone of his voice that he was a little rattled by whatever it was that had happened.

"There's a text message going around from Evan. It's a link to a rap video from YouTube."

I waited for him to continue... and then realized, after a few moments of awkward silence, that that was it. Show's over, people.

"I see," I said slowly. "What kind of rap video was it?"

I had a pretty good idea of roughly what kind of thing we'd be working with here. Evan had older cousins who listened to rap, and he idolized them, so it was clearly going to be something along those lines.

"It was an *aggressive* rapper, with lots of bad language and violence in the video."

Of course, I could understand this parent's concern, especially if he'd worked to keep his kid sheltered from that kind of shit. So, accordingly, I said, "I apologize for that. Evan has older cousins that he likes to emulate, but I'll have a word with him about sharing that kind of content with his classmates."

I personally don't subscribe to the parenting approach of censoring certain media, largely because I don't for one second believe kids subconsciously "absorb" depictions of violence or bad language or whatever and immediately want to emulate it (if anything, it can form a healthy outlet for those kinds of impulses), but also because I know from personal experience how therapeutic music can be. And who was I to take that away from my son, even if that did come in the form of gun-brandishing rappers?

Even still, I knew I couldn't put my own parenting style of anyone else's kids, nor should Evan have been subjecting his peers to music they felt uncomfortable with, so I called my sister-in-law and asked her to walk me through how I could put restrictions on certain apps on his phone. I also took Evan's phone from him after explaining the call I'd had the previous night. This would, at least temporarily, have to be our solution.

Little did I know that the fallout from this slight *faux pas* of Evan's was far from over.

Shortly after this phone call, I found out that the moms of the kids who'd been involved in this had all made plans to meet up the following night to "discuss" the whole incident. It struck me as a little strange that I hadn't been invited (it was *my* son who'd started this whole mess, after all), but oh, well. I invited myself along and figured anything they'd planned on saying they could say to my face.

Upon arriving to this "meeting", I found that the majority of the moms there were quite well-to-do (most were married to a doctor or a doctor themselves) and from a very different cultural background to me (Asian descent, wealthy upbringing, etc.). Naturally, I, rocking my associate's degree and managing my animal hospital, felt a little out of my depth here, but I pushed past this feeling of insecurity, brightly introduced myself, and humbly apologized for the entire situation. I could see genuine hurt in a couple of the women's eyes, so I made sure to go over to them and give them a personal apology. Truth be told, I hadn't considered the fact that Evan's classmates would have some very real and valid cultural differences to him, and so in that moment, I fully understood that the situation must have really stressed some of these women out. I explained to them that we hadn't meant for this to happen and that I knew Evan hadn't meant any harm by it, either. I finished by saying I hoped we could move past this, as Evan really was such a sweet kid.

A conversation naturally grew from there, during which we discussed what it was like raising kids in the digital era. I also took this opportunity to explain that Evan's phone had been taken from him, he was grounded, and I was in the process of putting limits on certain apps on his devices.

As we were wrapping up the meeting, one of the moms let slip the fact that there was another meeting taking place at the school the next day.

"What meeting?" I asked quickly.

"Oh, we're having a meeting with the principal about this tomorrow," one of the other moms piped up.

Uh, what? Yet *another* meeting that I hadn't been invited to about this "problem" of my son's? I'd come to this meeting after being shunned from it with nothing but sincerity and understanding, and while I hadn't exactly expected to get brownie points for this, I sure as hell would have expected one of the moms there to have had the courtesy to let me know another meeting had been set up with the friggin' *principal*. Was this a lions' den, or something? Had I just waltzed into a group of people committed to making the consequences my son faced for this mistake far more far-reaching than they needed to be?

I looked at the women before me, swallowed my anger, and said, "It was a pleasure to meet you all. I'll see you tomorrow bright and early, at seven-thirty."

When I returned home that evening, I asked John to attend the meeting with me, just to be on the safe side. I wasn't sure what I was about to walk into, and there was strength in numbers. So, John and I rocked up at school the following morning, Evan in tow. We of course dropped Evan off at his class first, and the moment those kids laid eyes on him, it was abundantly obvious that they thought he was just the coolest kid ever. Their eyes widened, and they started grinning like maniacs. Evan clearly hadn't traumatized anyone here, but I also couldn't help but feel re-irritated at Evan when I watched this unfold. He had no idea of the cult-like ramifications that could emerge from something like this, if taken too far. Then again, these kids clearly looked up to Evan as a leader of sorts, and I knew that could definitely be used for good. I made a mental note to have a conversation with him about using his power for good, and not being an absolute knucklehead. Life chats with Momma!

Child taken care of, it was now time to tackle the parents.

John and I had what felt like a pretty seamless plan of action for this meeting: he'd let me do the talking, and if he spotted me floundering, he'd chip in.

I took a seat at the head of the table in the meeting room and watched a group of ladies, the principal, some of the teachers, and a social worker walk in.

Jesus Christ.

One of the moms opened the conversation by saying, "Since Evan has been here, we've noticed *X, Y,* and *Z*…"

"I agree," another mom chimed in. "Since he arrived here, my son's started listening to rap music."

I listened to this attack on my son pretty calmly, if I do say so myself, before cutting in.

"Hi! I'm Felicity, Evan's mom, and this is John, his stepdad. I guess we all already know that this meeting has been called because of Evan sharing that rap video. I just want you all to know once again that I'm very sorry that this has happened. This whole digital era parenting is all kind of new to me, as I'm sure it is for all of you, too. Even still, I have grounded Evan, taken his phone away from him, and put restrictions on all his devices."

"Well, you know, we think something more should be done," one of the moms said.

"I agree," another stated. "What else can we do here?"

"Wait, why the rebuttal?" I interjected, floored. "Why are you going down this road?"

"Well, we obviously know *you're* done with parenting, but we want to make sure our children are safe from this in the future," one of the moms responded haughtily.

...Did I just fucking hear that right?

Instantly, it felt as though my whole body was ablaze. *Done with parenting?* Was this woman on crack? Had she just heard one single fucking thing I'd just said?

I looked at the mother who'd just finished speaking (who, by the way, was sat right across from me and was still somehow refusing to give me eye contact), pointed at her from across the table, and said, "You look at me when I speak to you!"

She jumped and, sure enough, met my eyes.

"Never *once* did I say I was done with parenting," I seethed. "*None* of us are done parenting until the day we die! This is a job we signed up for for a lifetime, so do *not* put words in my mouth again."

She had absolutely nothing to say to this. Shocker.

"There is nothing further this school can do except listen to our grievances," I pressed on. "Evan did not do this while on school property, nor with a school iPad or laptop. All *these* people can do is listen, and I've already told you what *I've* done as his mother. Anything else is unnecessary. And if anybody else has anything to say, I suggest you get it out in the open now. I've got to be at work in fifteen minutes."

A few moments of uncomfortable silence passed before the principal finally said, "Yes, the school has no connection to this issue and thus does not have the authority to suspend Evan or have him removed from the school."

Ha.

With that verdict, the ladies started filing out of the room. Equal parts smug and furious, I stood and began pulling on my coat and scarf when I realized I had John, the principal, the social worker, and two teachers staring at me from across the table.

"What are you all looking at me for?" I asked, scowling.

One of the teachers broke into a big old smile and said, "Nice job, Mom! You handled that crowd *well*."

I grinned. "I've had to deal with worse. That was nothing!"

Shocker number two: as soon as John and I walked out, we spotted a group of six or seven of the moms running their fucking mouths, as they all did in this neighborhood. I smiled at one of the women, put my arm around her, gave her a nice, good squeeze, and said, "It's a pleasure to meet you all! Can't wait to do it again! Have a good one, ladies."

Felicityspeak for *don't fuck with me.*

This right here is a perfect example of Evan doing something thinking it's going to be cool, only to quickly find out it was a dumbass decision. Which *would* be a pretty straightforward learning moment, *if* it weren't for this "cancel culture" that pervades our society nowadays. This whole ordeal was dragged out for long enough just by a bunch of lowlife women who had nothing better to do with their day than to drag a poor fourth-grader and his mom through the dirt for sharing a fucking music video, so I can only imagine what it'll be like when Evan makes an actual mistake on social media. Will he be paying the price for whatever that mistake happens to be twenty years down the line? All because his prefrontal cortex wasn't fully developed and he had a bunch of goofy kid hormones coursing through him? I have no idea, and I honestly wouldn't like to think about it too much.

So, yes, Evan was dealing with a lot of (semi-self-inflicted, but still unwarranted) bullshit during this time. The poor kid couldn't catch a break.

And this wasn't the only thing that arose around this time that had the potential to throw our (that is, the family unit's) world into chaos.

I was on the way back from dropping Evan off at school one morning when something deep within nudged me to go back home. The nudge was hot. It was as if heat had flooded my entire body.

I had an image flash of a woman.

What was my intuition trying to tell me?

My guides speak to me in images, and images of *go fast, hurry* kept hitting me.

Compelled only by this gut instinct, I pulled into the garage and opened the laundry room door. It was around 8:15AM, and John's car was still there. He hadn't left for work.

Strange.

I entered the family room... and found what I'd somewhat expected. Something that I do not feel the need to share here for the sake of John's privacy, but something that shook me to the core. This would be one of many incidents leading to me questioning John's faithfulness in our relationship, all of which he would deny.

All my feelings of *I am not good enough* were hardcore drilled into my head within our relationship over the years, and it wouldn't be until much later that I'd open up about this in family therapy.

In the meantime, I was reevaluating everything. We'd just moved, I'd just gotten a new job, and my previous home was already being rented. *What the fuck do I do?*

It would take me a good few years before I fully understood John's personality and why he sought escape in things like women, drugs, food.

Even still, why would he deny his actions when his hand had been caught in the cookie jar?

Unfortunately, the lack of accountability he had faced throughout his life meant he could still play on this side of the fence, and so I taught myself to separate John's inner child-led behavior from who he is as a man, in addition to holding up my ginormous wall of protection—the wall that exhausted everything in my body, but allowed me to still extend my understanding, empathy, and support. The hurt John led to me feeling over the years ultimately helped me move into an emotional space where I practice emotional detachment, which has formed a great part of my deeper healing and emotional freedom. But I couldn't deny that it was really fucking draining. During our "courtship", if you will, I'd totally let my guard down and felt free to express my inner child, be goofy, and tell him anything and everything that was on my mind without a filter. But now, I needed to distance myself for my own sanity and wellbeing. And this realization felt heavy. Loaded. Like something I didn't want to think about too much for fear of uncovering something I wouldn't be able to unsee.

Was this just part and parcel of marriage? Was I destined to be with someone who could make me feel on top of the world *and* the lowest of the low at the same time?

These were questions I wasn't ready to answer. And as the wedding crept closer, I couldn't help but feel that there was no true genuine happiness from either side of our families, although this feeling wasn't confirmed until our wedding day.

In truth, I felt exceptionally lonely during this time. Nobody expressed any genuine interest, never mind joy, toward the union, and this was a little crushing. On a day where I was supposed to feel enveloped by love, I felt only animosity.

Regardless, I looked stunning—like a glamorous queen—and my son and stepkids were all decked out, too! My stepson (the best man) had the most beautiful speech for his father about what an amazing man he'd grown into, and the small outdoor boho-city chic place in Chicago we got married in was just perfect.

Basically, everything went off without a hitch, including our honeymoon. Things felt complete.

Once we returned to reality, however, some of our wedding guests began to open up to me. "Felicity, what is *up* with the families? No one seemed thrilled this happened." One wedding guest actually told me they'd had to vacate the wedding because the energy was that toxic. "My apologies for dunking out after the ceremony. There's some deep dark bad juju going on, girl." Another one's response: "Did you just have a feast for your enemies? I'm confused."

Right after the honeymoon, I called Dawn for something and realized the opportunity to discuss how I felt during the wedding planning (i.e., alone) was there.

She responded, "I can't be happy for you. I feel bad for John."

I was speechless. "Dawn, why would you feel bad for John?"

She had no concrete reason, and I hung up the phone.

Full disclosure: this was probably one of the most deeply hurtful moments in my and Dawn's entire relationship. I was devastated. Perplexed. And deeply, deeply wounded. As we've established at this point, all I'd ever wanted from my sister—from my whole family, really—was approval. So, naturally, this was a *real* punch to the gut.

Dawn and I ended up sweeping this under the rug, and for now, I decided not to completely cut her and the rest of my family off. That would be for later.

And what was Dan's reaction to my and John's marriage? Perhaps unsurprisingly, not good. There were a few occasions right after the wedding when Dan and I needed to hop on a phone call to discuss something to do with Evan and he came out with random things like, "Why are you not dead yet?" or, "I hope you die soon."

Lovely things to wish upon the mother of your son.

To this day, I still have dreams of him trying to kill me—the direct result, I believe, of the energy from him I pick up on. In truth, I still do deeply fear that one day, he will try and come at me again, only this time, with the real intention of kill. I suppose that's a symptom of trauma that probably won't ever fully go away.

So, this was the reception of my and John's union.

And soon, COVID was going to rear its ugly head and change this world forever, including that of my family.

We needed to buckle up. We were sure in for a ride.

18

Healing Pitstops

————

OUR MOST SIGNIFICANT PERIODS OF growth, change, and development are almost always catalyzed by a very difficult decision, and that was definitely the case for me in the wake of COVID.

Truly, I think this was one of the times in my life where my healing was tested the most, and while I can now clearly see that absolutely everything happened for a reason and ultimately steered me in the right direction, it was very difficult to see the purpose in all the pain while I was wading through the thick of it.

Right before COVID hit, I queried my memoir (the one you're reading now). The response was along the lines of, "I am not saying no, but who are you? Memoirs are hard to sell, and nobody knows who you are." While Young Felicity probably would have taken this knockback hard, I thanked God for this amazing rejection letter, since it told me exactly what I needed to do next.

I ran straight for the closest notebook, called John, and asked if I could quit working at the clinic so I could begin building my dream.

"Of course, sweetheart."

I think it was at this point in my life that I truly started to understand what it is to *trust the process*. Yes, building a brand turned out to be far harder than I thought it would be, but this didn't discourage me. On the contrary, I relished the challenge. I was on the road to launching my magazine, *She Is You*, a project that little did I know would soon grow into the most beautiful community of women looking to consciously undergo their own journey of self-growth and -healing professionally, personally, and spiritually—a journey I had previously felt was out of my hands, but was now fast learning I had complete control over. I had learned that it was *my* choice if I let someone else grab the steering wheel for me.

I also didn't know we would launch incredible transformative programs for our clients that would prove truly life-changing for some.

All of this was to come. For now, I just had to trust in the process and operate on a basis of faith and inner knowing that all that was meant to be mine would be.

…And I had to reckon with the disease that was about to infiltrate the world and flip everything we'd ever known on its head.

The winter/spring of 2020 was, in all respects, an absolute fucking ride, and, of course, this kicked off with COVID.

A pandemic.

Fabulous.

Not only this, but for whatever reason, once fifth grade hit, Evan's rage toward me, his father, and the world was brought to its climax. He just hated everything.

Right at the beginning of COVID (specifically, St. Patrick's Day), Morgan moved in with us (as in, me, John, and Evan), which I was beyond excited about but, more importantly, Evan was thrilled over. Morgan was super-bubbly and had an absolute heart of gold, and we all looked forward to this change immensely. She'd previously been living in the city after graduating college, and didn't want to be on her own during COVID (and also needed some redirection in her life), so the plan was we'd temporarily move her back in. Once she settled in, however, it didn't take long before my eyes were *wide* open to her struggles. Her and John's relationship needed a *lot* of work, largely because his head was in the sand. In the end, it took a few years to get him to open his eyes and learn to be there for Morgan like a dad should.

Morgan's move started pretty unproblematically, however, with her and Evan (like many other people, I'm sure!) staying up late binge-watching *Stranger Things* and *Outer Banks*. They'd order a McDonald's and settle in together for the night, which was a pretty heartwarming thing to see. It felt really good to see their growth and how they supported one another.

Even still, my heart hurt for Morgan. You could see she wanted the attention of her parents, but they couldn't give it to her.

It was while I was simmering on this that a dreaded possibility washed over me: could this be what I was doing to Evan, too?

Once COVID was in full swing and all non-essential work and education started being done remotely, Evan declined fast. The lack of structure in his daily life threw him off massively. He, like many other kids, *depended* on that structure.

It was also around this time that he started having regular meltdowns about visiting Dan. I felt like I was in a complete Catch-22 whenever this happened. I wanted Evan to be happy, but in my mind, him going to his dad's was non-negotiable. This wasn't helped by the fact that his therapist was telling me that Evan was trying to manipulate me and that I should make him go to his dad's anyway.

Of course, I know now I was at complete fault for not listening to Evan when he voiced that he didn't like going to his dad's; for shutting him down and saying he legally had to. But looking back, I can still understand my actions. I could have been held legally responsible for not delivering on my end of the court-ordered childcare agreement, after all. Once again, I was stuck between a rock and a hard place.

Evan didn't mesh well e-learning, nor with being at home all the time, and as a result, he began to stop taking care of himself: poor hygiene (I was having to practically drag him to the bathtub), poor eating habits (again, it was war trying to get him to eat anything of nutritional value), insomnia... the works. I had a team comprised of a therapist, sports clubs, a psychiatrist, and school, and together, we were catering to anything and everything he needed. Yet nothing was working.

I dove into alternative parenting approaches, desperate for a solution, but at this point I was running on fumes, completely reactive. My head was spinning with stress. My son was mentally deteriorating, my stepdaughter was an emotional hot mess dealing with her own baggage, I was trying to build the magazine and my personal brand, *and* I was navigating a new marriage. I wanted to fucking scream. It all just felt like absolute fucking sensory overload.

We struggled on for the remainder of fifth grade and throughout sixth grade, trying solution after solution after solution, to no avail, before Evan rapidly declined (again) and began to threaten self-harm. Out of nowhere, Evan was now having one screaming meltdown after another, to the point where Morgan was asking to move out.

I felt truly horrible for the whole household, and Evan's entire team were perplexed at his behavior.

There's one story that springs to mind that I feel encapsulates the place he was at during this time. I picked Evan up one Sunday evening at around six from a friend's house, and once we were home and he was sitting at the kitchen island eating dinner, he, out of thin air, began one of his temper tantrums, this time about a pair of football helmets and pads that all his friends had and that he thus wanted. This was symptomatic of a recurring bigger issue: the kids out here got everything they wanted, and this was a philosophy I'd never adopted in my parenting—something Evan now rebelled against frequently, regardless of the price point of said item.

In the midst of this meltdown, John (understandably) decided he was over it, and so grabbed Evan's milkshake and demanded he go to his room if he was going to behave this way. Evan of course responded to this with a big, "Fuck you!" so John grabbed him by the back of the neck, yanked him right off the barstool, and screamed like an old-school dad would: "If you ever think you can disrespect me…" blah, blah, blah.

He literally put the fear of God in Evan.

Don't get me wrong, as a child of the eighties, my mother would have mopped the floor with me if I'd spoken to her like that, but this wasn't a parenting style I wished to adopt myself, nor was John Evan's biological father. It wasn't his place to discipline Evan like that.

So now, we had a shitstorm on our hands.

In the end, I decided to have Evan evaluated at a local hospital to see if he qualified for an inpatient program, simply because the verbal self-harm threats were becoming too frequent for me to feel confident that he was safe at home. After all, even though I had a safety plan (i.e., verbal threats = ER trip), that could only help us so much if it got to emergency level. I'd had enough and knew something serious needed to change if we were going to overcome this and become a stable, loving, communicative family unit, so I took him the following night, almost exactly twenty-four hours after his little meltdown and John's parenting *faux pas*.

It was surprisingly easy to get an immediate appointment, and once Evan and I were there, they proceeded to explain how it worked: they would interview him alone, then me, and then both of us together.

By this point, I was exhausted. I just desperately wanted some normalcy and for my son to have strategies in place that would allow him to better process, navigate, and communicate his feelings.

And then during the final interview, right there in front of me, Evan stated, "My stepfather choked me."

Yep, you read that right! Fucking *choked* him.

My jaw dropped.

I asked to go outside to have a cigarette so I could calm down.

"I'm afraid not."

"What?"

"You can't leave the premises while he is here."

"Okay, I understand that, but are you telling me this security guard"—I motioned to the hulking guy stood next to us—"can't come with me to ensure you don't have a runaway parent on your hands?"

"Nope."

Great.

Of course, I knew Evan was lying and that he'd done this on purpose, knowing full well what the potential consequences were. I also knew we would now probably have the DCFS involved.

Could it get any worse?

The hospital's final decision? A six-week outpatient program via Zoom.

Whoop-dee-doo.

The day after our appointment, a sunny Monday, I called for a family meeting with Dan at Tommy's house for that evening. I needed all the help I could get. In the meantime, it was a bright afternoon, and the sun was shining through my quiet home, Stevie Nicks was playing on the whole house radio, and I was in the process of popping a roast in the crockpot. Evan was e-learning upstairs. Basically, I was basking in a rare clean, quiet, peaceful moment, shedding the stress of the previous weekend, when the doorbell rang.

"Mom!" I heard Evan shout. "There's a lady at the door!"

I opened the door to the following introduction: "Hello, my name is Natalie, and I am with Child Protective Services."

My heart sank.

Honest to God, I am so over my fucking life right now.

By this point, I'd already asked God that he not let me come back as a different life form upon my death. This shit had already been way too painful the first time round.

Despite the growing pit in my stomach, I welcomed her in, advised her of our dog, and walked her to the kitchen so I could finish putting dinner on. I then called Evan down and explained who she was and what she represented. "Evan, if they don't think you're safe here, they will take you from me and put you in foster care."

In other words, you'd better come clean on your embellished statement.

Right at that moment, as I was speaking to Natalie, my phone rang. It was Samantha, Evan's therapist.

"Hey! Just checking in on you. How was last night?"

"Well, I can't speak right now. I have DCFS here."

She audibly gasped through the phone. "Oh my God, Felicity, are you kidding me? What did Evan say? Please call me back."

Natalie ended up staying for about an hour interviewing me and Evan separately and checking over the house. At the beginning of my interview, she looked at me, and I could instantly read her facial expression.

"I know you have more important things to do than be here with us," I said.

"Yes, you're correct, but I had two different calls reporting this concern."

Two?

Oh.

Fucking Dan.

"Look, Natalie, this is us. This is our household's vibe, as you can see." I gestured to the quiet; the chill music; the clean, organized home. "This is us."

"Felicity, Evan opened up and admitted he lied about the incident—

"

Phew!

"—but this doesn't mean you're out of the woods. I'll need to do another surprise visit in the future, but for now, I'm going to proceed by stating nothing was found."

"Thank you, God."

Perhaps unsurprisingly, all of this—Evan's mental health, Morgan's personal struggles, and my own responsibilities—led to me fully shutting down, my PTSD well and truly triggered. And while many may think this was not a very well-informed decision (and perhaps it wasn't), I had to send Evan to live with his dad for some time so I could get my head above water and figure my shit out. If I didn't do this, I ran the risk of fully losing the ability to show up for my family how I needed to, and I couldn't risk that.

During that one week of him being gone, I realized that the full team of support I had (John, Morgan, Dad, my siblings, Evan's therapist, and Evan's school) somehow just wasn't cutting it. He was in so much emotional pain by this point that weekly therapy was doing nothing but temporarily papering over the cracks.

I'd actually already researched residential treatment facilities a while back. I'm a worst-case scenario planner, so I'd already done my homework and knew where I'd want to send him if it ever came to that.

Of course, I'd hoped it wouldn't.

Now, however, I was honestly at a loss. I wanted—*needed*—Evan to be happy, yet I suspected his baggage was now so deep-rooted he'd need a lot of help to begin to let it go. I knew he needed impartial experts who could guide him through his own healing at his own pace. And I also knew that how he was—how *we* were—currently living was completely unsustainable. He needed help so he could embrace himself in all his wholeness and so he could see how truly incredible he was and how much he could achieve.

I didn't take this decision lightly. If there had been an alternative that would have allowed him to heal *and* stay with his loved ones, I would have snapped it up in a heartbeat. Yet it didn't seem such an alternative was feasible. And I was worried I was running out of time.

I knew what needed to be done. And I needed to get Dan on the same page. For the sake of our son.

Of course, nothing was ever going to be easy with Dan. And this was no exception. The moment I raised this with him (the same week Evan was staying with him), he stopped paying child support and started planning on moving and purchasing a new car.

At the end of the day, all Dan cared about was his money, not Evan's wellbeing.

I needed some moral support from someone who'd known and cared for Evan for most of his life, so I called Dawn and asked if she'd attend one of Evan's joint therapy sessions with me. I obviously couldn't go with Evan while he was with Dan, and my logic was that us three ladies (me, Dawn, and the therapist) could use this as an opportunity to brainstorm a treatment plan, and maybe even figure out how to bring up the prospect of a ranch with Evan.

Dawn accepted.

Once we all sat down in the therapist's office, Dawn proceeded to explain her solution for Evan: to take Evan and raise him herself, with Scott.

I was absolutely flabbergasted.

Thank God for the therapist, who responded by saying that that wouldn't happen legally, as in that situation, he would go to Dan.

"That won't be an issue," Dawn responded calmly. "Scott and I have already spoken to Dan, and Dan realizes he can't raise Evan and says he doesn't want Felicity to raise Evan, either."

What the fuck.

My sister—my own *sister*, who I'd called in my moment of need, expecting her to fully support me and Evan—had actually already gone behind my back and tried to take my son away from me. My *sister*. Of course, I'd had many (albeit smaller) signs along these lines before, but this was when my eyes *really* opened up and fully saw how truly evil and dark my "family" could be. And the worst part? This idea that I wasn't competent enough to raise Evan myself was a sentiment also shared by David: "Ya know, Wheezy, Evan is just like you were. I think it's best Dawn and Scott raise him, since you can't do a good job."

All I'd requested was some help from my family. I wasn't a crackhead or alcoholic or hooker, contrary to what their narratives suggested. I just had a child who'd experienced trauma. That didn't mean I wasn't capable of raising him, it meant we needed to find the right help so he could navigate what the fuck was going on.

My jaw hung wide open as I watched my family dig their hate deep into me. Their hostility left John and Morgan dumbfounded, too. Whatever fake picture of my family I'd tried to create for my husband and his family crumbled in that moment, and my family's true colors were shining strong.

They were out for blood, and I was to be hunted.

They'd not only crossed a boundary of mine, but of my husband's, too. John was fuming. "How *dare* your sister come in here and think she can do this?" he spat. "Does she not realize that *I'm* the stepparent, not her? What kind of family *does* this to someone?"

Morgan also had my back during this whole fiasco. She was appalled at what was happening, and always reassured me that I was doing the right thing. She'd witnessed Evan's meltdowns up close and personal, after all, and so she knew firsthand how stressful the situation had been for the whole household. And despite my "family's" horrendous reaction, I knew this was the right decision to make. Evan needed more than I could give him. I'd reached a point where I struggled to fully let my walls down around anyone, and so even though I was physically there for Evan, I couldn't be there for him emotionally in the way he needed me t0.

This is still a work in progress for me, and I often have to remind myself to not be so hard on myself for this and to give myself the grace I would give to anyone else in my position. I am also on a journey of self-healing, just like Evan is.

This is why breaking the cycle of intergenerational trauma is so damn important. I was desperate to keep my son close so I could be a pillar of security and reason for him, yet my *own* trauma meant I couldn't be that person. At least, not yet. I needed more time. And that wasn't something Evan could, or should have to, give to me.

And Dan was the icing on the Evan cake. He'd always shown up for Evan with a beer in one hand. I knew Dan loved his son deeply, but he couldn't conceive of doing the very basic job that fatherhood demands: putting Evan before his own superficial needs.

My family's behavior just added insult to injury. Evan would eventually open up about how confused he'd been throughout his childhood about who I, his mother, "really was", because every time he stayed at Dawn's house, she, Heather, and Rachelle would talk about me in front of him. They'd apparently discuss how I was neglecting him and how I didn't care about him. This naturally bred some doubt in his mind, and in my opinion, they knew exactly what they were doing.

This was no family. Really, it never had been. I deserved so much better, and so did my son.

Evan ended up staying at Dan's for a week or so after I made the decision to send him there so I could take a moment to breathe and get some mental clarity. On the last night, I received an unexpected call from Stacy.

"Hi, it's Stacy. Come get Evan. He's unhappy."

I was perplexed. Stacy had never once reached out to me.

I put the phone down, still confused, when my phone instantly became inundated with messages from both Evan and Dan. The latter was begging me to "give him a chance" to "prove himself as a father".

I was now even more confused, and more than a little concerned.

I responded to Dan simply telling him that Morgan and I were on our way to pick Evan up. My reason for bringing Morgan was simple: I was afraid of what Dan could potentially do to me. I knew his history, and knew bringing my husband could up the chances of this even more. So, Morgan offered to come.

To be on the safe side, I also called Scott, since he was a cop in the next town over from Dan.

Scott met us there after the hour-long drive. We both parked on the street, Scott talking to me through the driver's window (like a cop does). The three of us were engrossed in conversation when the back door driver's side opened and Evan and all his stuff was shoved in—hard. In the midst of the confusion, I heard Stacy's voice: "Get out of here. He's angry."

All three of us were still trying to get our bearings on what was going on when Morgan gasped. Behind Scott was a towering, drunk, angry Dan, and he was about to lunge at me through the car window.

Scott managed to physically push him away and yell at me to "get the hell out of here".

I was frantic. It was dark, and I had to ask Morgan to GPS us out of the subdivision so I wouldn't have to turn back around and pass Dan.

I called Dawn and suggested she call the cops, her response to which being that Scott was used to this and could handle it.

Driving away, all I could see was Scott continuing to push Dan away in the chest.

It turned out that Dan had (obviously) gotten drunk that night and begun calling Evan names before kicking him down the stairs. The violence would certainly have escalated if Stacy hadn't called.

In other words, that night, Stacy saved Evan's life.

19

An Intervention

A
ND SO THIS WAS THE climate in which the decision was made: Evan was to be picked up on April 9, 2021, to go to a treatment facility. And from this point, my life was forever changed.

During the week leading up to Evan's departure, I was sick to my stomach, praying hard for some sort of miracle. My family knew of my decision, and I had won my court case that gave me full parental rights to make any decisions for Evan that I deemed necessary *without* Dan's consent. In other words, I at this point had no obstacles preventing this from happening… except the very real possibility of me caving in. Of me falling short in being able to do this.

We (me, Morgan, John, and Evan) spent Easter (two days before Evan's departure) together, and throughout the day, I had to keep sneaking away to cry. My heart was in excruciating pain. And Evan was totally clueless.

Some may wonder why I didn't inform Evan of my decision before he was scheduled to be picked up, and this was for a few reasons. First, I was certain he'd try to prevent this from happening by pulling some strings (threatening to move out, getting my family involved, etc.), and I knew this intervention was the most promising route for his healing. Second, I thought there was a feasible risk he would run away (not something he'd done before, but certainly something he had threatened from time to time). And third, I simply didn't have the emotional capacity to deal with another layer in an already-emotionally grueling situation.

Do I feel like I made the correct decision in retrospect? Honestly, yes. Evan has told me since that he wishes we could have just spoken about it, but I know deep down inside that the Evan I have now is not the Evan I had then. Plus, if I *had* discussed it with Evan, it would have more than likely got back to Dan, which meant it would have more than likely got back to my family, which meant it was more than likely they would (at the least) threaten to take custody of him. Again.

Yeah, no.

Prayer was my anchor during this horrendous countdown. My communication with God was as strong as ever. "Why, God? Why does this have to happen? Why me? Please ensure his safety and wellbeing."

I kept the prayers going strong and fluid.

The day before Evan left was one of the last days of spring break. I remember going up to his room that day to find him singing and freshly showered. I was shellshocked at this image. The poor kid had been struggling so hard with his depression that I'd been having to drag him into the bathtub to bathe him, and yet here he was, clean and upbeat, excited to go to town with his friends and ride their bikes.

I asked whether he could squeeze in some Mom time, but he refused. "Mom, it's way too nice out! We can have dinner together."

With that, he left, unsuspecting, and I had the full day to pack all his belongings. I'd arranged for a service associated with the ranch to come pick him up the following morning, who'd requested a ton of documents and a travel bag with a change of clothes and some slides, snacks, and meds, plus anything else that would make him feel at ease.

I grabbed what I could, snagged Tigee (his favorite stuffed animal), and sat down to write him a letter explaining my reason for doing this.

> *Hello, Evan,*
>
> *I know you must be so scared right now, but please know you are in good hands with Tammy and Jeff. You are safe.*
>
> *Evan, your mental health has declined so rapidly. I love you so much, kiddo, but you need so much more help than that which we can give you here.*
>
> *You are going to Utah, to a place called a ranch. This is a safe place. You will be there with a good group of people so you can get to the core of what's going on. I need you to know how difficult this decision was to make and how heartbreaking it is to send you off like this, but I really feel this is the safest way for all of us.*
>
> *I love you more than words can express.*
>
> *You know of my love for music, and so I want to share these lyrics with you. This song helped me so many times when I felt like I was sinking fast.*

Let it go / Let it roll right off your shoulder / Don't you know? / The hardest part is over / Let it in / Let your clarity define you / In the end / We will only just remember how it feels…

> *The ranch will be in touch with me once you arrive, and we will see you as soon as we can.*
>
> *I love you very much, Evan. God bless your journey and strength.*

XO, Mom

Evening was fast approaching.

Morgan was home and just watching me pace back and forth, back and forth. I was fasting and chain-smoking.

I picked Evan and his buddies up that night from a local Babe Ruth baseball game, all the boys piling into the car. "Can we get McDonald's?" the boys called from the back seat.

"Of course we can."

T-minus twelve hours until the hardest decision of my life sprang into action.

It was 4:30AM the following morning, and I'd been tossing and turning for about an hour or two. I was so scared. What would happen when they woke him? I already felt overcome with guilt.

The ranch people who were picking Evan up any minute now had requested that our dogs not be in the house when they arrived, so the evening before, I'd had to make up some bullshit excuse to Evan to explain why they were gone. They'd also requested that no siblings sleep upstairs, so Morgan and the cat were currently sleeping in the basement.

Around an hour before, at 3:30AM, I'd received my first text from Tammy.

HELLO, FELICITY. THIS IS TAMMY FROM THE RANCH. WE HAVE LANDED. WILL BE THERE IN FORTY-FIVE MINUTES.

My chest felt as though it was physically clenching in fear, pain, and anxiety. I didn't want to do this.

John was up now, too.

I felt paralyzed and kept watching my ring cameras, praying Evan wasn't awake. It wasn't unlikely he'd be up at this time.

My phone buzzed with another text.

HELLO FELICITY, IT'S TAMMY. WE ARE OUTSIDE.

Fuck me.

God, please, I pray to you and Archangel Michael. Please, God, please protect this little boy on this journey.

I opened the front door, and there they stood. Tammy and Jeff.

I took one look at Tammy, who looked just like me: an average mom. Nothing alarming.

I began to explain what was in Evan's bag when I broke down in tears. She responded to this by immediately embracing me and reassuring me Evan would be safe.

With that, the three of us headed upstairs.

Evan's room was on the second floor, all the way at the back of the hall among three other bedrooms.

I entered his room. He was sound asleep.

I kissed his forehead and whispered, "Evan, it's me."

He instantly woke up, looked at me, looked at Tammy and Jeff... and knew exactly what was happening.

"I love you, Evan."

And with that, I left the room.

As I walked down the hall, I could hear him saying, "Wait, Mom, wait! No, no, no..."

"Put your slides on," I heard Tammy say. "We must go."

He didn't resist. He sobbed down the hall and stairs and yowled from the front hallway, "But Mom!" and "I love you!"

And just like that, he was gone.

I cried like someone had died. I just sat there sobbing.

When I speak about God preparing us to do hard things, I absolutely do believe He prepared me for this exact moment, despite the unbelievable pain I was in. I'd been through some tough shit, but this by far was the toughest decision to make. Yet losing my parents, going through a divorce, and all the other obstacles I'd conquered gave me the grit to think long-term and not so selfishly. To consider giving my son a second chance at life. Something my own mother neglected to do for her children.

Making the decision to send Evan off to heal was literally me breaking the generational trauma bond so we could be free from the negative, harmful family patterns we'd developed.

I was a hot mess, and I can only imagine how Evan was feeling, but Tammy kept me up to speed on how he was doing, and said she'd call me once they reached the ranch and was officially in their care.

All I could do was breathe. Breathe, breathe, breathe through the pain.

I can't imagine what a parent goes through when they physically lose a child, and I pray for all of them, because the adjustment period we underwent after Evan was taken was hell.

The pain I experienced was intense and heavy, even though I knew it was absolutely the right decision for him. His unmade bed and stuffed animals (yes, Evan still loved stuffed animals) remained scattered around his floor, and it took me months before I stopped crying whenever I went into his room.

Pain aside, I was completely and utterly perplexed as to what on earth my life could even look and feel like now that Evan was gone. He had been at the very core of every decision I'd made, every thought I'd had, every place I'd gone to, for more than a decade. What was left for a mother without her child? Would I take care of myself a bit more? Read more books? I knew these things would feel like mere distractions, a way to divert my attention from the constant countdown in my head. The countdown until I could see him again.

Around twelve hours after Tammy picked Evan up from our place, she called me to tell me he was in the care of the ranch. She said he'd been a good boy and had been scared—puke kind of scared—but that he hadn't resisted and had been speaking to Jeff about sports throughout the day.

The next time they called me was to inform me they were going to call Dan.

I hadn't told Dan I was doing this, only that I was considering it. I'd been afraid he'd show up and screw things up.

Naturally, once he received the call from the ranch, my phone absolutely blew up. I had to send him straight to voicemail and contact my attorney.

Of course, word then got out to my family. In anticipation of the uproar I was sure was coming, I sent a text to all of them simply stating Evan was safe in Utah and asking them to please be considerate of our space.

Basically, "Please don't spam me with hate mail."

Obviously, this request fell on deaf ears. I was absolutely inundated with texts saying what a horrible decision we'd made. How I was the biggest fuckup on Earth. How I was ruining Evan. How horrible of a mother I was.

This cemented another tough decision I'd known for a while needed to be made: I needed to walk away from my family. I truly believe that once we decide to truly stand in our power, God, the universe, whatever you believe in, will remove everything in your life that no longer serves you for your higher good. If it's meant to be gone, it will go. And right now, I could hear His message loud and clear: in order for me to fully grow into the woman I knew I was meant to be, I had to let my family go, regardless of how painful this would be. (I do love them all, after all.)

After acting on this decision, I did try to reach out to a few of the people who'd seemed less judgmental a couple of times, only to discover that everything we chatted about was going right back to the rest of them. That was my hard lesson to learn: the devil will always disguise himself. And he sure did.

The bottom line was, whenever I'd put my effort into a relationship with my siblings, I'd immediately assume the role of the wounded little girl who was constantly seeking validation and approval, and this ultimately prevented my growth. And thank God I recognized this when I did and was able to do the work to put her (my inner child) at ease! As much as I never would have wished for my family life to have come to this, this period presented the opportunity for me to really mull over my life and relationships. To grieve, process, and reflect. There were many times over those next few months when I simply sat at the kitchen table and cried, Morgan and John shaking their heads in disbelief at my family's (rather unsupportive, to put it nicely) response to my decision. Morgan was a particular savior for me during this time. Her understanding and support was limitless. She's an incredible young woman.

I love my family, truly, and I wish all of them nothing but the best, but, in the long run, I had to do what was best for me and my small unit. That was just how it had to go.

I gave myself a good week of sobbing and sorrow before throwing my all into creating the most dynamic healing team for the journey that would completely alter my life. I found a therapist and began to unravel my life in sixty-minute weekly appointments, and my functional medicine doctor got me registered for a medical marijuana card to alleviate the intense anxiety I was experiencing. (By the way, getting stoned when you're in this much emotional pain probably isn't the smartest decision, but yes, I did get stoned, thanks to Jesse at my local cannabis store, and it sucked.) I started really focusing on my health and once again battled severe intestinal issues that landed me in the hospital, where I was told my intestines were shot. "We could make this easy and remove them and put them in a bag," they offered.

When it rains, it pours.

I continued to sort through all the details of my life during my therapy sessions—my mother; my father; both sets of grandparents; my siblings—and it became clear to me that our parents greatly influence the character we adopt from a young age... *until* we begin healing. It was that last part that my family had seemingly failed to recognize. The fact that this predisposition of sorts to follow in our parents' footsteps *isn't a guarantee* but is something we can take control of and transform, if wanted, was mind-blowing to me.

This was a life changing realization for me. While I perfectly understood that we're a product of our upbringing (that's something I learned in school), the shock, awe, and disbelief I felt upon this discovery stemmed from me trying to wrap my head around the impact that this had on me emotionally and mentally.

Wait—I'm tough. "No, Felicity, you have strong walls up to protect you."

Wait—I battled way worse. "Felicity, you've been in fight-or-flight mode for most of your life. It doesn't surprise me you have the health issues you do."

Are you telling me that my mother's love was conditional? That my absent father affected my belief system and expectations of my future husbands? Wait a second—so my parents' children, me included, were all *groomed* into their roles, and their behavior is nothing personal toward me, but is just them acting out their feelings?

Yes, yes, yes, and yes.

This was a complete mindfuck... and yet these realizations helped to push me into a realm where I understood why we are the way we are.

I swiftly began to devour every Thich Nhat Hanh book. He taught me the best and most peaceful understanding of how we should approach life. Brené Brown's books, Bessel van der Kolk's *The Body Keeps Score*... anything and everything to help my brain understand the depth of my dysfunction.

I was trying to absorb it *all*.

It took a good slap or two from my therapist (verbal, that is) for me to wake up and realize I'd been in a bit of a stupor for... well, all my life. And once I did, I was back into self-starter/healing mode. *Okay, now I understand. So how do I operate in this culture out here? Where do I fit in in all this?*

Since then, I consciously and resolutely stayed true to myself and myself only. If I wanted to wear the same sweatshirt, jeans, and baseball cap for days on end, I damn would. I was a mom and a writer, and I didn't have to look my best to fulfil either of those roles well. This of course ran much deeper than whether or not I wanted to wear makeup on a certain day: I'd learned not to care, which is very powerful in a day and age where everyone wants something from you. I wasn't going to hold back my true personality for acceptance, and I wasn't going to kiss anyone's ass to try to fit in. I'd always been comfortable with flying solo, and that was damn well what I was going to continue to do, fancy neighborhood in the suburbs or not. We're all just doing our best with the resources we've been given, and I learned back then that just because someone beautiful and glamorous hasn't worked through their shit yet and still projects their own insecurities onto others, doesn't mean *I* need to throw myself back into that cycle just for the sake of... what? A brunch invite? A "friend" who doesn't like me for me anyway?

I believe that our role, as women, is to empower and lead ourselves and our families alongside our partners (if we have one. If not, we can be just as powerful alone). We should be clear on and live in accordance with our core values, and teach our children about these so that if they choose to adopt these same values for themselves in the future, they'll know exactly what that looks like and how to go about doing it.

I also think inclusivity (that is, bringing others up instead of constantly putting them down) is paramount, and it's very difficult to be inclusive when you're surrounding yourself with people who are operating at a low vibration. Truly, I don't think there's any excuse for the bullying I hear about through Evan that these grown-ass women put each other through. And the worst part is, this culture has become so entrenched into so many women's "normal" that their moms, their sisters, their aunts, and their friends are only further encouraging this toxicity.

To "zoom in" on this further, there is a certain character archetype, if you will, that I have experienced and come to know time and time again during my time living in a fancy Chicago suburb, and that is The Leech. (I'm sure you can see where this is going!)

The Leech is a woman who feels entitled to a life in which she is taken care of by her man, regardless of whether she is married or divorced. (Yes, a *divorced* Leech will expect her ex-husband to continue supporting her, period.) She feels no desire to have a job or to do anything remotely productive in her life, and, to look at the problem a little deeper, has a very minimal sense of agency. She relies on the goodwill (or the idiocy, depending on how you look at it) of others in order to keep afloat, and she has no problem with staying that way. In fact, she probably fears any alternative.

Note that I don't believe there is anything at all with wanting to be a stay-at-home wife, nor is there anything wrong with having a "breadwinner" in the household. What *does* gross me out is a) the entitlement these women exhibit and b) the fact that The Leech doesn't genuinely crave to be a stay-at-home mom/wife. She just wants to do *nothing*. And that's a very big difference. It's the difference between agency and passivity. It's the difference between being privileged and being spoiled. It's the difference between maximizing on your situation and taking advantage. And The Leech is everywhere, raising her daughters with the message that it's okay to go about life with no aspiration or drive, and not only that, but to leech off other people.

I try to look at these women with sympathy, but I must admit that the façade of luxury and glamor really irks me when I know that deep down, if that woman's circumstances had been different (that is, if she hadn't had the privilege so many would kill for), she'd be doing what just anybody else would have to do to get by: waiting tables and living paycheck to paycheck.

There's absolutely no shame in that, mind. My point is that these women are so out of touch that they can't even conceive of them being "demeaned" in such a way. Such a fate is for the lowly "others". It could never possibly touch *them*. And if it did... well, it would scare the shit out of them.

My point? I think Mrs. Leech should muster enough humility to put the bottle of wine to the side, show a little kindness, and extend a warm welcome to the new mom in town.

Just a thought.

I quickly learned I wasn't going to see eye to eye with any of my new neighbors in this respect, however—at least, not anytime soon—and so once I embarked on this healing journey (for real this time) and got over my own sense of low self-worth, I learned to entertain myself through my deeper loves. It certainly helped that it felt as though I'd been let into some sort of enchanted forest (a beautiful house? *Acreage?* Um, hello?), and this gave me the room (both physical and spiritual) to connect with myself. I immediately set about gardening and reading, and I even hosted a gong bath in our backyard. Turned out there was a not-insignificant number of women out there who were all experiencing the same thing: disillusionment with our increasingly superficial world, and a craving for something deeper. Something more spiritual, intimate, and meaningful. They didn't want to grow fat and happy; they wanted to open up and explore the innermost parts of themselves in a safe space. And it fills me with warmth to be able to say that I managed to create that safe space for some of those women.

There was also a Buddhist temple in my neighborhood that opened up for meditation sessions after the COVID lockdowns, and I can't even begin to describe to you the peace that would envelop my very being whenever I sat down with those other people and chanted and meditated in their presence. All very high-vibration, good vibes shit.

So, essentially, despite the insane decisions I'd felt forced to make and the chaos of the preceding months, I was slowly but surely building my tribe and inviting people I trusted into my circle. And they were definitely *not* the people who side-eyed those they called friends. And I say that as someone who's met some *real* powerhouses—badass women who've been in the thick of hardship and struggle and yet forged on, and created something amazing for themselves in the process. Trust me when I say *these* women aren't sitting around belittling one another. They're too busy enjoying the fruits of their labor with their families. And why shouldn't they? Why *wouldn't* they? Who has time for concerning yourself with others when you're already so secure in and grateful for this reality you have constructed for yourself?

The bottom line: in an ideal world, all these women I knew would direct their energy they currently used for belittling others into a passion; a purpose; a journey. And then they'd take all that experience and not only revel in this new life they'd created, but also teach the new young ladies of the world to do the same; to be strong, open-minded, and inclusive.

Until that day, I thought, *I will continue to sit over here in my bubble with my land, dogs, son, and garden, and any women out there who are aligned with a life of spiritual development and self-actualization are always welcome in that bubble.*

Basically, I dove headfirst into my own healing work, and fasting, writing, and quitting smoking were first on my self-healing list.

I nailed the fasting and writing. Quitting, on the other hand, took me a hot second, but I did.

Next was taking care of myself much more, which meant really focusing on my health. My health over the years had really been compromised: I had high blood pressure, polycystic ovarian syndrome (PCOS), and metabolic disease. Basically, the American diet (and my stress) was killing me, and I knew that. So, as previously mentioned, I adapted to long-term fasting and slowly healed all of the above.

My next area for focus was my business. My magazine needed a *lot* of TLC, so I dove right into that and began to chip away at the to-do list—and quite successfully, if I do say so myself. The magazine grew nicely and steadily, and I loved throwing myself into it. Our community was flourishing, and all around me I was seeing women who were just as dedicated to their rebirth as I was. It was beautiful to see.

Next, I opened my home up to new Reiki coaching clients. I enjoyed welcoming the energy that came with this. It was something I'd missed very much. The past two years had been utter chaos, and so I hadn't been in the right energy space to continue, yet as the weeks went by, it got ever so slightly easier, little by little.

Every day after I woke up, I journaled, starting by jotting down my wins to show me that I *was* succeeding, and then did some gratitude and manifesting practice. I'm a huge believer in manifesting, or what I call vision-creating. I firmly believe we can speak the life we want into existence.

After this, I conquered my morning chores to sit down in my office by 9AM.

So, my routine was down. So now, how could I keep my morale up—or, more accurately, conceal my depression and soul-crushing longing for Evan?

I created a meditation space in my family room, where I went for a break twice a day, once in the morning and once by mid-afternoon, after my daily workout. I love, love, love to meditate. Bringing in that good energy with breathwork and releasing all the tension and stress on a release, breathe, and repeat basis has been my savior.

Spiritual practices are *important*. I harp on to my clients about this, so it wouldn't be right if I didn't mention this here. If you don't have a spiritual practice, create one. If you don't know how, research, because when life gets rough, we need to turn inwards, toward our god, soul, source—whatever you believe in. Just do it. Your mind, body, and soul will thank you for it.

Weeks went by before I could speak to or see Evan, and during this time, I slowly began to feel sorry for my family.

I struggled with anger for a long while. I won't hide that. To this day, I still have moments of anger. My journey to forgiveness is still a work in progress. When it came to Dan, I made peace quite quickly, but when it came to my family... well, there's still blood in it. These are the folks who should have your back, after all, not stab you to fuck with a pitchfork. The pain inflicted by my blood relatives is *much* more deep-rooted than that inflicted by Dan. Indeed, my radical awakening (or second awakening) proved profusely more painful than anything I'd ever endured, and maybe this was because my inner child was still wounded and heartbroken and still craved the attention of her siblings. After all, I'm a born and bred (or groomed, rather) people pleaser; that's my trauma response. And the ten-year-old Wheezy within was feeling abandoned once again.

Upon recognizing this, I spent the course of that year encouraging her independence and emotional growth. Sometimes, I even spoiled her with cotton candy and non-stop gabbing with my husband.

And yes, John stood strong beside me the entire way, never once considering changing course.

We were coming up to week six of no communication with Evan when I received an email from the ranch stating he'd passed his value and we could have a Zoom session together.

That first session was very hard. Evan was harboring a lot resentment toward being sent to the ranch, and his main goal of the call was to convince us to let him come home—all stuff they had prepared us for. Overall, though, he looked good, and, interestingly, the ranch was offering parents the option for them to attend what they called a parent seminar: a weekend of walking you through the work they do with the kids to get them to open up.

I spoke to John about this, and we signed ourselves up for the early summer session, knowing this would mean we'd be able to see Evan for the first time in twelve to thirteen weeks.

It took us roughly twelve hours from leaving home to arrive in Utah, and my first impression was that *everything* was red. It was the desert, alright. And holy shit, was it *hot*. It was easily one hundred and ten degrees of dry heat. Even still, I couldn't help but admire our surroundings. This was my first time out west, and what beautiful landscape! The cliffs, the red mountains... We definitely needed to squeeze in some hiking.

We arrived at the hotel and took a stroll in downtown St. George, a super-quaint, lowkey, chill town. The first thing I noticed was how low-maintenance everyone seemed there. I loved it. A far cry from Fakesville back home.

After our stroll, we headed out to dinner for a steak and glass of wine, wondering what the next few days would hold.

Lord knows I was in for a huge awakening, because this trip was *not* going to be hikes, strolls, and luxury meals.

By the time 9AM on the following Friday morning rolled around, John and I were standing in the hallway of a hotel in a group of thirty adults. We cordially introduced ourselves and chitchatted, as parents do, and once the doors opened up, the room was filled with about ten staff members awaiting our arrival.

We had notebooks and pens on each chair. Our first instruction: don't sit next to your partner. Get yourself uncomfortable.

Wait, what?

The next three hours were dedicated to walking each and every one of us through our psyches—the dark parts of ourselves that we had allowed to lay dormant. The bad memories, the hurt, the neglect, was all resurfacing for me and some of the other parents.

When it came time for lunch, I was emotionally exhausted. John, meanwhile, was his typical self—"That wasn't too bad"—and we skated off to grab a bite. Our return brought on another four hours of digging.

By the end of the first day of the seminar, we were sitting in a circle with our backs to one another. I had just discovered the extent of my mother's neglect and impact on me. We were told to hold our mothers in "light", which I just couldn't do, so I sat there, frozen in pain and anger, with a staff member rubbing my back.

I was in awe of what the past eight or nine hours had opened up to me. I felt shaky and had a hard time breathing. I was emotionally exhausted. All I wanted to do was crawl into bed and sleep this off, but John's go-getter, push-through-things attitude insisted we still go out for dinner, as planned. So, dinner and a stiff gin martini in the intense dry heat of St. George, Utah, it was.

Day two of the seminar held no prisoners from the onset. From the very start of the session, we were digging into our innermost difficult feelings. At one point, I asked to leave, and they said I was "running away". That I needed to confront this.

After lunch, I told one of the staff members I felt like I was going to pass out. This was just becoming too hard for me. I requested that I be granted permission to sit some of the seminar out if it got too difficult. I hadn't been prepared to unpack forty-four years of trauma and abuse in one intensive weekend. The staff member could clearly see the worry in my eyes, and responded, "Of course. If you must."

We ended day two by standing in a circle facing one another. I distinctly remember the song *You Say* by Lauren Daigle playing. We'd all just accomplished two days of deep, intense healing work. I stood there crying to myself. I was in so much pain. Deep-rooted, visceral pain. What a mindfuck these days had been! As the song continued, the staff members kept guiding us with positive affirmations before they (finally) said, "Okay, open your eyes." And there he stood, right in front me, his big brown eyes staring up at me, grinning ear to ear.

I melted down so hard and pulled my son in.

You know the scene in Disney's *Dumbo* where Dumbo's mom is rocking Dumbo in her trunk while she stands in jail? That was how I felt. I had just had an absolutely unbelievable experience—an experience that still rocks me to the core every time I think of it.

I cried. Like, ugly cried. I couldn't control myself. In fact, I couldn't speak when they asked me for my thoughts. Everything felt unreal. Like it was a dream.

Evan looked good. He'd dropped some weight, which was good, his hair had been cut off, and genuine happiness seemed to dance in his eyes.

We got to sit with Evan for fifteen minutes before the group was ushered back. We also had a three-hour visit scheduled for the following day.

I was numb from head to toe, and desperately wanted to crawl into bed, but, yet again, John kept me going. "Sweetheart, we have dinner plans. Let's go."

The first on-campus visit we had took place in one of the family rooms, where we could chat, eat, and play board games. We brought Evan's favorite food, which he just picked at. He asked a couple of questions and started to get frustrated with our answers, which we'd expected. Over those three hours or so, we played a couple of games, and I reassured him, over and over, that we'd done the right thing; that he'd do great here.

As a parent, it's hard to see your child in pain, physical or emotional, and as a mother, your very intuition, your core, your *bones*, are screaming at you to fix it. We put band-aids on bruised knees. We cuddle our children when they're scared. We lend our confidence to them while they have none in themselves on their first day of school. Bottom line: our job as a mother is to be there for our kids in any way they need—and to do so one hundred percent of the time.

On the flipside of all of this, helicopter parenting doesn't make for resilient children. And I knew this journey was Evan's to navigate. I had to back away and develop a healthy boundary around his mental health journey rather than trying to bear his cross myself. This was unbelievably difficult for me to wrap my head around, never mind do, yet I knew that if I really wanted to act in accordance with Evan's best interests, this was the only way.

This was what I had to remind myself of when I boarded that flight back to Chicago. This was what I had to hold onto if I was to encourage, rather than jeopardize, my son's healing. And I knew he could do it. This conviction was as clear, as self-evident, as my love for him. I just had to hold onto that faith.

20
Emotional Walls

———

ONE COOL FALL MORNING, JOHN and I were having coffee (a pretty standard part of our morning routine), chatting and enjoying the sun streaming through the windows, when I asked, "So, what's your day looking like?"

"Well, I have a meeting. The board has to get together and make some hard decisions. And I might need to do a walk-through for one of the plants."

I nodded along, and, once he ceased speaking, waited for him to return the question.

To no avail.

Instead, he picked up the conversation by talking more about himself, and before I even knew what was happening, he was rising from the table and dashing off to work.

What?

Suffice to say that I was hot under the collar and pretty damn annoyed by this whole conversation.

Why, you ask?

Well, to be honest, I'd been harboring the feeling that John had completely stopped showing up in the relationship how he used to. Typical mid-relationship male complacency. This one example of a one-sided conversation was just one of many (and I mean *many*) that had occurred of late. It seemed we only ever spoke about what *he* wanted out of life and how *he* was currently the best version of himself anybody had ever seen, and so on and so forth. Don't get me wrong, I of *course* admired the fact that he was so driven and self-certain, and I obviously wasn't mad about the fact that he felt he'd done a lot of self improvement over the years, but I always came out of these conversations feeling so damn *alone* and unheard. Like, yes, I wanna hear about your day, and I wanna know where your head's at in all respects, but isn't that curiosity even a *little* bit reciprocated? Don't you want to know how *I'm* doing? Where *my* head's at? What *my* day's looking like?

This kind of emotional neglect buried deep *fast*. I couldn't help but feel as though I was over here doing the growing for him, always pushing him to be the best version of himself, and was getting quite literally nothing back. Not even a, "Thanks, babe." And I *certainly* wasn't getting the favor returned. It was all about *his* life and *his* mindset and *his* goals, and I was getting pretty damn tired of it. He was taking way more than he was giving back. Period.

Obviously, I continued to go about my day, still pretty pissed about this exchange (stroke monologue), and allowed this moment to create a ginormous story in my head—a story about how John wasn't being good enough; about how I wasn't really ever being *listened* to. And in this latter point, I do believe I was validated. For the past four years, I'd say something, and he either wouldn't respond, or he'd circulate and find a way to resume talking about himself.

So, by the time 5:30PM rolled around, I was *very* keen to address this with him.

Naturally, he strolled through the door in his typical boisterous "John" fashion: "My sweetheart! I'm home! How was your day?"

"Not bad. I had a couple meetings. Worked out."

"Well," he pressed on, "I met with this person, and I walked through some of the plants, and…"

And off he went.

I sat in silence for a good few minutes until I heard the words, "So, what's for dinner?" followed by a pause. The first question he'd asked since he began speaking.

"John, can I ask you something?" I said suddenly. "Do you realize that you rarely ever respond to the things that I say? And do you understand that when you do this, it makes me feel like I'm not good enough? Do you understand that you do this *all the time*, and so *all the time*, I don't feel good enough? Do you see how one-sided this marriage is?"

Okay, so maybe that wasn't the best way to approach this conversation with someone who was exhausted from a day at work. I know myself that when I've had a full and tiring day, the last thing I want to do is be bombarded by question after question about my performance in my marriage, or any equally heavy subject. Even still, I'd been sitting on this all day—no, for several *years*—and had decided I'd had enough. It was time for a grownup conversation.

Now, one of the biggest struggles in our relationship had always been the fact that John felt the need to constantly defend himself, and this had been the case for his whole life, with family and friends and romantic partners and so on and so forth. So, he immediately went on the defense. Clearly, a constructive conversation about this wasn't going to happen, and we weren't going to get anywhere by trying to have one while we were so easily bristled. So, to me, the obvious next solution was to bring up the prospect of marriage and family therapy, something that was an *extremely* wise move.

I share this story because when reflecting on my relationship with John and Dan, and even with Evan and my mother, I realized that all of my relationships had always had some level of emotional unavailability to them. This, of course, begged the question of why I was constantly attracting all these vastly emotionally unavailable people, and why *I* was often accused of being the emotionally unavailable one.

I have pondered this in great depth over the years, both in therapy and out, and the conclusion that I have come to is that when you have emotionally unavailable parents as a child, you become a problem solver yourself. You learn to self-soothe. You come up with your own coping skills. You find ways to navigate the highs and lows of life alone, without any emotional support or a safety blanket, physical or metaphorical.

This was difficult for me to come to terms with in relation to my own life, and this was primarily because I knew, when being honest with myself, that these childhood experiences (all with a running theme of no emotional security or support) culminated in me often being very emotionally unavailable for Evan. (There goes that vicious cycle of intergenerational trauma again!) And, of course, I have also been hugely emotionally unavailable with my romantic partners, including Dan and John, at certain points, and that was because I'd surrounded myself with unimaginably huge walls my entire life so I could protect myself for being hurt.

Sounds obvious, but it took me a long time to come to terms with this fact.

Mexico had been my and John's go-to vacation ever since that first trip away together. We turned this into a family holiday on occasion, but generally speaking, Mexico was our escape from reality; from the demands of work and family.

Mexico had always held a special place in my heart, not just because it was there where I really fell in love with John, but also because I felt a very strong spiritual tie to it. I wouldn't be surprised if I had a previous life there.

We had one of our couples' trips to Mexico booked for a couple of months before Evan was due to return from the ranch. We'd both been working like crazy, and we knew we'd need to be giving Evan our full attention upon his return so he could adjust back to living at home smoothly. So, we really wanted to squeeze in a good week of some real good rest and relaxation in one of our favorite spots in the world. By the time you get through the shitshow that is customs, you're plunged into Paradise... and God, did we need some of that!

Upon arriving, we were surprised by how busy the resort was. January and February was definitely not peak season, yet the place was bustling. And I hate to say it, but as soon as I saw all those women with their drinks and bikinis, laughing and having a good time in the sunshine, my heart completely sank. Not because there was anything wrong with what they were doing or because they made me feel insecure (I was way too deep into my healing journey for that shit now), but because I was accustomed to John's less-than-cOnsiderate behavior toward me whenever we were out in public with beautiful women hanging around.

I didn't want to kill the mood, however, so we checked in as normal, grabbed a drink, and looked for a place by the pool to chill.

It didn't take long for John to get talking to every resort worker under the sun, though this was pretty normal for us by this point. We knew a lot of the staff by name from our other trips. Plus, John was a pretty social, charismatic guy anyway, so it wasn't unusual for him to knock back a few drinks and find someone to chat shit with wherever we went.

I watched this happily enough, but not without a little unease. I was extremely cautious and mistrusting at this point in our relationship, and I knew his "John-isms" often led to him doing something he knew would make me (and, I'm sure, ninety-nine percent of the other people on the planet, should they ever find themselves in my position) feel insecure or uncomfortable. Plus, I was in the (unhealthy) habit of panicking as soon as I found myself "getting comfortable" and putting my walls right back up, convinced that the next nasty surprise was right around the corner.

Again, though, I didn't want to allow my own trepidation to taint the vacation, so we enjoyed our evening together, as well as the next few days, without a hitch.

By the time we were about halfway through the trip, I found myself slipping back into that place of serenity, security, and trust. My cheeks ached from smiling so much, the drinks were flowing, and we were both super-chilled out and happy.

Now, it was custom for us to have a couples' massage whenever we were on vacation at this resort, and during this trip, one of the other couples mentioned to us that if we went to a neighboring resort for the massage instead, it'd be way cheaper.

Obviously, John and I were sold.

As was also custom for these massages, we had a few cocktails in us by the time we went to this resort for our appointment, and as we walked, I realized, in the midst of the fog that was my tipsy happiness, that it felt as though something was... off. Alarm bells were suddenly ringing in my mind, and I had a deep-set gut feeling that something was going to go wrong.

It didn't take long for us to realize that this other "massage place" was actually just a canopy, beneath which a bunch of people were getting massages. Not too weird, I guess, but again, the alarm bells were ringing loud and clear. My intuition wasn't too happy about this change of plan.

We checked in and got comfortable on our beds, and as soon as the massage therapists arrived (a young woman for John and a man for me), the alarm bells only grew louder and louder. The massage therapists introduced themselves and directed our attention to a laminated piece of paper with a list of types of massages and asked us which we would like.

"I'll do the full-body massage," I told my massage therapist.

John pointed to the massage he wanted on the list, chuckled, and gestured with his hand obscenely. Gestured in a way that suggested it was a good ol' happy ending massage that he was wanting.

My heart sank to the floor.

Did he just do what I think he did? I glared at the young Mexican massage girl as she chuckled—though she immediately stopped laughing once she saw my look of shock. *On our vacation? With me right here?*

I felt utterly sick to my stomach. Physically ill. My head swam and my stomach felt like a swirling vortex of hurt and shame and mortification.

I was lying on my stomach at this point, and throughout the entire massage, all I did was strain to hear every tiny noise that came from next to me. Would she oblige? If he'd been so shameless to ask her right in front of me, who was to say he wouldn't follow through with it with me in the very same space as him?

What was even weirder was that my own massage therapist seemed very intent on keeping me facing away from John during the treatment. There was even one point when I turned over (so I was lying on my back instead of my stomach) and my massage therapist immediately draped a warm towel over my head (including my eyes), blocking my view from John entirely.

Panic really started to set in. What was this guy trying to stop me from seeing? What was my husband doing? What the everliving fuck was going *on* over there?

At this point, I was so stressed and convinced something must be happening that I couldn't figure out whether I could actually hear anything suspicious or whether my brain was just filling in the blanks. I *thought* I could hear something strange, but...

I tried to lift my head and see for myself what was happening again, but my massage therapist physically pushed my head back down on the bed. *"No,"* I said, more than a little panicked, and tried to rip the towel from my face—only for *him* to tell me "no" and put the towel back over my eyes.

A few moments later, the massage was over, but not soon enough. My heart was pounding and my fists were clenched the entire time. I felt betrayed. Doubtful. On edge. Certainly not the relaxing massage I'd signed up for.

As soon as that goddamn towel was finally removed from my face, I sat straight up and looked over at John. He was lying still on his bed, and was clearly still drunk. Other than that, I couldn't really read his expression, and certainly couldn't tell whether he'd got the happy ending he'd requested.

He handed over the cash, and as we walked back to our resort, I was still almost shaking with anger and uncertainty.

"Hey, that wasn't so bad!" he chirped as we walked. "What do you think? Did you like the massage?"

My frosty rebuttal: "Yeah, it was great! How was your happy ending?"

Pause. "What do you mean, sweetheart?"

I was infuriated. What was he playing at? "Well, you *did* ask for a happy ending, didn't you, John?"

He furrowed his brows and remained mute. He seemed, quite literally, lost for words. Which, again, set alarm bells ringing, though I didn't know how to interpret this. If *I* had been falsely accused of something, would I be shocked into silence? Or was it the opposite? Would I struggle to find words if I knew I was guilty? Which one was it? I had no idea. All I knew was that my intuition was still telling me loud and clear that something was off.

And then, he launched straight into his defense. "I don't know what you're talking about. I never asked for that. You must have misunderstood."

My heart sank because I was already familiar with this little routine of his, and I knew it screamed guilt. Whenever his hand had been caught in the cookie jar, he was in the habit of completely switching the situation around on me and, yes, gaslighting me. It must be that I had *remembered* wrong, not that he'd fucked up (Heaven forbid). It must be that I had misunderstood, misheard, misinterpreted; that it was *me* who was now causing an issue, who was going a little crazy, not him who had made a huge mistake and been caught red-handed.

And it seemed this situation was going to be no different. He wouldn't be caught dead admitting to a mistake, no matter how obvious or blatant.

Naturally, from this point, I was counting down the hours until the end of this vacation. I was still seething with anger, betrayal, and hurt, and to be honest, I felt very done. With the trip. With my marriage. With him. Frankly, I was sick of being walked all over and taken advantage of, and, at the end of it, treated like a fool, *every fucking time.*

That vacation was the point where I truly mentally shut off from our marriage.

I share this not to villainize or shit all over John (I adored him, after all) but to illustrate the fact that when you have two people who haven't worked out their stuff, they can trigger each other *constantly*, and that was definitely the case with me and John (hence why it's so important to actually own up to your shit, do the work, and move on with your life).

This definitely brought me to a point where I felt it would perhaps be easier to just leave the relationship and be single than to constantly deal with all this hurt and pain, and this honestly said more about me than it ever did about John. Sure, I didn't appreciate his behavior, but I'd known exactly what I was getting into when I chose to be with him. *I*, on the other hand, had moved the goalposts and decided I was *tired* of this shit.

Yet at this point, I also felt that it *was* John that I wanted to be with, and so I discussed with my therapist how I could directly but constructively address with John the pain and hurt I was dealing with. And through those therapy sessions, I was able to reflect on some *insanely* valuable lessons from my and John's relationship.

Firstly, you should *never* seek validation in or base your self-worth around your partner. I know I'm beautiful and deserving of a whole, peaceful life, and I don't need confirmation from anyone else for me to firmly believe that.

Secondly, emotional freedom is *critical* in any relationship. This lesson is still a work in progress for me, but ultimately, learning how to adapt to somebody else's (radically different) emotional needs *while* not neglecting your own is a critical skill.

So, where was my head at after that trip to Mexico? Well, I knew my walls had shot the fuck back up, that was for sure, and I also knew that I was now feeling an emotional disconnect that was perhaps bigger than I'd ever felt toward John. But I still viewed our situation optimistically. *This is recoverable*, I thought. *I just need to be gentle and patient with him. And figure out how I can guide the both of us through this shitshow.*

In the end, though, I had very little time to process this vacation or what the fuck I even wanted to do in my relationship, because Evan was soon due home after taking the entire course at the ranch—almost a full year—and my focus of course needed to be fully with him as he readjusted back to life at home.

Before his return, we ended up going back out there again for part two of the parent seminar, which proved to be nowhere near as difficult for me as part one. (Thank God for my therapist!) We also visited Evan again, which went much better than the previous visit. He was working hard, which culminated in him being permitted to do off-campus visits. This meant he was able to come back home for a week.

He was turning over a new leaf, he looked *so* much happier, and his emotional intelligence spiked.

He was going to shine.

Evan and I conquered some of our greatest fears and accomplished wins we'd never thought we were capable of over the course of that year. John and I were overjoyed at this progress, and anticipated him graduating the program at the end of March. This would mean he could return to school in April, after he'd got reacclimated to home, friendships, and, of course, baseball.

In the meantime, before Evan's return, I was determined to continue what had been started during the ranch's parents' sessions: unpacking my forty-four years of insane nonsense.

This was never going to be any small feat, yet I don't think anything could have quite prepared me for what this process was going to be truly like. To put it nicely, it completely saps you of energy. Your life is turned upside down, with everything you thought you were and your values, morals, goals, and beliefs all being reevaluated. I had some of the most intense experiences I've ever had in my life while unraveling my past. But I persevered. I dove deep into some good inner child work and worked with shamans, therapists, and doctors—all natural, holistic approaches to healing. While the process was often horrendously difficult, I built an amazingly supportive community along the way that carried me towards my goal of a life not in survival mode; a life of healthy, meaningful relationships. I discovered how selfishly I had been living, aiming for goals that were not aligned with my deepest intentions.

I also truly learned how none of us has any room to judge the next person. We're all sinners and degenerates on some level. None of us are really truly worthy of the Lord's presence. We simply pray he surrounds us and forgives us for the shit we do.

Overall, 2021 was very much so a year full of firsts. I enrolled in and completed a *very* good course and cranked out some serious business growth, I co-authored a book and signed a publishing contract to facilitate you holding this bad boy in your hands right now, I cried when no one was home and learned to release my pain alone, I journaled and wrote a ton of shit, I tried to convince John to let me play the drums (yes, that's my inner child needing some good grounding sound. I have a secret dream of having a drum-off with Dave Grohl!), and I ventured outside my comfort zone and did things that I'd previously feared due to my mother's beliefs.

I often daydreamed of the day Evan would come home; the warm sun that would shine on my face as I'd watch him play first base or pitch. I missed the sounds of a group of beautiful boys playing in my home. I loved all of Evan's friends, and I missed seeing their faces, but was comforted by the fact that Evan was safe, happy, and healing where he was, and that his life would be so much richer and he would be so much more equipped to deal with life's hardships after his return.

This was what I held onto during those nights when the silence in the house felt physical and oppressive. This was what I held onto when I desperately wanted to just give my little boy a squeeze and bury my face in his hair.

Basically, my radical awakening led me to take a much humbler, kindness-driven approach to life. Don't get me wrong, I'm still unpacking and learning to let go, but my progress has been exponential.

While this may sound dramatic, one of the truly most liberating physical things I did was cut all my hair off. Much like when my niece accidentally lopped a little too much of my hair off after I'd left Dan, this new style felt like a physical marker of the new me. I still bawled my eyes out when my super-fabulous hairdresser, George, created a gorgeous Audrey Hepburn-esque pixie, but I also acknowledged that this was the sign of a beautiful new beginning.

It may take a long while before the hard, protective exterior I have always worn comes off completely, but for now, I know for sure that the soft, warm, compassionate Felicity is still there. And I'm starting to fall in love with her, just a little bit.

March 2022 eventually rolled around, and Evan's return was blissful. His friends rejoiced, surrounded him with love, and picked up like nothing had happened. My heart swelled with joy at this.

His return to school was a little rocky, as we somewhat expected. Kids can be (and often are) real douchebags, and insisted on starting a rumor that the reason for Evan being "sent away" was him beating me. Not the welcome committee I would have wanted my kid to have been greeted with, of course, but a first test for Evan's newfound resilience, nonetheless.

His return home also marked the beginning of him having to make some difficult decisions. Specifically, he still held a huge grudge toward his father because, as he saw it, Dan had not been there for him properly during the times he'd needed support. As of right now (at the time of writing), I believe Dan and Stacy are separated, and Evan refuses to see him. I know Evan's relationship with his father is something that haunts him a lot, and so I desperately hope, for the sake of his happiness and spiritual growth, he can find some peace in this soon, whatever that looks like.

As for Sherry, she sent Evan a postcard every day while he was in the ranch, and I know she loves him very much. They have recently started seeing each other again, and I'm happy to say Evan has firm boundaries in place and has communicated to her that he wishes to not see his dad, and she's respecting that. So long as that continues to be the case, I have no problem with Evan and Sherry having a relationship.

In the late summer of 2022, we saw my family for the first time in two years to visit my Nan (who is still going strong!)—which, by the way, was eventfully uneventful: the visit was pleasant, but *everything* was swept under the rug. Dawn literally walked in with an upbeat, "Hi, guys!" as if nothing at all had happened.

Evan enjoyed seeing them, but with everything they've done, he'd allow few to have a relationship with him, and even that relationship would have firm boundaries in place.

During that visit, I kept everything polite, but simultaneously realized this: while the door is open for Evan and me to walk right back into their lives, the moment we do, my family will always ensure we're where *they* want us to be. Our relationship with them would always have to be on *their* terms. So, to be frank, I don't fancy having anything to do with them, and nor does Evan.

This doesn't go for Tommy, of course. He's the best.

Basically, Evan and were working on building our tribe. We're not close with my or John's family, so we worked on building new relationships instead. This is a journey that we both decided to go on as individuals. It's a decision I came to in light of my radical awakening, and it's a decision Evan came to because of the perspective and tools the ranch gave him. Of course, it was tremendously difficult when he wasn't here, and I missed him like crazy, but sometimes, we have to do hard things if we want to reap insanely good benefits, and sending Evan to the ranch ended up being one of those hard things. The ranch gave Evan the resources he needed in order to fully deal with life and all its ups and downs. I constantly see adults that don't have the emotional awareness that he has, and it amazes me when he calls me or someone else out for negative coping mechanisms and behaviors with a, "Hey, that kid is showboating over there, Mom. What an attention seeker," or, "You're making it personal, Mom."

Sending him away allowed me to pull away from that exhausted, reactive parent headspace and approach him with understanding and compassion. Don't get me wrong, this is still a work in progress, and I'm still learning how to let my walls down and welcome in the soft, compassionate mother, wife, and woman I dream of being. And to be honest, I'm not quite sure why embodying this version of myself has been so difficult. I don't know if it's a safety or security issue, or if it's just a part of my makeup to default to a strong, tough, vocal trailblazer. I envy (in a good way!) those women that you see and hear that are so very feminine, soft, and carefree, and I dream about what I'd look or feel like if I could fully embody that energy.

That's my next big goal: to step into that feminine. To let go of the tough exterior and let others fight my battles for me every so often, rather than constantly feeling the need to prove my resilience, time and time again.

And when you have a big goal like that, there are usually a whole load of realizations that bubble to the surface.

It took me an *especially* long time to come to terms with the fact that me regularly telling Evan "I love you" did not take away from the fact that I was extremely emotionally distant from him. I now know that it is essential to be emotionally vulnerable around your child and to teach them, through your own behavior, that being emotionally vulnerable is okay, and actually a strength. But I instead kept up those walls—that impenetrable front—and compensated for my distance with physical affection and "I love you"s.

So, as I sat there in my therapist's office trying to digest the reality that it had actually been *me* who had been emotionally unavailable the whole time and who was responsible for attracting equally emotionally unavailable people, these were the thoughts flying through my mind.

Thoughts of parental and marital inadequacy. Thoughts of guilt and sadness.

Because the truth was, deep down inside, I was *yearning* (and still do yearn) for that deep commitment; that feeling of surrender; of true intimacy. Yet in reality, I was scared shitless of it. So scared that just the *thought* of laying myself bare in that way literally triggered my fight-or-flight response.

Yeah, this shit went deep.

I knew that wasn't an excuse, though. The bottom line was, it was my role as a mother to work on my shit so I could become more emotionally available for Evan. So, I continued to work on it.

Evan himself was going through a year of intense therapy at this point, so in a way, he was able to be my teacher, which definitely helped things. I think he understood the true extent of what I was battling mentally as soon as I opened up and told him that it was hard for me to be vulnerable around him or anybody. And, sadly, I think he'd already picked up on this. Shortly thereafter, when Evan came home from the ranch permanently, he had a complete mini meltdown, crying and screaming that I "wasn't there for him" and that I "wasn't listening to him".

I pulled myself away from that moment and to my bedroom so I could process everything, John right behind me, and this was one of my "ah-*ha!*" moments. A very humbling "ah-*ha!*" moment, at that. What I'd been exploring in therapy suddenly clicked for me in that moment, because in between all the screaming and crying, there had undoubtedly been truth in what Evan was telling me: "You're not listening to me. You don't understand what I'm saying. *Why won't anybody understand what I'm saying?*" The bottom line of everything coming out of his mouth was that I was emotionally unavailable to him, and I was a part of the reason why I'd ultimately had to send him to the ranch.

This was a crazy moment for me. In a way, it was grounding and enlightening, but it was also a massive mindfuck. And a huge guilt trip.

So, there I sat on my bedroom floor, having a little meltdown myself as I processed this lightbulb moment.

Meanwhile, poor John was sitting there, perplexed, probably wondering, *What the fuck is going on now? I've got my stepson melting down in the family room and my wife is now crying in the bedroom!*

Of course, super-grounded, problem solver John got right in there. "Sweetheart, what's going on? Why are you crying?"

And it all came spilling out. Through my tears, I told John that the reason Evan was the way he was because he had a mom who'd been unable to be emotionally available for him, because I didn't know *how* to be emotionally available.

"I wasn't taught how to be," I sniffled. "My mother never taught *any* of us how to be vulnerable and present."

And then I continued to sob.

While painful, that "ah-*ha!*" moment was the pivotal point of my personal life. It was the moment when I knew I needed to begin to take the walls down in earnest.

And it wasn't just Evan I needed to work on this with. I needed to fix this with John, too.

But it turned out my relationship with John was a whole other beast. In fact, I'd even venture to say that at this point, it was even more complicated than my relationship with Evan. Shortly after my "lightbulb moment" on the bedroom floor, John and I ended up outlining some really clear boundaries in our relationship—something John struggled with massively (John didn't respect boundaries within any kind of relationship, within our marriage and otherwise, and I say that with love).

And boy, was that struggle about to become evident.

It was shortly after this conversation and agreement that we planned a date together, and I was excited to see if or how John's behavior would change now that I'd made it clear what I needed from him in order to feel secure in our relationship.

I got more dolled up than usual for the occasion, and by the time we'd been seated in the restaurant, we'd proceeded to do what we do best: people watching. (Don't judge; it's intriguing stuff.) As we laughed and chattered together, nursing our drinks (mine a gin martini with a twist of lime, his a vodka martini), I looked into his eyes and realized that for the first time in forever (perhaps since our trip to Mexico), I was fully letting my walls down in the presence of one thousand people (well, not quite, but you get the point); that I was laughing and happy; that in this moment, I had full trust in this man that I'd married.

At one point, I looked up mid-laugh to look at the group of people I'd just heard walk through the door... and there happened to be a beautiful woman among the group. Cindy Jones.

I glanced back at John. His face was flushed and donning an absent, stupid grin, and not because of the vodka. He was staring right at Cindy. It was as though I was watching a sixteen-year-old schoolboy watch his crush walk into the room.

Without a single glance at me, he rose clumsily from his seat with a harried, "That's Cindy Jones! I've got to say hi!"

For context, Cindy Jones was a divorcée from the area, and was a name that had come up in many a "nudge" to John from family and friends. And here she was, gorgeous and single. And my husband was ogling at her.

You know when you're suddenly so upset that it feels as though your chest is physically welling up with pain? That was how I felt as I perched on the edge of that barstool, watching my giddy husband wrapping his arms around and kissing on the cheek another beautiful woman.

I would have felt hurt and betrayed if we *hadn't* just had a conversation very clearly outlining my boundaries, but the fact that we *had* only added insult to injury. It was gross. Hurtful. Asshole behavior.

Basically, it took a lot of self restraint to not just burst into tears there and then. But, of course, I kept my cool, and watched as a few moments later my dumbass husband came bounding back, seemingly on Cloud Nine. "Cindy's out to dinner with a group of friends," he said happily. Obliviously. There was not an iota of shame, embarrassment, or sheepishness on his face.

In that moment, all the boundaries we'd discussed and agreed upon as a couple mere days before were trodden over. My trust was dashed, and my walls shot right back up.

Of course, we ended up discussing this incident with our therapist afterwards, who did their best to a) explain to John how this was breaking a boundary and how this will have made me feel, and b) get me to understand that it's okay to keep my walls down, even if the person who made my put my walls *up* in the first place continued to hurt me.

Of course, I rebelled against that last point. I couldn't see how letting someone hurt me over and over just because they couldn't understand what a fucking boundary was was the way forward. How would I know when enough was enough if I just let myself be walked all over all the time?

As a write this today, further down the road and with a fuck-ton of therapy and a huge third awakening under my belt, I'm still no closer to an answer for when enough is enough and when we should just let the people we love do their own thing, even if it hurts us. I didn't marry John so he could eye-fuck someone across a bar right in front of me, but then again, I understood he had a ton of his own shit to work through from his own life and that sometimes, compassion was the way forward. Plus, I suppose it kind of was a mistruth to say that I didn't sign up for this, because I'd been under no illusions about John's character—the good and the bad—when I'd married him.

Still, something about this whole ordeal didn't seem right. It was settling badly with me, that's for sure. All the positive affirmations I'd recited to myself over and over during my intensive healing period while Evan had been way came flooding back to me in one huge wave, and I suddenly realized, with startling clarity, that this very, very far-removed from what I knew I deserved and what I knew was acceptable.

The walls were up, and a seed was planted. I didn't have to stay in this. Not if nothing changed.

Then again, I loved the idiot. And so I hoped, feebly but desperately, that our relationship would never come to that.

21

A Change of Heart

I T ALL STARTED WITH A conversation in the pool over a game of tug-of-war... with a pool noodle.

Why were we playing tug-of-war with a pool noodle? Simple: I was trying to show John what an energy vampire does. The effects of being around an energy vampire were self-explanatory in my world, but to John, this was a completely foreign concept. The blessing was that he was open and willing to understand what I meant by people being "energy vampires", and so commenced our lesson.

I'd tried to explain without the pool noodle, of course. I opened by explaining the basics of what being around an "energy vampire" (those who use you almost as a power outlet to restore their energy, leaving you depleted) feels like, and then went on to explain the imbalance I felt was present in our relationship. But he wasn't getting it. He could kinda understand in theory what this would look and feel like, but my explanations were doing nothing to *really* bring him into "my world" and drive the lesson home.

Inspiration struck when I saw the pool noodle floating along. (In case you didn't realize this by this point, we were in the pool. Just to clear that up.) I grabbed it, turned to John, and said, "Hey, here. Grab the other end of this noodle."

Once he had a good grip with both hands, I said, "Okay, now ask me how my day was."

"Okay, sweetheart. How was your day?"

"Oh my *God*, John, it was *hideous*! I had meeting after meeting. And can you be*lieve* that Joann didn't show up again?"

He frowned slightly. He looked confused, that's for sure.

"How was your day?" I asked.

"Oh, it was great. I—"

I gave a good tug of the noodle so it almost slid out of his grasp and cut in, "Wait, I didn't tell you. I went out to lunch and I was mischarged. But the good part is that during the meeting, everyone was, like, really proud of me for all the work I'm doing." I paused for emphasis. "Isn't that *great*, John?"

He smiled indulgently. "But sweetheart, I wasn't d—"

I tugged the rest of the noodle out of his hand and interrupted him once again. "John, what do *you* think I should do about this situation with Janine?"

He smiled again and shrugged. "Nice job. I get it."

"Yes, you see? I've sucked all your energy, and every chance you have to dive back into your world I take as an opportunity to bring back to me."

Looking back on this now, the underlying problem in our relationship (well, one of them, at least) was that we'd met each other as "unawake" people, and now, I was slowly waking up. He was certainly open to doing "the work", but he was still rooted so deeply in his intrinsic beliefs and habits that it didn't take long for us to end up on totally different pages.

Plus, my tolerance for bullshit, manipulation, and wrongdoing was definitely getting lower and lower with every day that passed.

As an "unawake" couple, we were amazing together. But with this mental and spiritual shift I was going through… well, we were getting to a toxic place, fast.

John was an egotistical man when I met him. An *incredible* man with innumerable attributes, but still fundamentally egotistical (as many of us are), and us people pleasers cannot resist someone egotistical; someone who is so easy to please and who thus gives us that validation and love we've always craved so readily. But this "awakening" of sorts suddenly turned me off from this constant ego-massaging. Like, big time. You're telling me you cannot stand to hear a simple fact about my day without redirecting the conversation back to you? Yuck. And it wasn't just me who was becoming increasingly "turned off". I could tell that the more I stepped into my power, did "the work", and became an overall stronger, more beautiful, and more successful version of myself, the less John seemed to want to engage with me.

Interpret that how you will.

How could I tell? There was all of a sudden a *huge* energy shift in how he addressed me. All of a sudden, comments like, "Sweetheart, you'll never be as successful as me," and, "Yes, you look lovely, but how do *I* look?" became the norm. Textbook narcissism. And I don't say that with any shade or malice. He was just so used to always being at the top of his game that his woman suddenly stepping into her own set a whole load of alarm bells ringing in his head about his place in the world and his self-worth. This is an easy trap to fall into and one that I empathize with, but that ultimately wasn't my problem. You feel threatened by your wife being independent and fulfilled and successful, with or without you? Oh, well.

I don't say all this to suggest that I pieced all of this together at the time. On the contrary, these are only things I've realized after lots of reflection and hindsight. At the time, all I knew was that these comments set off a strange chain reaction in me energy-wise, and that after a day, week, month of lots of success, I'd end up feeling inexplicably emotionally and physically drained... and it took me a hot second to connect the dots and realize this sense of exhaustion only came about after I'd expressed my happiness to John and, inevitably, received one of these comments.

This culminated in an exhaustion that was... no fun. In fact, it was utterly debilitating. All of a sudden, I was struggling to function.

The classic symptom of unwittingly falling victim to energy vampires.

And it wasn't just me who was noticing all the bad energy I was suddenly absorbing. I had quite a few healers in my community by this point, and they all agreed there was some negative juju being slung my way. "Felicity, if you can't feel this, I need to warn you that there are a few people—names I won't mention—that want this relationship and your success to be over."

Yikes. But also sort of validating. I'd known I could feel something (I was literally receiving messages in my sleep), but having this confirmed by my fellow healers at least put me on solid ground and gave me a clear(ish) idea of what was going on.

One thing was for sure: I would never give up my power just because it made others feel uncomfortable or intimidated, or whatever. I would just continue doing my shielding and protecting.

Though then again, should you have to heal and protect yourself from your husband?

These were the questions I was contemplating. And while the answer to such a question may be obvious when laid out in black-and-white terms like this, our situation was actually far from simple. John was a fundamentally selfless man whose sole mission was to make others happy... yet that was his very problem: he always thought he could "fix" the people he loved (almost always with material items, no less), and this (not least the fact that he'd pursued the career he had solely so he could "make sure everyone else was happy") had sucked all the joy out of him for the last two decades of his life. The problem was that now, I'd shown John he could still have the happiness he'd been missing all that time, and in the process, I became his power source. The wall plug. The vat of energy he had to take, take, take from in order to feel whole again, and which he had nothing to give back to.

This is what happens when a people pleaser who doesn't know when to stop giving becomes deeply involved with someone who has been emotionally neglected (and is thus vastly emotionally unavailable). The "taker" awakens each morning feeling energized and brimming with life, blessedly healed from a lifetime of emptiness and filled with a sense of abundance, while the "giver" sits feeling depleted and disorientated, wondering how the hell they got here and why people pleasing suddenly doesn't feel so good anymore.

John, at his core, cared for me more deeply than anyone ever had. But the man just had no fucking clue how to be there for me in the ways that really mattered. What good was a ten-thousand-dollar bracelet when he couldn't bring himself to listen to you tell him how your day was?

I felt like leftovers. I think Evan did, too. Along with all of his kids. I wasn't the only person feeling like the only choices were to have a one-way relationship with John or no relationship at all.

A lightbulb moment I had during my healing journey was this: John loved my qualities, but not *me* as a whole. He loved the sum of my parts, but not who I actually was at my core, in my essence.

He only loved the pieces of me.

And ultimately, he was always looking to paper over the cracks (normally with a pretty hefty cheque) instead of addressing the core issue. Yes, he was going to therapy and open to some inner work, but these beliefs and habits were so deeply entrenched in his DNA at this point that

I was faced with the inevitable question of, *Are we definitely going to grow together, or am I going to outgrow him?*

I think I already knew the answer to that one.

John sure knew how to foster a relationship financially, but spiritually, emotionally, mentally, and physically? Forget it.

So, here I was, at yet another crossroads, depleted of my very lifeforce and back to craving the simple things in life: solitude, good food, good books, rest, peace, and privacy.

Realistically, we needed to have some difficult conversations.

It was 10PM on a Saturday night, and I was picking Evan up from a friend's house.

As I was walking back to the car, Evan in tow, I noticed a group of boys riding down the middle of the street in the pitch dark on motorized bicycles, flying across the sidewalk and the railroad tracks.

"That's it!" Evan suddenly exclaimed, voice practically tremoring with excitement. "That's the bike I've been telling you I want! Isn't it awesome, Mom?"

All I'd thought when I'd seen those maniacs speeding down the street was that I'd be fucking *pissed* if any of them had been my kid. Yet in Evan's eyes, these were basically the coolest kids on Earth, and he wanted to do anything and everything they did, period.

This is the problem when you're trying to raise your kid with common sense and healthy boundaries in a very privileged, materialistic, out-of-touch neighborhood. Unfortunately, it seemed these other kids sucked all the good judgment out of him.

"You've got to be kidding me," I responded, frowning. "You know damn well you wouldn't be allowed to ride that around like that at night. These kids are lucky they're still alive! Plus, it's, like, a two-thousand-dollar bike, and you have two legs that work just fine. No, I don't think so."

"You suck!" he suddenly burst out. "I can *never* get anything I want!"

This heated response completely bewildered me. Sure, we'd been having some behavioral issues with Evan as of late, but just seven months before, he'd been at the ranch with nothing more to his name than the bare necessities. And now, he'd already reached a point where his mind had been re-polluted with materialism and entitlement.

"Whatever," he said a few moments later. "I'm going to save up for the bike myself."

I considered this answer for a minute or so and then responded, "Evan, really think about this. Do you understand the full picture here? You're fifteen in a few months, and you're going to be driving soon, so why would you save two thousand dollars for a motorized bike when that could be two thousand dollars toward a car? Do you understand your own logic here?"

Now, of course I understood that he was only fourteen and that he just wanted to be like the other kids and have the "big cool thing" they were all talking about, but I also wanted to encourage him to connect the dots here. Save a little longer, and you can get yourself a beater car that can take you to and from your sports meets (which were basically all he cared about at this point in his life). Considering that and the fact that he'd almost certainly hurt himself if he was recklessly running around town on a motorized bike, I just wasn't going to understand him making any alternative decision.

Perhaps unsurprisingly, this conversation deteriorated into a back-and-forth argument. Emotionally, Evan had been doing alright since his return from the ranch, but I was seeing a very real sense of entitlement and lack of motivation creeping in. Take the fact that because Evan had sports, school, homework, and socializing to do, I'd agreed I'd still clean his bedroom, do his laundry, etc. and give him a twenty-dollar allowance (something that seemed like a fair deal)... yet slowly but surely, Evan was doing his sports and homework less and less and was spending more and more time out with his friends. At that point, I (and I see this is entirely my fault) took it upon myself to still do his chores and give him his allowance, *and* to give him extra money for his outings—because I didn't want to leave him high and dry, right? Yet whenever I did this, the "thank you" I got was always Evan trying to take more than I'd offered (which was already more than we'd originally agreed).

In other words, for him, the agreement became less about allowing him to have balance in his life and more of an opportunity for him to take advantage.

Lovely.

Basically, for all the discourse I was hearing about "hustle culture" and "putting less pressure on our kids", all *I* was seeing was an increased sense of entitlement and lethargy among our youth... and I think this was quite simply because *we did too much for them*. It took a whole team of therapists to get me to pull back, leave him to figure out his own time management, and to give him the space to understand that work = money, and no work = no money, but once I finally did this, I could suddenly see, with vivid clarity, just how *handicapped* this generation had become. I don't care how our kids spend their spare time so long as they're still open and willing to help out and earn their keep when the time comes, but the problem is, I think we're raising a generation that instead feels entitled to all the luxury in the world *without* any of the graft that comes with it.

Essentially, the gap between my generation and Evan's feels huge and gaping. If I'd said, "Eh, I'll think about it," to my mom after she'd asked me for some assistance with some housework, I would've got the shit slapped out of me. And while I'm most certainly not advocating for *that* style of parenting, I feel the completely lax, "anything goes" parenting approach of today was also an evil, just on the opposite end of the spectrum.

So, after I had this realization, I pulled Evan to the side after one such incident and said, "Buddy, I love you, but life is going to hit you so damn hard if you don't take control of this entitlement you've got going on. You're not going to be handed *anything* in life. You're going to have to work your *ass* off. Do you understand that? Do you understand that yes, you are privy to certain privileges, but that doesn't mean you are entitled to or owed anything?"

I paused, taken aback but relieved by the fact that he was suddenly listening to me very intently.

"I will no longer make you your school lunches or your breakfast. That is on you. As for your room and laundry, you need to figure out how to manage your time. This is where a schedule comes into play. You plan out your week. You've been taught this, so use the tools you've been given—from the ranch and from me."

This may sound harsh, but the bigger picture of this exchange was a mother who desperately wanted to keep her child safe, secure, and on the right path, while the child in question wanted to lose control and have a complete "YOLO" mentality.

As you can probably tell, there was a huge tug-of-war in our family that had been going on for far too long, and I was just trying my darndest to keep Evan grounded and focused on the things that mattered.

Here's a classic Felicity hot take: I really think the messaging that we receive about being endlessly selfless and sacrificing for our families, only to receive *nothing* in return, is completely skewed. And I do wonder quite how many women there are out there, both today and historically, who, propelled by this messaging, completely pulled the short end of the stick in life and, critically, *didn't question it*. I mean, really, how did we get here? *Any* idiot can see that preventing someone from voicing their struggles is just going to lead to a buildup of resentment and, ultimately, a breakdown. So how has it become taboo for mothers to stand in their power, take back control of their homes, and set healthy boundaries and expectations upon their kids?

Note that this isn't me trying to excuse moms from the work and responsibility that comes with motherhood. On the contrary, I believe that if you make the decision to bring another human into the world, you are obligated to address your own toxic traits, go to therapy, and do the hard work, just like I did. You're not responsible for your kid's every action, but they *do* learn by example, so go about your life as you would have them go about theirs. If you want your kid to have high-vibrational energy, then guess what? *You'll* need to cultivate that energy for yourself so they can watch, observe, and absorb. Of course, this won't guarantee that they enter their eighteenth birthday a well-rounded or flawless human, but it'll certainly increase their chances, and that's all you can try to do as a mother.

I can only imagine what Dr. Laura Markham would have to say about my approach. *Huh! You expect kids to give back? Well, they don't do that. They're natural little takers, and it's your job as a mom to fulfil their needs.* But hey, I know what's worked for me and what's aligned with my philosophy. I may be no Dr. Laura, but what I can tell you is that I have a whole lot of life experience, and from that, I know that if we do not set our own boundaries on how much we are happy to give and show up in *any* given relationship (mother-child relationships included), we will reach a point where we feel completely sucked dry. As a mother and a *person*, you deserve to have balance and appreciation in every corner of your life, and if that isn't your reality right now, it's okay to step back and *put yourself first*.

When I became a mother, I made the decision to be completely and utterly selfless within my relationship with my son. I opened up my energy, mind, body, and soul completely to Evan, and he responded by tapping into an energy source that had remained buried within me that felt comforting, familiar, and, honestly, ancient. It is because of this that I am pretty convinced Evan and I have a soul contract of some sort, or that at the very least we have had a past life together. I got this feeling the second I laid eyes on him after giving birth, and the feeling was so poignant and uncanny that it took me a while to properly wrap my head around it.

And yet. I say this with love (Evan is and always will be the light of my life, and I adore the young man he has become), but Evan had definitely developed the habit of gaslighting me and John whenever we were in a conflict. This problem reached a boiling point right after what, as I am writing, is our most recent court hearing with Dan. We needed to discuss a large sum of money that was owed to me (I'd financed the ranch, and wanted to see what Dan would be willing to cover), and by this point, Evan hadn't seen Dan for about eighteen months. This was in direct opposition to our divorce decree, which was a big problem, but who was I to overstep one of (no, the *biggest* of) Evan's boundaries and force him to have a visiting relationship with someone who ultimately made him feel like shit? I'd already sent him to be with Dan against his wishes for legal reasons before, and I feared it had done more harm than good. So now, Evan got to decide who he did and didn't have a relationship with, period.

I also knew Evan felt bad for Dan's other kids (Evan's half-siblings). I feel he likes them, but he doesn't see them anymore. Evan told me recently (in so many words) that he felt like he needed to protect them; that he felt bad for them when he went over because the house was a mess and Stacy would be sleeping, not watching the kids.

Basically, Dan wasn't exactly looking to create a warm, fuzzy, loving atmosphere as Evan's home away from home.

I feel that, to look at the "bigger picture", Evan is being spiritually tested. It's as though the universe is asking him, "Will you upgrade and increase your vibration, or will you continue operating at a low vibration?" To tell the truth, he's definitely thrown himself right into "verbal abuse" territory and hurled all his anger and resentment my way as of late, so as far as his behavior goes, things aren't looking too great. I feel Evan is a very lost soul at the moment, and has reached a fork in the road. But, should he continue on the warpath, I at least have the tools I need in order to keep myself spiritually well. As a person who's also had a difficult life and as his mother, I completely understand all of the anger he's clinging onto, yet I cannot afford to let my boundaries slip at this time. My role as his mother will continue to be to guide and support him (within reason), and what he chooses to do with that is ultimately in his hands. If he chooses to walk the same path as his father, then perhaps with his father is where he'll end up, should he wish for that. All I know is that toxic abuse will not be welcomed in my home.

This may sound harsh, and perhaps it is. But if I have learned anything over the course of this life of mine so far, it's that I would only ever be doing myself and my life a disservice by "zoning out" my higher self and not pursuing what she so desperately needs and envisions for herself (i.e., a life of peace, alignment, and ambition). God is good, and He has never abandoned me (it has only ever been me who has abandoned *Him*), and so I trust wholeheartedly the guidance I receive and the fact that things will pan out precisely in accordance with God's plan. And at this time, Evan was constantly fighting back, regressing, and manipulating, and so it seemed I was just going to have to let go a little bit, relinquish our control, and see what he made of a life without any of my input, guidance, or support. And it was with that reasoning in mind that we, regrettably, came to a point where we were seriously considering sending him to military school so he could get some time away from us, clear his mind, and, critically, re-learn the discipline and structure he clearly so desperately needed.

It was for these reasons (and that's putting aside his tendency to manipulate and abuse) that we put all our cards out on the table for Evan and gave him ample warning for what his options were if there was no change in this respect in the near future. Sure, it's probably going to be a tough year for Evan, but I think this is just a matter of needing to be cruel to be kind, and I hope that one day in the future, when he's healed and thriving and all of this is a distant memory, he'll be able to look back on all of this and understand why we came to the decision we did. I hope he'll be able to understand that I really did all of this out of love and because I could see ever-so-clearly how bright and vibrant and amazing his future was going to be if we could just get through this rough patch in one piece.

I was sat in a therapy session when my therapist turned to me and said, "How have you been handling everything that's been going on with Evan?"

I took a deep breath. It was time to speak it into existence outside of our family unit.

Once I'd collected myself, I told her what had transpired over the weekend. Me and John had made the decision that Evan would be going to military school.

She nodded slowly. "So, how do you feel?"

"I had a ton of pizza, binge-watched *Gilmore Girls*, and spent about one thousand five hundred dollars at TK Maxx. And yes, I realize I'm not coping in the best way, but I'm very, very sad."

I settled back into silence, sat with the echo of the words I'd just said, and allowed the sadness—the deep, hollow sadness—to envelop me for a moment. And, of course, I began to cry.

"It hurts," I told her. "It hurts to know I have to send him away again. As a parent, I don't want to do this. I want my child *close* to me. And it hurts to know that maybe Dawn is right. Maybe I *can't* raise my kid."

"How does that make you feel? Thinking about your sister's comment?"

"It makes me sad and angry. They have no idea how *hard* I've had to fight to keep Evan protected and safe. And it makes me angry to know that I don't have a family that comes together to support each other when the going gets tough. Instead, they want to pull you apart, tear off your clothes, and stomp you to the ground."

After a few beats, my therapist continued, "So, do *you* think you can't raise your kid?"

I thought about this for a second. "You know, if I hadn't gone through so much trauma and wasn't so emotionally and physically exhausted to the point where my soul just wants to lay down forever... then yes, maybe I would have been more equipped to handle Evan's shit. And if Dan wasn't such a legitimate *psychopath*, then we may not be in this situation, and we'd instead be able to co-parent in such a way where Evan never would've gotten to this point." I exhaled shakily. "My heart is heavy, and it hurts for Evan, but I have to step away and allow him to figure out his life path."

My therapist nodded, and then said, "I hear you, but you still haven't answered my question. Do you think you can raise your child?"

"No," I said immediately. "I'm giving it my all. I've given him everything I have. Yet he's still resisting. So no, I can't. At least not right now. He needs someone around him who's stronger and has that dominant, masculine energy that he's projecting right now."

"I think the best thing to do is to have a conversation with Evan after I speak to his therapist and once his application has been approved. Do you think you'll be able to fully explain why you feel the need to make this decision?"

"He pretty much knows already. I've mentioned it a few times in conversation, and deep down, he knows. Trust me."

She nodded again. "So, how do you think your family will respond to this?"

"I don't care what they might think or say. They are the evilest of evil when it comes to this. I know in my heart that what I'm doing is right and is what's best for my son, and I know that as a result of this, he'll have way more awesome opportunities at his disposal."

This situation had been made all the more difficult by Dan's role in Evan's life—or, should we say, lack thereof. As I've mentioned, he based his parenting solely around whether or not it was "convenient" to be and act like a dad at any given moment, and he was just as precious with his money as he was over his time. This had culminated in the aforementioned court case over the vast amount of money he owed me.

At this point, my therapist smiled sadly and said, "You know, Felicity, my heart hurts for you. You've been hurt your entire life, and I don't seem to recall any point where you were granted a moment to get your head above water. But you know what, Felicity? You're a fucking warrior, and I love that you've done so much emotional growth as a result of what you've been through. You haven't allowed this to consume you, and I'm so proud of you."

When I've felt as though I've had nothing, it's been amazing to have my therapist in my corner, cheering for me and validating me. And you know what? She was right: I *did* need to raise a glass to myself and acknowledge how much I'd fought my way through. I, and I alone, had gotten *myself* out of some of the deepest, darkest, ugliest holes, and there was certainly something to be said for that, even if I was still imperfect and riddled with self-doubt at times.

22

The Final Act

———

I KNOW THAT AS I write, there are innumerable women out there who are currently grieving their relationship with one or more of their children, and though our suffering will of course differ, I can definitely relate to that struggle.

I should mention that, to Evan's credit, he does respect my rules. Which, to me, shows that it isn't your typical teenage rebellious phase he's going through. Instead, his misbehavior is that which is characteristic of struggling adults (manipulation, verbal abuse, low self-worth, etc.), which means what we're dealing with is something really quite complex. And, as you'd probably expect, the result of that has been a time period that has all round been really quite emotionally charged, stressful, and draining.

This may sound selfish (and honestly, maybe it is), but when I was in the thick of this period, all I could think was, *I didn't do all of the work I've done just so I could be stuck in this abusive cycle again.* I'd done so much therapy, established so many boundaries, climbed so far, cut off so many people... and yet here I was, stuck in the same old situation again, although, arguably, a much worse version of it, since this time, it was my own child putting me through the ringer.

My objective in sharing this is *not* to villainize Evan. On the contrary, we've had many a conversation with him where we have explained how his behavior comes across, and he is truly horrified and humiliated whenever he grasps the gravity of what he's done. "I can't control it. It just *happens*," is a very common response from him, and I feel that neatly encapsulates where he's at: lost, confused, and desperate for change.

So, I'm incredibly empathetic with where Evan's at. God knows I haven't always been the easiest to live with during the various phases of my life, and so I'm glad I can be here to offer that validation and solid support network to Evan. Deep down, though, I know that in the same way that the ranch did Evan a world of good, so will military school. He thrives on routine and direction and masculine energy, and that, I believe, is what makes him so suited to the kinds of experiences he'll have there. It killed me to have to make a decision such as this (much like it did for me to send him to the ranch), but if we're just on a treadmill, walking the same path over and over and just not getting anywhere, I'm not sure what other choice I have. And that makes my heart hurt for him in a way you wouldn't believe, because I really feel he's been robbed of so much purely because he's not had a stable, consistent father figure in his life. John has done as much as he can to at least partially fulfil that role, but I fear this is a case of "too little, too late". So, regardless of how things pan out in the near future, one thing is pretty obvious: Evan needs the opportunity to become the man he was always destined to become. And if his home environment is not conducive to that, then that's not something I should take personally or try to ignore.

I don't want anyone to think this is a conclusion I've come to lightly. While the decision to send Evan to the ranch turned out to be probably the best one I ever made, I still fully grasp the gravity of what "sending your child away" can do to them mentally, at least in the short-term. I love that boy with all my heart and soul, and would go through anything in order to have him here with me and have us both go through this healing process together, but at the end of the day, if that's not what he's needing right now, then it's my role to honor that and do anything and everything in my power to maximize his chances of long-term happiness and fulfilment. Plus, I don't want to *fight* him anymore. Love isn't always enough, and right now, I think we both have our own respective journeys to go on.

Something I also feel the need to mention is that, unlike when we sent Evan to the ranch, Evan has had fair warning this time of the prospect of him being sent away somewhere else if his behavior continues. I should also mention that his entire therapy team is on board and think it will give him a strong foundation upon which to commence his healing journey in earnest.

Again, I do not share this to villainize Evan or to victimize myself, but to give a well-rounded view of the situation we're dealing with and why we've resorted to such extreme measures yet again. I tried other means of working through this with him before we made this decision, of course—I had him come to church with me, was encouraging of him connecting with God, and engaged him in many deep chats—but the bottom line is that he is just depressed, anxious, angry, and resentful, and he doesn't yet know how to channel those emotions into something positive and not self-destructive. And really, who can blame a fifteen-year-old kid for that?

What I'm trying to say is, I feel deeply for all those mothers out there who have had to walk away from their children due to toxic behavior, addiction... whatever it may be. Considering we are constantly force-fed the narrative that mothers should primarily be self-sacrificing and put their kids before everyone and everything else, it feels *really* painful and counterintuitive to allow yourself to take a step back and say, "This is wrong, and it isn't my job to be hurt like this."

And to those who judge those mothers who decide to take a step back for their mental and emotional wellbeing: you have absolutely no idea what happens behind closed doors and, critically, what it's like to live with that day after day. What may look like a straightforward, easily rectified situation to you could actually be a whole emotional rollercoaster and trauma-fest behind closed doors. No mother makes that kind of decision lightly, you can be assured of *that*.

This is one of the reasons why we need to squash this narrative that mothers are selfish if they think of themselves above their children, and why we instead need to create a culture of support where we embrace the mother out there who is struggling to move forward. Such a culture wouldn't demand much: just an open heart and mind and a willingness to understand the fact that you can't ever fully grasp someone else's circumstances and mental headspace.

So, what's the status on Evan? As of right now, I've got him on a boys' and girls' club waiting list, so we'll see how this situation pans out. For now, I have made it very clear to him that we will continue to support his journey so long as he treats me and John with respect and maturity. If not, we'll consider him a "free adult" at the age of eighteen: free to make his own decisions, but not welcome to live under my roof. From that point, he'll be completely independent and left to figure his own shit out. No financial support or deference in the face of a torrent of verbal abuse and manipulation. He can pick which road he'd like to go down, and I'll stay true to this promise either way.

Of course, I have thought over and over, in excruciating detail, of what Evan's perspective on all of this must be. He is a boy who is in pain and just needs structure, discipline, and empathy, yet he has a father who is uninterested and a mother who is so exhausted from the chaos that she's considering (at least temporarily) walking away. I get it, and I desperately wish things could be different. And, of course, there's still time for things to be turned around. For now, though, I'm loosely planning for the future and keeping my mind open to all possibilities so I'm not caught completely off-guard and find myself knocked back in my healing journey.

Regardless of what decisions we end up having to make, I will hold on to the image of me reaching a place of being able to fully trust Evan with my heart again. I will imagine us playing board games and cuddling up and watching movies together. I will imagine us talking about our days and laughing about small, silly things. And, as Evan awaits the beginning of his new journey (whatever that may look like) and as we continue to complete court-ordered therapy with his father, I will continue to check in with my higher self and ascertain whether or not I am doing the right thing, by myself and by my son. I will evaluate the system whose hands we have been put in and consider whether they really have our best interests at heart. I will again reconsider my planned course of action: is there anything I can do that I haven't done already to mold Evan into the hard-working, disciplined young man I know he is deep down? Is it right for me to let him go off and face his demons alone? Will he thank me for this in the future and attribute this decision to his independence and sense of agency, or will he blame me for it and become even more disillusioned and directionless than before?

I have no idea, and I think that uncertainty is, without a doubt, the scariest part of being a parent.

Yet we forge on, because what else can we do? And we hope we are doing right by our children and by our spiritual selves.

Speaking of doing right by our spiritual selves: I also had some shit to figure out where John was involved.

The truth is, I spent a long fucking time feeling *angry* in mine and John's marriage—though that word doesn't seem to cut it. My soul's very essence and energy felt depleted, for longer than I care to admit.

How I look at it is, you can navigate life's many curveballs, injustices, and heartaches in one of two ways. You can use it as fertilizer—as an opportunity for growth—or you can let everything pile up and fester until you become a bubbling ball of pessimism and mistrust.

I'd be lying if I said I didn't take the latter route for a long-ass time, and I feel like this really culminated during the peak of my frustration and insecurity about John's behavior. My narrative was that I had been walked all over and abused by everybody that had claimed to love me, and that I was sick of everyone as a result, including John. (Inaccurate? No. Unproductive and pessimistic? Yes.) I adored him, but it felt as though there was never any comeuppance for his fuckups. He'd blatantly cross a boundary, and I'd ultimately move on for the sake of keeping the peace. That's not to say there weren't wonderful aspects to our relationship, too (he'd cared for me and Evan as though he'd known us forever from the onset, and he'd given me the grace and space to work through my shit), but the bottom line was that it felt as though every time I voiced my needs, concerns, or boundaries for regards our relationship, everything fell on deaf ears. And that was eating me alive.

Of course, I knew that the main culprit for this was his inability to be held accountable. John couldn't physically bring himself to own up to his mistakes, no matter how big or small. It was like he had some sort of spiritual block; something that demanded he never "admit defeat", as he probably viewed it. Even in our counselling sessions, he always managed to skirt around how he'd contributed to a given problem. I now know (with the blessing that is hindsight) that John was just the product of the system in which he'd always functioned—namely, one that was fundamentally superficial and that valued ostentatiousness over actual spiritual wellbeing—and that, critically, this was a system he *liked* to function in (probably because it felt safe and familiar and predictable). He was cognizant of the fact that his behavior was repellant to me, but on any meaningful level, he did not have his eyes open to the damage he was causing.

Obviously, I, too, had my own rather unhealthy coping mechanisms, and I was more than open to giving him the time he needed to work through his, but I also couldn't help but ask myself: when would I just have *peace* in my life? Would I ever reach a point where I could just work on myself and not have to worry about everyone else around me, too? Was I really content with being taken advantage of time and time again until John finally worked through his six decades of emotional baggage and started treating me how I deserved to be?

When was enough, enough?

This may sound harsh, but, rightly or wrongly, I felt as though I was reaching the same spiritual and emotional place I'd been in when I was with Dan. Only this with John *hurt* so much more, mainly because I'd initially allowed myself to trust him so deeply and freely.

And so here I was, in the same mental headspace I'd fought so hard to claw out of all those years before, faced with the daunting question of, did I leave my marriage and start over with just my son all over again? Or did I stay put and hope one day, things would magically change—and that that day didn't come when I was already too far gone to fully recover?

If there is anything I have learned from John, it is that our "earthly selves" struggle with forgiveness. Like, a lot. Maybe more than anything. And this situation was no exception. There was so much hurt in our relationship on *both* ends (for me and for him) that ultimately meant we never felt heard, by each other or in our family dynamic as a whole... and several months or years of not feeling heard is damn difficult to recover from. And this was even further complicated by the fact that our communication styles (again, our "inner child") differed massively, especially when hurt was at play. I, for one, am known to have a bit of a mouth on me and to be very vocal when I have an issue with someone or something, whereas John remains silent, suppressed, terrified to rock the boat or "create a situation". I did my best to adapt to this when possible, always (well, almost always) conscious of not "attacking" him or being overly confrontational with my tone or approach, but sometimes I would just succumb to my own emotions and go right for the jugular, and I fear this caused a lot of damage for both of us.

In a nutshell, I had to consider, quite simply, whether John and I were compatible anymore—and whether we ever had been. We'd both contributed to one another's healing immensely, and of course we had shared innumerable happy times, but I also knew (when being honest with myself) that I was partial to overgiving, and I knew that if I wanted to stay present—for myself; for my peace; for my son—that wasn't an option anymore.

That isn't to say John wasn't pulling his weight. On the contrary, John was doing "the work" at the age of sixty-three, and while I was very much so emotionally done with tiptoeing around him and catering to his needs (as I'm sure he was with me), it would be remiss for me to not acknowledge that he was trying his hardest through therapy and such. With every day that goes by, he is more introspective and reflective and (productively) self-critical, and even if his behavior is not justifiable, that kind of frankness with the self *really* demands you set aside your ego in a way that most people never do in their lifetime. *That* deserves recognition.

Again, though, this doesn't mean that this relationship was right for me or that I had to, or should, put up with any of his behavior. But I still have to give credit where credit's due. And John was busting his balls to heal that neglected little boy he still had inside. I say this not to point the finger at him or his family (almost all trauma, in my experience, is generational, so playing the "blame game" would just be pointing out the obvious), but the bottom line is that I feel he was "lost in the mix" in his (very big) family, and that this ultimately led to him being attention seeking, needy, and emotionally unavailable in his adulthood.

And God knows women love to fix things. Hence why he was such a babe magnet, even (and maybe even especially) when he shouldn't have been (such as—ahem—in the sanctity of our marriage). This may even be, at the root of it, how he attracted me to start with (I adore healing, nurturing, growing), but the constant give and take eventually wore me down and sucked all the lust for life I had out of me. And both he and I are to blame for this: he for not reciprocating my love and affection and having some self-awareness, and me for not outlining clear boundaries from the get-go.

Basically, at this point in my life, I felt hurt and betrayed, my thoughts a constant clusterfuck of pain and resentment and chaos... yet spiritually, I felt strangely clear on what was happening here. I'd pledged I'd never allow myself to go through abuse and mistreatment by the hands of others again, and in voicing that pledge, I had created a boundary that God wanted to test. This wasn't karmic punishment, or the actions of some sick-minded higher power who just wanted to see me suffer. I was being guided on a path to even more empathy, growth, and clarity than I'd ever experienced before.

What I'm saying here is, I could very much so see the wood for the trees in my current situation, and I had my eyes wide open to everything that was happening. That didn't mean it didn't hurt like shit. That didn't mean that most of the time, in my mental headspace, I wasn't resentful and solemn and sapped. My spiritual self might have understood the "bigger picture", but that didn't mean my earthly self wasn't still going through the motions of suffering and heartache and *anger*.

I explain all of this so it doesn't seem like there's a weird dichotomy in everything I'm saying here. After all, it's a little counterintuitive to say in one moment that you have nothing but profound love and compassion for someone, and then in the next moment to say that you despise their behavior and what they've put you through. Yet what I'm trying to illustrate is that these thoughts and feelings very much so coexisted for me at this time. I wasn't exactly jumping for joy when he was entertaining other women right in front of me at social events, but I also understood this was his inner child seeking warmth and security and validation. I abhorred the culture of shallowness and superficiality he'd cultivated, but I also knew this was just what he was familiar with; what felt safe to him. And I knew I deserved more than this, but that didn't mean I didn't feel he was truly deserving of a lifetime of peace and happiness with someone that operated more naturally in his orbit. My spiritual clarity cohabitated with my mental anguish, and while that may be difficult to understand, that was the space I was in.

So, what has this "earthly" anger taught me? It has taught me that whenever we're feeling this, something is out of alignment. It has taught me that boundaries are either not being set or are not being respected. It has taught me that God is steering me down a path that will make sense to me when the time is right, and that I have to trust in that process. It has taught me that it is time to focus inward; to identify the underlying issue, rather than getting swept up in the heat and outrage of the moment. It has allowed me to both witness and experience firsthand what happens when you allow unhealed emotions to build. This reminds me of the poem *Harlem* by Langston Hughes: *What happens to a dream deferred? / Does it dry up / Like a raisin in the sun? Or fester like a sore— / And then run?*

In my experience, anger festers. It festers in a deep, oozing, volcanic sore, constantly ready to rupture. Specifically, for me, it manifested in me emotionally shutting down and becoming pretty unapproachable, and that is something I massively regret.

And so I am doing the work. I am identifying and talking to and appeasing that anger. I am taking all the emotions that come with doing "the work" in waves. I am acknowledging them as the spiritual purges and cleansings that they are. I am journaling; meditating; actively requesting that the energy I have given out over the course of the day comes back to me. And the more I learn, the more I realize that enhancing your earthly experience is less about "letting go of the baggage" and is more about coming to a place of empathy and understanding and asking, calmly and openly, for peace. I am still human and will always experience these waves of anger or hopelessness or panic, but these spiritual tools will see me through these times of trial and tribulation, and I know I will emerge uplifted.

As I write, I cannot help but notice that there are a few key messages that are making a reappearance in my life—a sure sign that there is a lesson I need to learn that I haven't previously heeded.

The first one: who is making the final decision? When confronted with a difficult choice, I have always felt "stuck" in some way, or convinced myself that it isn't my decision to make. And right now, it was purely finances that were tying me down. I'd cut off all my financial ties before, of course (when leaving Dan), but this situation felt very different. Times were different, the economy was tanking, I didn't have much in retirement or savings (it had all been invested into my business)… and did I mention the prenup?

Technically, if I was to stand in my power and lovingly let John go, I'd walk out with what I'd walked into the relationship with (which wasn't exactly much), plus two dogs. It wasn't that my safety net was insecure; it was that there was no safety net to speak of.

The second message: are you abiding by your boundaries and standing in your power right now?

Hm.

And the third message, which was coming through loud and clear: what are you willing to walk away from in order to save yourself?

What are you willing to walk away from in order to save yourself?

Well, I certainly wasn't going to allow whether or not I fulfilled my spiritual blueprint to be dictated by something as temporal and meaningless as money.

I looked out of the window on a glorious, golden fall day (October 10, 2022, to be specific), sunlight streaming through the windows, and allowed recognition to dawn on me with the midday sun.

I would do whatever was necessary in order to step into my power and embody the fullest, most radiant version of myself.

And financially... well, the dominos will fall where they will.

Afterword

After going on the crazy journey that has been revisiting and penning the life story enclosed in these pages, I wish I could provide an "ending" that is satisfying. Neat. But that would be a total deception. We may try to categorize the many stages of our lives into themes and patterns and eras, but really, we are all on one continuous journey that ends randomly, haphazardly. And so it is only appropriate that this story ends in the same way. Because ending it with a "flourish", or attempting to "tie up loose ends", would be a total fabrication.

Then again, we all love an ending, whether happy or sad. So, here is where I am at in my journey as of early 2023.

So much of my reclaiming my power and building my confidence has come from growing my business; my empire; my road to personal and financial freedom—a freedom I only ever dreamed about (though desperately craved) not many years ago. I've taken a pipe dream that took root in my mind fifteen years or so ago and created a platform where I can share my story and support other women on their respective journeys while they learn to embrace doing the exact same thing. I can now say that all those years spent hustling and getting my hands dirty in pursuit of a better life have culminated into this: a business and platform I always felt I could, yet never knew how to, launch and manage. Scrubbing floors like I did reinforced to me why my plan was so important. It gave me the drive to want more for myself and Evan.

I will admit that establishing a clientele out here has taken a bit of time—a bit of a blessing in disguise, since I don't know how I could have handled a full list of clients while all of this was kicking off! It was with this in mind that I initially decided to be practical and only open myself up to a select few people as and when I was available. This has proven to be a beautiful, rewarding way of navigating things and managing my time, and the success stories of my clients only serve to spur me on.

Evan is my reason for all of this. If that little guy hadn't come into my life, I know for a fact that I wouldn't be where I am today. If I could wish for anything in this world, it'd be for him to truly understand that you should *never* let anyone dictate to you or tell you you're not good enough or that your goals are unfeasible. I want him to know that we, not some jackass friend or family member or teacher or boss, are the creators of our own destiny.

Evan has had probably the hardest year of his life, but he's a born survivor, and he'll thrive over the course of the next year. I know it. He's made difficult decisions, developed a self-awareness that most grown adults don't have, and had many challenges, and so letting go of control and anger will, for him, be a lifetime battle, but I believe in him and his strength and healing power.

As for my magazine, *She Is You*... well, this is everything I ever wanted to do and more. This isn't just a business; this is my passion. My *calling*. *She Is You* is a community for midlife women seeking a sisterhood bond, and they accompany one another on their own healing journey of reinvention. The gals call themselves "midlife warriors", and that's what they are! They are women who are looking to reinvent their lives through better health, professional fulfilment, rewarding relationships, and spiritual exploration, and all is falling right into place, prospering with growth and opportunity. We offer monthly workshops, classes, and get-togethers, including monthly group Zoom calls. There is such a need for female friendships that are authentic and genuine; ones that can embrace adversity and help you along without judgment. And *She Is You* has now become that for so many women.

I have everything built out for my long-term plan, and I keep chipping away at it daily.

I truly feel God brought everything into my life as lessons, and me as a teacher. My journey with Evan is one that will last a lifetime (and I am at peace with that), but my job with John feels done here. That doesn't mean there is any resentment on my part, or that I wish him any misfortune. On the contrary, I truly believe John to be deserving of a wonderful woman that is wholeheartedly accepting of who he is, but the reality is we have simply outgrown each other. Unfortunately, that is just the long and short of it.

I now know why I, like so many, was put on a path of pain and hardship: because it was what I needed in order for me to develop the grit needed to get to where I am today. It has also gifted me with the tools I needed to mentor other women that want the same out of life. I absolutely have been and, at the time of writing, absolutely am being "victimized". There are no two ways about that; no way to make that truth prettier or more digestible. But I am *not* a victim. I am very clear, confident, and assured in the fact that the behavior of those around me, including that of Evan, Dan, John, whomever, whether positive or negative, is absolutely no reflection of who I am or what I am worth as a person.

I hope that whoever is reading this can see the overarching message in all of this: that *we hold the power to change our own lives*. That *we can redeem ourselves and recreate that second act.*

God gave me this life for a reason, and even though it has been a very painful life at times, I've found my silver lining by realizing that I went through the pain that I did so I could teach others. So I could give them the courage to undergo their own healing journey. I may not be uber-accredited in scholastic knowledge, but mine is more: it's the firsthand blood, sweat, and tears of experience; the kind that would make most people run and hide.

I remember that I'm my mother's daughter. I'm a born warrior, and will always stand strong in my storm, no matter how tired I am.

This life has taught me the hardest lessons, and yet I will continue to accomplish my dreams and create new ones, always.

Acknowledgments

I would like to thank Rebecca Perry for helping me write my story and holding space when I couldn't control the tears. You have been beyond kind and generous.

Thank you to John, my rock, best friend, husband, and most excellent teacher! You, my friend, have taught me some of the hardest lessons and given me some of the greatest gifts. Keep pushing through your healing journey; you deserve happiness and joy.

Evan, this book is all for you. One day, I hope you realize that we can overcome our struggles, regardless of what life hands you. My love for you is more than words; you are my heart and soul. It's been you and me, kid, this whole time. You make me proud every day, and you will always be my little boy (and my all-star baseball player). Keep aiming for the stars, kiddo. I know one day, I will have the chance to watch you play on the Cubs' field.

To my family: I hope you will find peace in your life one day. I love you.

Tommy: I love you, man. You will forever have a place in my heart.

Keep being a beacon of light for the people around you. I know life has been challenging, but you have a gift that is yet to be fully realized. You are meant to help broken children with your gentleness, so tap into this potential, kid. It's your calling. I love you. Wheezy.

About the Author

Felicity Nicole is an author, speaker, and coach, as well as the creator and owner of *She Is You*, a brand for midlife women seeking transformation and healing through a community of togetherness. Her second book, *Pieces of Me*, is a stunning memoir chronicling her life, from growing up in a dysfunctional family, to finding herself married to an abusive husband as an adult, to gathering the strength to start over and pursue something more. Now a thought leader for other midlife women who have found themselves in similar situations, her passion project, *Sisterhood of Midlife Warriors*, is a program for women seeking healing in a group setting.

In her free time, Felicity hunkers down with her family, plays the cello, gardens, and reads.